Honor First:
A Citizen-Soldier in Afghanistan

Thanks for your
support of the
United States
Armed Forces.

Honor First!

Matt B. Mongin III

Honor First:
A Citizen-Soldier in Afghanistan

Lieutenant Colonel
Platte B. Moring, III (Ret.)

The views expressed in this book are those of the author and do not reflect the official policy or position of the Pennsylvania Army National Guard, Department of the Army, Department of Defense, or the United States Government. Some of the names of the soldiers referenced in this book have been changed in the interest of maintaining their privacy. I would like to thank Colonel Steven Mahoney for assisting me with the technical aspects of this book and Kerry Ann Kollhoff for editing the manuscript.

ISBN : 1-4196-3759-2
Library of Congress Control Number : 2006904251

To order additional copies, please contact us.
BookSurge, LLC
www.booksurge.com
1-866-308-6235
orders@booksurge.com

Honor First:
A Citizen-Soldier in Afghanistan

TABLE OF CONTENTS

PREFACE

The older I become, the more value I place in the quality of honor. More than wealth, fame, or power, it is honor that gains the genuine respect of others. Honor allows us to live our lives with pride and a clear conscience regardless of our circumstances. When we honor our God, our family, and our nation, we honor ourselves. Honor is a gift that no one can take away.

Honor First is a story about a Philadelphia trial attorney who is called up for active duty as a National Guardsman for the first time in his life at age 45. This book chronicles a journey from the mobilization station at Fort Dix, New Jersey, to the Hindu Kush Mountains of Bagram Airfield, to the diplomatic maneuvering of Afghan reconstruction in Kabul. It is a lawyer's story, but it is much more than that. It is about how citizens who become soldiers at a time of war can do things that they never thought possible.

Those readers looking for an account of combat activities in Afghanistan will not find it here. I never fired my weapon or saw anyone who did. Those readers seeking a cynical anti-war saga post Vietnam need not read this book.[1] Although I am skeptical about everything in my life, I am cynical about nothing. Those readers wanting the complete history of Operation Enduring Freedom will need to consult other sources. Even though we made history at the Office of Military Cooperation-Afghanistan, I make no effort to chronicle all of it here.

This book concerns the lives and interactions of ordinary citizens making the transition to military life after September 11, 2001. It is a story of family sacrifice and personal duty. This book is about rebuilding a nation and creating a foundation for a just society. It demonstrates how individuals can make a difference in this world. Most of all, this book is one soldier's account of his trying to do the right thing. In short, it is <u>Honor First</u>.

THE CALL TO DUTY

To all men and women in our military . . . your mission is defined. Your objectives are clear. Your goal is just. You have my full confidence, and you will have every tool you need to carry out your duty . . . . [T]he battle is now joined on several fronts. We will not waver, we will not tire, we will not falter, and we will not fail. Peace and freedom will prevail.

President George W. Bush
October 7, 2001

MISSION EXECUTION

The people of Afghanistan are a world away from the nightmare of the Taliban. Citizens of Afghanistan have adopted a new constitution, guaranteeing free elections and full participation by women. The new Afghan army is becoming a vital force of stability in that country. Businesses are opening, health care centers are being established, and the children of Afghanistan are back in school, boys and girls.

The progress is a tribute to the brave Afghan people and to the efforts of many nations. NATO—including forces from Canada, France, Germany, and other nations—is leading the effort to provide security. Japan and Saudi Arabia have helped to complete the highway from Kabul to Kandahar, which is furthering commerce and unifying the country. Italy is working with Afghans to reform their legal system, and strengthening an independent judiciary. Three years ago, the people of Afghanistan were oppressed and isolated from the world by a terrorist regime. Today, the nation has a democratic government and many allies—and all of us are proud to be friends of the Afghan people.

President George W. Bush
March 19, 2004

"THE FIRST DEFENDERS"

The concept of armed citizenry providing collective security for the homeland predates the foundation of the United States. In fact, the idea of the citizen-soldier has its roots deep in ancient Anglo-Saxon tradition. It is hardly surprising then, that when 18th Century Pennsylvania was threatened by bands of Native Americans, it would react by forming companies of organized settlers, known as "Forrest Runners," to protect the settlements.

While the official lineage of the 213th Area Support Group starts in 1849, traditional history begins with these "Forrest Runners," and covers the period of the French and Indian War, the ensuing campaigns against western Indians, and the eight long years of the American Revolution. Among the first militia units to report for service with the Continental Army was a company from Lehigh, Northampton, and Salisbury Townships, Pennsylvania, known as the "Northampton Riflemen." Again during the War of 1812 and the Mexican War in the 1850s, these same Pennsylvania Militia companies rallied to federal service.

It was not until the founding of the "Lehigh Fencibles" in 1849 that a unit was formed totally of Allentown men. From 1849 to 1922, Allentown provided Infantry units to the state and federal governments as part of the organized militia. The original unit was reorganized in 1850 to become the "Allen Rifles." It was one of several eastern Pennsylvania companies, which were the first to respond to President Abraham Lincoln's call for troops to defend the nation's capital. Arriving in Washington on April 18, 1861, the Allen Rifles were personally greeted by President Lincoln, who proclaimed the unit as "The First Defenders."

This designation, as well as the motto, "Honor First!" are ones that the unit has used proudly ever since.

Following the Civil War, the Pennsylvania Militia was renamed the Pennsylvania National Guard. Upon declaration of War with Spain, the 213th mustered into federal service as part of the force that captured Puerto Rico. The unit then reverted to its citizen/soldier status until 1916 when it served with General John "Black Jack" Pershing at the onset of World War I. In 1940, the 213th was among the first National Guard units called upon for World War II. Deployed overseas in 1942, the 213th participated in the invasion of North Africa and Italy.

Headquartered in Allentown, Pennsylvania, the 213th Area Support Group provides command and control for 1700 National Guard soldiers serving in twenty separate non-divisional units dispersed throughout Pennsylvania. During peacetime, the First Defenders have responded to state emergencies including truckers' strikes, floods, and blizzards. During wartime, the 213th is designed to control five to ten battalions that supply logistical support for up to 30,000 soldiers located within or passing through the Group's assigned area of operation.

Recently, units of the 213th Area Support Group supported soldiers participating in the peacekeeping mission in Bosnia. Other units of the Group helped liberate Kuwait as part of Operation Desert Storm in 1991 during the First Persian Gulf War. On March 15, 2003, the Headquarters and Headquarters Company of the 213th Area Support Group was mobilized for Operation Enduring Freedom. Honor First tells the story of the First Defenders in this campaign and the role played by its Command Judge Advocate in the reconstruction of Afghanistan.

I dedicate this book to my wife, Susan, and my children, Leigh and William, without whose support my contributions to Operation Enduring Freedom would not have been possible.

Chapter I.

The Order for Mobilization

I t was just another day at the office. I had my first cup of coffee and was reading my e-mails. There were very few people at work at the Allentown office of White and Williams LLP. No one was required to be at the law firm until 9 A.M. Camille Stockdale, a secretary for the Worker's Compensation Practice Group, was always one of the first of the staff to arrive at the firm. She never entered my office in the morning, but on this day she did.

"A plane has hit the World Trade Center in New York," Camille said.

I looked up from my computer and turned to Camille and asked, "Was it an accident?"

"The people on the news are saying no," she answered.

Trying to impress her with my knowledge of warplanes, I volunteered, "It must have been a small commuter plane because no fighter jet from a foreign country would be allowed to enter our air space unchallenged and would not have sufficient fuel capacity to fly here from abroad."

"Platte, it was one of our 747's," Camille stated with exasperation.

"Oh, my God," I said.

That night, as our family gathered at the dinner table, I offered a solemn and emotional prayer. "Dear God, please do not let this horrible tragedy affect my family." However, deep inside, I feared that it would.

Ever since the fateful day of September 11, 2001, I knew it was likely that I would be called to active duty with the Armed Forces of the United States. The world was different now. The old assumptions about National Guardsmen were no longer valid. A citizen-soldier was expected to do more than weekend drills and be available to assist with blizzards and floods. The continental United States had become a battlefield, and I was one of America's warriors.

At the first staff meeting of my National Guard unit following the collapse of the World Trade Center towers and the attack on the Pentagon, my unit Commander, Colonel Marshal Eward, a decorated Vietnam War hero, told us to prepare for active duty mobilization. Eward speculated that the 213th Area Support Group ("ASG") might be needed to provide logistical support to the troops fighting the Taliban regime in Afghanistan. He felt that there was a mission for the unit in Uzbekistan of pushing supplies south into the war zone.

The Pennsylvania Army National Guard was no longer one weekend a month and two weeks of active duty for training in the summer. I now could be called to full-time active duty. My unit, the 213th ASG, was on a war footing and I was part of the expeditionary force of the United States Army.

My wife, Susan, thought my National Guard involvement required me to spend too much time away from home. Even though she had the utmost respect for the military and commended my volunteer service, she felt that my legal career was more important to our family. I was the Managing Partner of a regional office of a major Philadelphia law firm. White and Williams LLP had required that I spend a countless number of hours at the office in order to serve clients and make Partner.

When combined with my law practice, "Weekend Warrior" duty took me away from her and the children too often. Susan frequently said, "Do you know what price your family has paid as a consequence of your National Guard duty?" I never had a good answer for that question. I am not sure that I had one. Instead of trying to explain to her the pride I felt in wearing the uniform, I tried, albeit inadequately, to thank her for the sacrifices she and the children had made during my continued participation in the program.

Ever since 9/11, I had prepared Susan as best I could for the possibility of military deployment. I kept her posted on every command briefing and rumor of potential mobilization. I spoke to her parents at length and tried to explain why I might be forced to leave her and our two children for over a year. We discussed whether it would be better for Susan and the children to stay in Pennsylvania or move in with her parents in Virginia Beach in the event of a call-up.

Ironically, the 213th ASG received the alert order to prepare for mobilization on her birthday, February 14, 2003. For some reason unknown to me, the full-time staff at the Armory had not bothered to call the soldiers in the unit to inform them of this news. I did not learn of the alert until the following Tuesday when I called the Armory to find out if anyone had heard anything about an alert. I had a trial in state court in March and wanted to know if I should prepare for it or send the case file to someone else in the firm. When Major John O'Boyle notified me of the alert order, I made the first call to Susan. She was concerned, but not alarmed or angry. She gave me her support.

On March 4, 2003, I was called to active duty. During my tenure with the ASG, the unit had been mobilized during the first Persian Gulf War in 1991 and then again as part of the peacekeeping forces in Kosovo. However, both missions did not require an Army lawyer, so I stayed home. Now, at age 45, I was being called to serve as a full-time soldier for the first time in my life.

The most difficult task confronting me was finding a way to tell the children that their father was leaving. As it happened, the day of my receipt of active duty orders from the Army was also the date of my son William's first Boy Scout meeting. The week before, my heart had been filled with pride as he "crossed over" from Cub Scouting to Boy Scouting. I am an Eagle Scout and had always hoped that my son would also become involved in the Scout program. He was now standing before me, beaming with self-confidence in his new Boy Scout uniform.

As we sat in the living room getting ready for the meeting later that evening, I helped him learn the Scout Oath. It begins, "On my honor, I will do my best to do my duty to God and my country . . ." All of a sudden, it became clear to me.

Later, at dinner, I asked Will and my teenage daughter, Leigh, to explain to me the meaning of the introductory words of the Scout Oath.

We began, "On my honor."

Will said that it is like making a promise.

"I will do my best."

Leigh said that that meant a person should try her hardest.

"To do my duty to God and country . . .."

"Isn't that like a job?" Leigh asked.

I answered "yes," but questioned her whether it was like getting up and going to work each day.

Will then offered, "It is more like a life long task."

And with that, I hoped that my children understood why their father was leaving home.

This soldier's story begins at Princeton University in 1976. At that time, America's involvement in Vietnam had ended. Only a few years earlier, militant students had firebombed the Princeton Armory and spit upon ROTC cadets. The military was generally in disfavor in this country. Very few young men and women entering college had any interest in the armed forces.

The summer before my freshman year, I had been sent literature from the Reserve Officer Training Corps ("ROTC") offering the opportunity to become a commissioned officer in the U.S. Army in exchange for fully paid tuition and six years of active duty. This package was of no interest to me. I had too many important goals to accomplish to be burdened with six years in uniform. I was going to graduate from college, attend law school, and then run for the United States Congress. I threw the literature in the trash.

It was my father who prompted me to give some thought to the Army. He had served in 1952-54 with the Army in Germany after the end of World War II. Upon graduating from the University of North Carolina, he became drafted in the Army as a Private. Life was difficult enough in the military, but serving as an enlisted soldier with a college degree was debasing in the old "brown shoe" Army. He wanted something better for his son.

My dad told me in 1976 that America would be involved in other wars. The Cold War with Communism was not over. The old Soviet Union was a threat to national security. The military draft had ended, but the prospect of future use of force was still real. When I received a second mailing from ROTC during the spring semester of my freshman year at Princeton, Dad pulled it out of my trash can at home and advised me to give it some thought. Twenty-seven years later, I was a Lieutenant Colonel ("LTC") in the United States Army serving in a combat zone as part of the Global War on Terrorism.

Although I had been a commissioned officer in the Army for 22 years, nothing I had done in the National Guard was anything like what is required of a soldier at war. After finishing my Officer Basic Course in 1979, I had spent four years as a military policeman in the Army Reserve. My duty simply involved performing two weeks of annual training at Fort Knox, Kentucky, and Fort Meade, Maryland. Upon graduating from Vanderbilt University School of Law in 1983, I transferred to the Judge Advocate General's Corps. The rest of my military career was largely spent representing soldiers on weekends. I was soldiers' counsel in the District of Columbia Army National Guard while I was working as a trial attorney with the US Department of Justice and then in Pennsylvania as a member of the National Guard in Allentown. The most difficult cases I handled were discharges from service for absence without leave ("AWOL") and for positive urinalysis.

When I received the mobilization order, I was a trial attorney defending doctors in malpractice lawsuits and corporations in products liability cases. War had now called me to service as the Command Judge Advocate of the 213th Area Support Group ("ASG"), Pennsylvania Army National Guard.

"Soldier first, lawyer always," is the motto of the Judge Advocate General's Corps. I hoped that it would be soldier for now, lawyer always.

Chapter II.

Leaving Home Station

On Monday, March 17, 2003, President George W. Bush appeared on national television to address the nation. He gave Iraq's dictator, Saddam Hussein, forty-eight hours to leave his country or face the full fury of the U.S. military and its allies. Two days later at noon, the 213th ASG left Allentown for Fort Dix, New Jersey, in a convoy. On the evening of that day, the coalition began the invasion of Iraq.

March 19 was a glorious day. In my desire to spend just a few minutes more with Susan before leaving my home for a year, I arrived at the Armory late and missed roll call that morning. The building was filled with sobbing family members clutching their cameras as they stood against the drill floor walls. Chaplain Dale DiBernardinis was holding his Bible and giving the morning prayer. He told all 132 members of the 213th ASG that God's love would bring victory.

The entire staff of the Allentown office of White and Williams was at the Armory to see me off. My dad, Susan, Leigh and Will came to the Armory wearing red, white and blue. My children were wearing my dog tags that I had given them the night before. Somehow they remained upbeat and cheerful while most of the well-wishers had eyes swollen with tears.

Susan had given me the most beautiful letter that morning. It read:

Dearest Platte,

You have demonstrated your love for me in so many ways in recent months. My birthday weekend was so very special and one that I will remember fondly for a long time. I thought we all had such a relaxed, fun time together and your interest in my happiness made me feel loved. I truly feel as if we are growing closer. Also, I know that you have worked very hard to make this situation as comfortable for me as possible. I love that about you. You have been so thoughtful with regard to my needs. Please know how much that means to me.

Your whole family is very proud of you. From me to the children to your Dad, sister, from my parents and brother and to all the aunts, uncles, and nieces and nephews who care about you – we are all proud of your willingness to serve your country, our country, and your commitment and dedication to your values. Please carry these thoughts with you as you carry out your daily duties.

In some strange way, I feel a little that this has been good for our family. I think we have all grown closer and all realize that what is so important is just family and loving each other. I know that you will do a terrific job over there and then will come home safely. Then I believe we will enter a "second chapter" in our lives, one that will be richer because it will draw upon our earlier experiences and one that will be sweeter because of our renewed appreciation of the many blessings that we have.

Love always,

Susan

Susan and the children joined my law office staff on the street just outside the Armory gate. Before we mounted our vehicles, I went to the Armory fence to say good-bye to Dad, who was standing on the other side. He was the first to cry. I had only seen him cry once before. It was the day that my mother, his wife, had died of breast cancer in 1985. He wished me well and said, "I love you, Bud."

I had decided the day before that I would ride in the convoy with the troops. Lieutenant Colonel Steve Mahoney, who would become my best friend in uniform, had offered to drive me to Fort Dix in his car. I politely declined the offer, realizing that riding in the Hummer out of the Armory gate was a lot more "cool."

The convoy was triumphant. It gave me a sense of what the Allied Forces felt while marching by the Arch de Triumph after the liberation of Paris during World War II. Family members and Allentonians lined the street as we proceeded through town with a police escort.

Flags were waving and "Good Luck," "Come Home Safe", and "We Support You," were shouted. The entire student body of the Trexler Middle School stood along 15th Street holding banners and yelling for us. I was impressed with the diversity of the school and the patriotism they exhibited that morning. It was a far cry from the hatred and distrust I had experienced while a Princeton ROTC cadet. We were now on active duty and on our way to the mobilization station.

The Hummer was filled with the Command Judge Advocate section. Sergeant Mona Cramden took the wheel. She is a thin brunette with a warm smile and gentle nature. Sergeant Cramden had last seen active duty service with the Air Force as a stateside recruiter in 1994. Mona was eager to please and worked hard. She was married, but rarely spoke of her husband. All I knew was that he had some ownership interest in a winery and that I had gotten a gift bottle of wine at the unit Christmas party.

Specialist Jane McFadden sat in the rear with Sergeant First Class Michael Hoffman. The convoy trip to Dix gave me time to learn something about McFadden who had just been transferred to our unit, the headquarters company, to fill a vacancy in our section after the receipt of the alert order. McFadden described herself as a "very bad kid" in high school. She was naturally intelligent, having scored a 1430 on her SAT, but presented herself as a street-smart teenager.

Complete with tongue piercing, acne, and tattoos, McFadden said she had rarely attended class in high school and almost flunked out. She wasn't rebelling against anything in particular, but was obviously underachieving. McFadden joined the Army to give herself a kick in the pants, and she told me it had worked. Before receiving her active duty orders, she had been employed for a few months as a paralegal for a law firm.

SFC Hoffman was another story. Now age 54, he had last been on active duty in Vietnam in 1968-69. He had served as an infantryman in the jungle, experiencing all the atrocities and frustrations of that conflict. Hoffman had a bad heart from smoking and reported to the mobilization station with three stints in his coronary arteries. In the civilian world, Hoffman was a Detective with the Whitehall Township Police. I valued his experience and good nature. Mike had overcome a lot. A year earlier, he had lost his daughter in a parachuting accident. His true pride and joy, Mike's daughter, had been a student at a prestigious cooking school when her parachute did not open and she fell to her untimely death.

Captain ("CPT") John Barrett spent the morning with his wife and family and was driven separately from the rest of the JAG section to Dix. My junior judge advocate was having trouble with his wife, an Israeli national. Kidding, Jack, said she threatened to poison his food or expose him as a homosexual so that he would be ineligible for this deployment. The Barretts had two small children, aged three and seven months. Having a husband away from home was particularly tough on young mothers.

Jack was concerned about his medical condition and thought it might serve as a hardship excuse to avoid deployment. Prior to becoming an officer for the first time at age 33, Barrett had a knee reconstruction. He had recently developed a Baker's cyst on a ligament that was painful at times. In the weeks after the alert, the National Guard had given him conflicting information about whether he was deployable as a consequence of this knee condition.

Jack is somewhat of an enigma. He has intense pride in his Irish heritage, telling me that Catholics had beaten him up many times in his youth for wearing the Protestant orange. Jack graduated from Cornell University and Widener Law School. He enjoyed playing rugby and performed as a clown in some Philadelphia Mummer's Parade drinking club. Jack had previously worked for my law firm, but had moved on to Rawle and Henderson, one of the oldest law offices in Philadelphia. Before the deployment, he was doing insurance defense work and was the owner of a partially renovated bar in South Philly.

While we were at the Allentown Armory, we had heard stories about hundreds of soldiers on gym floors in sleeping bags awaiting transportation to theater out of McGuire Air Force Base. After arriving at Fort Dix, we were pleased to learn that we would have two-per-room barracks. We had two single beds, desks, and wall lockers. There was no telephone, television or Internet. At first, it appeared that we would have no information about the war while we were training for it. We then discovered a cable hook-up for a TV in the dayroom.

The unit poker players had looked forward to a game on our first night at Dix. We converted a desk into a table by covering it with an Army blanket. The beer flowed. I was told we were limited to three duffle bags for all our uniforms, equipment, and personal comfort items. However, some of the full-timers with the unit had arranged for Igloo coolers that were now filled with beer. I had prepared for poker by bringing a small cloth bag loaded with loose change. Within two hours, I had won only one pot and was borrowing money.

At 9:50 P.M., Sergeant Major John Gurganus, a crusty Vietnam War vet, told the Poker Club that the President was coming on the air in twenty minutes to announce the start of the war. Gurganus was nicknamed "Tonto" after the Native

American who accompanied "The Lone Ranger" on the television show. In a scene reminiscent of some old World War II photo, the officers of the 213th sat on the floor and beds in the room of the Sergeant Major to listen to the radio and hear the President of the United States address the nation. At 10:15 P.M., George W. Bush announced that American and coalition forces had commenced military operations aimed at the overthrow of the Iraqi dictator, Saddam Hussein, and the liberation of the people of Iraq.

One of the members of our gathering, Lieutenant Colonel James Buggy, the 213th ASG's Director of Security, Plans and Operations, remarked that he would always remember that he was "in bed" with Major John O'Boyle when the war started.

Chapter III.

Ground Hog Day

Every day here seems like Ground Hog Day," LTC Colin Hannings said to me in a chance meeting my second day at Fort Dix. Two lawyers, with offices only one block away from each other in Allentown, shared breakfast together. Colin was house counsel with Allstate, handling automobile insurance defense in Lehigh County. We knew the same judges and had litigated against the same plaintiff's lawyers in automobile accident cases. And yet, we had never met.

Hannings was 48 year-old Army Reservist who was part of a Legal Support Organization stationed in Norristown, Pennsylvania, now destined for the Persian Gulf. Colin had been at Fort Dix for three weeks. His unit had just been validated for mobilization to Operation Iraqi Freedom. He shared with me some of the aspects of his pre-deployment training.

"Everyday we get up at the same time, put on the same clothes, and do the same thing. Just like Bill Murray in the movie, 'Ground Hog Day,'" he said.

Colin told me what to expect in the weeks that lay ahead -- Arab culture briefing, Smallpox vaccination, legal orientation, first aid, weapons qualification, a mobilization readiness field exercise, and nuclear, biological, and chemical training. Meals Ready to Eat ("MRE"), pre-packaged food, would be handed out for lunch. Combat exercises would be performed in "Full Battle Rattle" -- Kevlar helmet, load bearing equipment, gas mask, and individual weapon. Colin joked, "It is just like the life of an insurance defense litigator."

Hannings said, "You have the same routine every day. The first formation of the unit is at 0700 hours. The classroom training begins at eight o'clock and lasts until 11:30 A.M. Lunch is from noon to 1 P.M. The second formation occurs at one o'clock. More classroom or field training until 3:30 P.M. Final formation for physical training ("PT") happens every day at four o'clock. Dinner service starts at 5 P.M. Lights out at 10 o'clock."

"Sounds exciting," I said. "Is there anytime for golf?"

"I have not had a free moment since I got here," answered Colin.

During the first week of training at Dix, I had lunch one day with Colonel ("COL") Scott Wagner, who had succeeded Eward as Commander of the 213th ASG. I observed that the unit had many young females. Fifteen girls in our unit had joined the National Guard in order to receive monies to attend college. Now they were training for war in a foreign country. I remarked to the Colonel that it must be especially tough on these young women as they prepared for overseas deployment.

Wagner, a consummate family man, looked at me with a serious expression and commented, "In many ways, it is tougher on us older guys." "When I was twenty," he said, "I did not fear anything, and life was an adventure. I did not have to care about anyone but myself." The Colonel continued, "I now have a lot more to worry about. My wife wants to know why I have to go away, and I have to consider what life would be like for my three sons without me."

I stopped worrying about the young females so much.

After one week at Dix, the ASG assembled with nine other units at Timmerman Theater for a briefing on the Uniform Code of Military Justice and the Law of Land Warfare. Reserve Officer Major Giblin, a New York City plaintiff's lawyer with an office two blocks away from the World Trade Center at the time of the attack, gave the presentation. Giblin had volunteered for active duty following September 11.

He asked the over 250 persons gathered in the auditorium how many soldiers were Reservists. There was an enthusiastic show of hands. Major Giblin then asked the members of the other reserve component, the National Guardsman, to identify themselves. After receiving a loud response of "HOOAH" from the assembled weekend warriors, Giblin said, "You are all wrong. You are all now on active duty!"

The Director of Support Operations, LTC Dennis DeMara, had spent most of March 23 on his cell phone. He was 54 years old with a wife and three grown kids. Dennis was my oldest friend in the unit. He had been with the 213th ASG when I had joined the unit back in 1989. We had come to know each other when I had helped him with several legal problems with equipment accountability over the years.

Now his daughter was expecting a baby any day. The grandmother-to-be, Mrs. Dennis DeMara, had never driven alone more than 60 miles away from her home in Jim Thorpe, Pennsylvania, and was fretting how she would be able to get to her daughter's home in Wilmington, Delaware, without her husband. The telephone call to Dennis came late in the day. We now had a grandfather in our unit! DeMara's first grandchild, a boy named Zachary, was born while his grandfather was on active duty.

After I had been away from home for several weeks, the excitement of the events leading up to my reporting to active duty had ended. Susan, who had been a pillar of strength, was now left alone. Her husband had left his successful law practice and family for a volunteer assignment. The novelty of the deployment had worn off and the reality had set in: One year without Platte. Three hundred and sixty five days of taking care of two children without any help. Twelve months of parenting, house cleaning, and paying bills with no husband to share the load.

What was worse was that Will was having trouble at his private school. A classmate since second grade, Judas Jones, was harassing him. He told my son's friends that he hoped Will's dad died in Iraq. Several of Will's classmates reported this curse to their parents. These students' moms, in turn, felt compelled to call Susan. Susan was rightly upset and outraged and called

Judas' father. The father showed no concern or remorse for the comment.

The next day, Will received an anonymous retaliatory and threatening e-mail from what we knew to be Judas' home. The e-mail said Will "would be watched and he better look out or else . . ."

Susan could not sleep. She heard every sound in the house. She felt afraid. Susan did not know what to do. I was incensed by the cruelty of the child who would say such a thing and the callous insensitivity of the parent. We decided to report the incident to the school. Susan and I did not know what might happen to Will at school. I called the Lower School Director, requesting protection for my child. The school did not seem to care. The Headmaster weakly stated that he would do nothing in response to the e-mail without proof of the identity of the sender. He would do nothing to determine the name of the sender. We were on our own.

My first thought was to retain counsel to make sure that all legal means were pursued to secure the safety of my wife and child. I called a friend from my old law firm and asked for assistance. I then realized that my own law firm had a specialist in information technology, and White and Williams had previously offered to do anything to assist me during my deployment. I called the Managing Partner of the law firm, Allan Starr, for help.

Allan had a Marine son-in-law and had been a long time supporter of mine. He jumped into action. Starr said he would immediately subpoena the Internet service provider to ascertain the identity of the person who sent the threatening e-mail to Will. "Just give me the word and I will march into that school and demand action," Starr said. The subpoena confirmed that the e-mail came from the Jones home. Still, the school would do nothing.

Fortunately, Susan had the support of a loving family and one very good friend, Marian Bressner, during this crisis and at all times I was away. Marian was someone who lived relatively close by and who could always be counted on to listen. My wife also drew strength from daily telephone calls to her parents living in Virginia Beach, Virginia. Her brother and sister-in-law in Wisconsin offered comforting words by phone. The physical distance of her family from Pennsylvania made a support network difficult to obtain even in the best of times. However, the deployment made the separation from family even tougher. Without the everlasting love and concern of a good friend and the immediate family, this war would have been intolerable for my family and my service abroad impossible.

The war with Iraq was not having the outcome most expected. President Bush and Secretary of Defense Donald Rumsfeld had led the nation to believe the war would be over quickly. A "shock and awe" campaign was planned to undermine the Iraqi Army's resistance by destroying its command and control with a massive bombardment. An immediate surrender would ensue and an outpouring of support for the coalition. The bombs fell, but the war continued for weeks. A weeklong sandstorm had slowed the movement of the Third Infantry Division from its staging base in Kuwait to Baghdad.

American soldiers were now casualties and several personnel from a Maintenance Company, including Private Jessica Lynch, became prisoners of war. My unit followed all the developments on a television set up in the first floor dayroom. Every waking moment not spent on training was consumed by the war.

Chapter IV

The Apology

One of my duties as a Judge Advocate was to train the members of my unit on the Law of War and the Rules of Engagement. It was my intent to offer the very best classes that the unit had ever seen. I spent days working on a multi-media presentation to include film clips, photographs, and the most up-to-date PowerPoint graphics. To start the class, I felt I needed a really good joke or humorous story.

After considering and rejecting some "Saddam Hussein" jokes that I had heard recently, I decided that I would make fun of the Army for its excessive use of acronyms. It was one of my pet peeves that active army officers would converse in acronyms as if it was some special language reserved for only the military elite. At staff meetings, I frequently had to interrupt the discussion to ask for an explanation of an acronym so that I could understand what was going on at the unit.

Ever since the unit's arrival at Fort Dix, we had been overwhelmed with acronyms. I had to purchase a "Staff Battle Book" so that I could translate into English the acronyms that were being thrown around by the Fort Dix trainers from the 78th Infantry Division. I then arranged the acronyms I had heard during mobilization in a logical manner and incorporated them into my introduction to a class on the Law of Land Warfare. Before the start of my formal teaching, I read the piece called "ACRONYM MANIA":

When I got my MOBE[2] Order from STARC[3], NGB[4], FORSCOM[5], and SIDPERS[6] to go to DIX[7] and then CENTCOM[8], I was HOOAH[9]. I could not take my POV[10] because it was not MTOE[11], so I rode in the HUMMWV[12] after PMCS[13] along with females with PMS[14]. At the DIX BOQ[15] and BEQ[16], we met our UA[17]. We did CTT[18] in BDU[19] and LBE[20] with KPOT[21]. We learned about WMD[22], NBC[23], SINCGARS[24], OPORDER[25], and OPSEC[26]. After SRP[27], we did CIF[28]. Top then said to do PT[29] in IPFU[30] and I said FU[31].

We went to the ISB[32] in JLIST[33] with M16[34] and LSA[35] after doing METT-T[36] and IPB[37] in MOPP4[38]. At the MRE[39] we ate an MRE[40]. I stayed in the GP Medium and TOC[41] with my RDL[42] while others did MDMP[43], so that I would not be MIA[44] or EPW[45] at the PEHA[46] and be SOL[47]. Some soldiers got the UBL[48] at the ATP[49] and ASP[50] ASAP[51]. The OPFOR[52] was a NO GO in NVGs[53] while acting as COBs[54] without MILES, C2[55], GPS[56], and SOI. The ASG[57] HHC[58] had an AAR[59] with the CSM[60]. I learned that the ASG is a BOS[61] EAC[62] with help from the DISCOM[63] and COSCOM[64] re CSS[65] and CCIR[66]s.

If I do not get to the TSC[67] at the SWA[68] RSOI[69] in DCU[70] with TAT[71] and TACLAN[72] in accordance with the TPFDL[73] PDQ[74], I'm going AWOL[75]. Enough of this BS[76]!

The presentation met with huge applause. However, a few female soldiers did not clap. They looked like they were ready to explode. Major Pam McTish, Captain Myra Crouse, and Captain Latinya Danner saw no humor in the acronyms after the utterance of the term "PMS". For some female soldiers, even the inference that women are less mission-capable than men due to a gender difference is politically incorrect, sexist behavior.

I used to admire Major McTish. She is a somewhat attractive former company commander who had earned a combat patch in the first Persian Gulf War. Pam was able to maintain her femininity in a male dominated organization. I thought she knew when to laugh with the boys and when to stay with the girls. However, the acronym incident changed everything.

McTish made it clear that she did not like the reference to "PMS." Somehow she convinced the other females and some of the leadership that this type of humor was offensive to women. And so, despite receiving high praise for my two-hour block of instruction on the Law of War, it appeared that all that would be remembered from that presentation was my allegedly sexist reference to pre-menstrual syndrome.

The next week I was tasked with giving a class on Military Justice and Fraternization. I spent numerous hours preparing for the presentation, including reviewing three feature films that had court-martials for law of war violations. Having not learned anything from the fallout from the prior week's class, I decided again to interject some humor.

I solicited the opinion of LTC James Buggy, who coordinated all training. The son of a PA National Guard General Officer, Buggy is bald-headed, with a hawk nose and an easy-going manner. Buggy's guidance was, "Fuck them if they cannot take a joke."

At breakfast on the day of my second presentation, I engaged McTish in a conversation concerning the Army Fraternization Policy. This policy is intended to discourage sexual relationships between officers and enlisted personnel. Within seconds, she made me feel uncomfortable. In her view, all such relationships were strictly prohibited and there were no exceptions.

Despite my best efforts, I could not make her understand that every relationship between a man and a woman from the enlisted and officer's corps was not a court-martial offense. For a violation to occur, I explained that there must be some adverse effect upon the good order and discipline within the unit. It was useless. She had made up her mind and was not listening to reason or the public policy behind the regulation.

McTish was a feminist. She would not even acknowledge customary practices of civility between men and women. She felt it was sexist for a man, especially a senior officer, to open a door for her. She would insist that the senior male officer walk into the room before her.

I should have known that it was not a good day to provoke Pam McTish. However, once again, my vanity and desire to make people laugh overcame my prudence. I decided to open my class with a brief recap of my Princeton Debate Team experience. I wanted to demonstrate that, despite my academic background and profession, I was an officer who had a less serious side.

"During my junior year of college, I became Captain of the Princeton University Debate Team," I proclaimed. "I was feeling very good about myself. Then, a senior on the team called me a 'Master Debater' and a female underclassmen thought of me as a 'Cunning Linguist.'" Emboldened by the laughter and giddy applause of the crowd, I went on to countdown, in David Letterman fashion, my "Top Five" debate topics while at Princeton:

Number Five: Resolved: A drink before and a smoke after are the three best things in life.

Number Four: Resolved: The United States should erect firmer penal institutions.

Number Three: Resolved: A woman is just a woman, but a good cigar is a smoke.

Number Two: Resolved: The 1980s was a decade of women on top.

Number One: Resolved: Princeton women will not go down in history.

Each recitation of a resolution met with even greater applause. And yet, the big three females, McTish, Crouse, and Danner, were not pleased. In fact, they were pissed off -- more sexist humor from the Command Judge Advocate.

During the question and answer session following my substantive presentation, McTish raised her hand high in the air. I tried to avoid calling upon her. I could sense trouble. Finally, it became obvious to everyone in the auditorium that McTish had a question. I held my breath and recognized her.

"Sir, could you tell all the soldiers in this unit how to report a claim of sexual harassment," she asked. *I could not believe she was suggesting that my recounting of Princeton Debate Team topics amounted to sexual harassment.* However, I kept that thought to myself.

I responded in a very serious manner, "You can report sexual harassment to the Commander, the Chaplain, the Equal Opportunity Officer, or the Judge Advocate."

McTish was not going to leave it alone. She wanted me to sweat. She asked a follow-up question. "What if the Judge Advocate is the perpetrator of the sexual harassment? What do you do?"

I quickly replied, "Find another lawyer." The flip answer drew howls of laughter and some applause. The comic relief, nonetheless, was short-lived. I knew the damage was done.

To make matters worse, a female newspaper reporter from The Morning Call, Wendy Solomon, attended the class. Ms. Solomon was seeking to become an embedded reporter with our unit on the deployment. She did not quite know what to make of my humor. Solomon knew little about the Army and less about acceptable military behavior. At lunch after my class, Wendy asked McTish and Major Bridget Widdowson, the Director of Personnel and Administration, what they thought about my humor. To their credit, they just squirmed and said, "No comment". However, their uncomfortable silence spoke volumes.

At the next unit formation, Colonel Scott Wagner approached me and said: "We need to talk. I cannot believe you used the words masturbator and cunnilingus in class today." Colonel Wagner is a six foot two tall, West Point graduate, with a shaved head. As a commander, you could not ask for someone any better. He has many outstanding qualities, but a sense of humor in the face of a reporter is not always one of them. After dinner that evening, the Group Commander told me I had brought discredit upon myself and the unit in front of a newspaper reporter and he wanted me to make an apology to the entire unit.

I did not want to apologize. Moreover, I did not think an apology was necessary. I had only made a few puns and repeated some actual Princeton debate topics that made fun of both men and women. I discussed the pros and cons of making an apology with the other Lieutenant Colonels and the Command Sergeant Major Mike Wevodau. Mahoney and I discussed the situation for almost four hours while driving to and from Allentown and Fort Dix on our first weekend pass home.

Late on Sunday night, I met with Colonel Wagner in his barracks room. I wanted to make a last ditch effort to appeal his order for me to make the apology at the first formation in the morning. We had a long discussion about what was actually said, what my intent was, and how my words were interpreted. In the end, Wagner said, "Platte, I am absolutely convinced that this is the right thing to do." The West Point graduate wanted to set a tone. I saluted the Colonel and said, "Honor First."

The next day at formation I walked to the center of the U-shaped rows of soldiers and apologized to the 132 members of the unit:

> It has come to my attention from the Group Commander that some soldiers in this unit were made to feel uncomfortable by the statements I made before Friday's class. Upon reflection, I know in my own heart that the remarks I made were inappropriate given the time and place they were made and my position with this unit. Those of you who know me well understand that I am very sensitive to the feelings of others and

take great pains not to offend anyone. In my vain attempt at humor, I simply wanted to make the point that I am a regular guy, someone you can approach, that I am one of you.

In my presentation last Friday, I said that I did not know the definition of "an officer and a gentleman." Well, that's not entirely true. In my mind, the definition of a gentleman is someone who tries to make the people around him feel comfortable. I was not a gentleman to some persons in this unit on Friday and I apologize for that.

The apology was met with a huge round of applause. Soldiers shouted, "HOOAH" and "You the man!" When I got back into formation, Widdowson shook my hand. First Sergeant Steve Moyer approached me and confided, "I do not know what you said in class last Friday, because I was not there. But, I now know more than ever before that it is a pleasure to serve with you." Several females in the unit of all ages came to me and asked me why I felt it was necessary to apologize. I did not speak to McTish for two weeks.

Chapter V.

Operation Enduring Fort Dix

From the very first day we arrived at Fort Dix, my unit was treated poorly. We came to the mobilization station with the expectation that we would train for ten days to three weeks and then fly to Kuwait for Operation Iraqi Freedom. Instead, we stayed at the "mobe" station for 97 days and took it upon ourselves to re-name the mission "Operation Enduring Fort Dix."

Although they had processed many troops for the war, the Fort Dix chain of command had never mobilized a unit quite like ours. Unlike most deploying units, we arrived at the mobilization station at full strength. Moreover, the 213th had one full bird colonel, five lieutenant colonels, and four sergeants major. Usually, a company shows up for training with one captain and three lieutenants. Fort Dix was not accustomed to Field Grade Officers and Non-Commissioned Officers ("NCO") questioning their policies and procedures.

Within minutes of our arrival on post, buck sergeants approached our convoy and told us it was time for "amnesty." We did not need to be told that we could not have loaded weapons or illegal narcotics on post. No one in the 213th had these things anyway. However, our Fort Dix unit administrators told us that installation policy required us to surrender our prescription medicines and knife blades over three inches long. This exercise deprived us of our medication and pocketknives.

We then had to turn in all our vehicles for technical inspection. Every one of our Hummers and two and one-half ton trucks ("deuces") had to be given to the mechanics on post to see if they were fit for deployment. This made some sense, but what followed was chaos. The Fort Dix Maintenance Company did not even look at our vehicles for over a month. We understood that operational priorities mandated that units mobilizing before us had their vehicles inspected ahead of us. But in the early days of Operation Iraqi Freedom when we were a priority unit, no one at Dix made any effort to determine whether the ASG vehicles were mission capable.

By the required load date for placement of the vehicles on a boat for shipment to theater, the Hummers were not inspected. Our mission required the unit to drive our vehicles from Kuwait through hostile territory to a logistical support area in the vicinity of Baghdad. When confronted about the urgency of the situation, a Fort Dix staff officer nonchalantly stated, "If we do not get to your vehicles, then we'll just push back the load date." The fact that there was a war on did not seem to bother him one iota.

When the mechanics finally looked at our vehicles sometime in late April, they determined that the vehicles needed parts. Fort Dix did not have the parts. The smart people in the ASG Maintenance Section suggested that we call back to Fort Indiantown Gap, Pennsylvania, and request the repair parts from our state National Guard headquarters. Fort Dix would not allow this easy fix. The Dix mechanics had to order parts from the active army inventory.

Additionally, they would not allow the 213th mechanics to assist in the process of making repairs. ASG personnel could not even work on their own vehicles. What made matters worse was the fact that Fort Dix told our unit that we could not perform certain training activities because we had no certified vehicles to use and the post had no available HUMMVs to lend us.

After we had been at Fort Dix for two months and overstayed our welcome, the post needed our barracks for incoming officers participating in a Command and General

Staff Course. Dix required us to relocate our unit's billets. And so, the ASG packed up all our personal gear and moved to another barracks one mile away. These barracks were not nearly as nice as the former and required, in some cases, eight soldiers to occupy one 20 by 30 foot room.

The medical services were another nightmare. As soon as the state headquarters learned that the 213th was going to mobilize, it ordered the unit members to undergo two days of Soldier Readiness Processing ("SRP") at Fort Indiantown Gap. This SRP included complete physicals for soldiers and inoculations in late January 2003. This prior planning should have reduced the time necessary for medical processing at Dix. Instead, the SRP at Dix was a miserable redundant ordeal.

First, the active duty army had not transferred the National Guard medical test results from Fort Indiantown Gap to the ASG soldier medical files at Dix. As such, Dix medical personnel decided to create new files. Unit members had to have blood work done again. Others had to have a second inoculation of the same shot they had gotten in the arm at the Gap.

Second, there was no medical case management or coherent recordkeeping at Dix. We had no way of getting accurate and timely information on whether ASG soldiers were medically deployable. A call to the SRP to determine the medical status of a unit member often resulted in the responses: "We don't know." "We don't have any records under that name." "Can you call back later?"

Third, the post medical staff had no standard protocols on the conduct of clinical examinations and records reviews. Each doctor (or more commonly nurse or physician's assistant) did it differently. Thus, there were inconsistent standards of medical fitness for duty.

Fourth, the quality of medical treatment provided to soldiers was poor. Many soldiers chose to seek treatment off-post due to the failure of Fort Dix medical personnel to diagnose illnesses or because Dix lacked the required medical resources.

Chaplain Dale DiBernardinis was a case in point. The Chaplain is a registered nurse. He was having trouble with headaches, fever, and loss of hearing. According to Fort Dix procedure, DiBernardinis reported to sick call at the SRP and was examined by someone purporting to be a nurse. The nurse looked into the Chaplain's ears and took his temperature. The Chaplain insisted he had a bacterial infection and required an antibiotic. The SRP nurse said there was nothing wrong, gave him an aspirin, and sent him back to training.

Without getting permission from the Fort Dix training commander, DiBernardinis drove off post in his private car to see a trauma care doctor. As he expected, the Chaplain had an infection in his chest and in both ears that was at a critical stage for the preservation of his hearing. He paid for the doctor's visit and medication with his own funds.

Fort Dix calendared routine follow-up appointments for soldiers for dates many weeks after the day of our scheduled departure for Iraq. And so, soldiers could not get necessary treatment and medications before deployment. Additionally, the excessive length of time between the date of arrival at the mobilization site and actual day of deployment to theater was compromising strength maintenance. While undergoing training at Dix and awaiting deployment orders, the ASG lost the services of one Major who suffered a back injury during a field exercise.

Despite the unnecessary hassles imposed upon the ASG by the mobilization team on post, there were some good times. Command Sergeant Major Wevodau called us the "ASG Fraternity." On most nights, drinking for some would begin after dinner and continue into the wee hours of the evening. The number of trash containers in the barracks filled with beer cans the morning after was a testament to the revelries.

The most fun at Fort Dix for me was the time spent on the golf course and off-post. Jim Buggy and I joined with Sergeant Majors Werley and Wevodau to form a team for the weekly nine-hole golf league. We thought we were only going to stay at Dix long enough to play two weeks in the league. As it turned out, we recorded seven nine-hole scores and were in second place in the tournament when we left for the war in late June.

Our favorite off-post dinner spot was Chickie and Pete's restaurant in North Philadelphia. This seafood establishment was the Tuesday night meeting spot for the "Council of Colonels". Buggy, Deputy Commander Ferdinand Janze, DeMara, Mahoney and I enjoyed the fellowship, beer, and crab legs it offered once a week. On one occasion, we asked the waitress to guess the nature of our profession as the Council sat there in civilian clothes. She could not even guess. When we told her we were soldiers awaiting deployment to Iraq, she said, "No, you can't be. You are all too old." We felt it.

Chapter VI.

"Tell That Nigger To Mind His Own Business"

One of the most admirable achievements of the Army is equal opportunity. Ever since President Truman ordered the integration of the armed forces in 1948, the military has led the effort toward racial equality in America. More than any other public or private institution in the United States, the military has been able to achieve racial integration. For the most part, soldiers of all colors enter the ranks, work together as a team, and obtain positions of leadership. There are, however, some incidences of stupidity and prejudice.

All sorts of relationships are formed in the Army. The 213th ASG was no exception. Female soldiers engaged in lesbian relationships consistent with the "Don't ask, Don't tell" policy. Other soldiers formed more traditional girlfriend-boyfriend relationships. One young soldier got pregnant shortly after we received our mobilization order. She so wanted to deploy with the unit so bad that she had an abortion while we were training at Fort Dix.

Specialist Narcy Systick is the most attractive woman in the unit--at least in her own mind. Systick frequently wore a T-shirt with a warning on its front, "Don't bother—I'm out of your league." She has an angelic face, auburn hair, great wheels, and a body quite frankly that deserved attention.

Systick, unfortunately, is not very smart. Her father had left her mother while Systick was an infant. In fact, Systick met her father for the first time when she received her orders to go to war. The man who lived in her house with her mother while she was growing up used racial slurs all the time. These caustic comments were part of her upbringing.

Systick had a baby-faced friend in the unit named Private First Class Howard Romans. One week before deployment, Systick and Romans were having a quarrel at the rifle range. It was the wrong time and place. Systick's squad leader, Staff Sergeant ("SSG") Leonard Blue, overheard their conversation. SSG Blue, an African-American soldier, had been transferred to the 213th from another unit just months prior to mobilization because of inappropriate sexual conduct with junior enlisted females in his former unit. Blue told Systick that he sided with Romans in her disagreement with Romans.

Systick, who had several run-ins with Blue during our stay at Dix, had now had enough of Blue. She stormed off and barked to two other female soldiers, one white and one black, "Tell that nigger to mind his own business." Blue did not hear the racial slur. It did not matter. The damage to unit harmony was done. Specialist Jacqueline Bertlam, the African-American, had heard the remark and she repeated it to Blue.

Blue was livid. He immediately went to the ASG Equal Opportunity ("EO") Officer, CPT Latinya Danner, and registered his outrage. He wanted a pound of flesh. Danner, still stunned by my inappropriate sense of humor from the Law of War class, was a receptive audience for Blue.

The Army Command Policy includes equal opportunity. The regulation requires that the EO officer attempt to resolve the situation at the lowest level possible. The EO officer is not supposed to initiate an investigation of the situation. Instead, the EO officer is to advise the affected soldier concerning his rights and remedies.

Nonetheless, Danner, a Philadelphia social worker in civilian life, launched a full-blown crusade. She repeated Systick's mean-spirited comment to all soldiers of color in the ASG and solicited their feelings about the remark. Within hours of its utterance, every member of the 213th knew about Systick's use of the term "nigger".

First Sergeant Moyer took immediate action. He counseled Systick on her racial slur and told her that he expected her to apologize to Blue. Moyer prepared a formal counseling statement for Systick's signature warning that similar behavior would result in non-judicial punishment, an Article 15.

Neither Danner nor Blue was satisfied with the actions taken by the command. Danner obtained sworn statements from every soldier involved in the incident. Blue then retained CPT Barrett as counsel. Danner recommended that Blue prepare a written EO complaint.

According to regulation, all written EO complaints needed to be reported to the first General Officer in the soldier's chain of command within 48 hours. Further, the regulation required the commander to initiate a formal investigation leading to the preparation of a report containing findings and recommendations.

Colonel Wagner and I met with Danner the night of Blue's submission of the EO complaint. I asked Danner for her recommendation concerning the resolution of the matter. She stated that Systick had deep emotional problems stemming from her childhood. Systick had learned prejudice from her stepfather and needed extensive training on equal opportunity. Danner said Blue was not be satisfied with an apology. Systick should receive an Article 15 and be made to read a book on race relations and write an essay.

Wagner asked Danner if she had obtained sworn statements from soldiers before Blue had submitted the written EO complaint to the command. I had previously told the commander that such a procedure was contrary to the regulations. She lied and said "no."

I had reviewed the EO complaint for legal sufficiency before the meeting. I explained to Danner that Blue had not signed the EO complaint under oath as was required by the regulations. Further, CPT Danner had signed the complaint in the block reserved for the company commander. Finally, a racial slur, no matter how despicable, really was not evidence of Blue being denied equal opportunity. After all, Systick was a private and Sergeant Blue was her supervisor. Danner said she would speak with Blue and let us know what he wanted to do.

The next day at formation First Sergeant Moyer asked all members of Systick's squad to gather in the commander's office. The command had investigated the issue and made its decision concerning the appropriate remedy. Behind closed doors, Systick issued an apology to Blue and her entire squad. She expressed genuine remorse.

Blue was still hopping mad. Systick was not getting what she deserved. He wanted her to get an Article 15. Danner helped him prepare a revised EO complaint. I met with Jack Barrett. I explained to him that the command had decided to require Systick to apologize to her section, had given her a written counseling statement, had required her to write an essay, and had warned that further racial remarks would result in an Article 15. I further stated that the EO complaint as originally submitted was legally insufficient and requested that it be withdrawn.

Barrett was back to me within hours. His client was not buying it. Blue wanted to negotiate the type of punishment given to Systick with the command. He would withdraw the EO complaint on the condition that Systick apologize to the entire unit. Barrett said, "With all due respect, sir, Wagner set the precedence when he made you apologize to the entire ASG." I told Barrett that I would report his client's demand to the command group. I sensed trouble.

Colonel Wagner went ballistic when he learned of Blue's demand. "This command will not have its disciplinary decisions questioned by an NCO! Let him submit the damn EO complaint," said Wagner.

When he cooled down, Wagner called a meeting of the entire command group and Blue's chain of command. Twelve of us met in Wagner's barracks room. Coincidentally, the ASG had just been notified that day that it was to deploy to theater in four days. I explained to the group that if Blue did not get his unit apology from Systick, that Barrett was going to prepare a formal written EO complaint for his client. The 213th would have to report the EO complaint to First United States Army at Fort Meade, Maryland. And then, Captain Timothy Brooks, the company commander, would need to start a formal investigation. Sergeant Blue, Danner, the appointed investigator, and all the fact witnesses would have to stay at Fort Dix under the command of First Army until the complaint was resolved including any appeals. In short, the ASG might deploy under the cloud of an EO complaint at less than full strength.

Colonel Wagner surveyed the senior officers and NCOs in the room and asked, "Can anyone give me one good reason why I should not transfer Blue for permanent duty at Fort Dix?" At first, no one spoke. Then, I mustered up the temerity to take a contrary view. I spoke about the concept of retaliation and explained how Blue, Danner, and Barrett could misinterpret the transfer as revenge for filing a written EO complaint. Sergeant Major Michael Wevodau suggested that this was sergeant's business and asked for an opportunity for the NCO chain of command to speak with Blue. Wagner agreed.

The NCO chain of command for Blue was his section sergeant, Susan Brown, and First Sergeant Moyer. They decided to speak to Blue about what it meant to be a Non-Commissioned Officer in the U.S. Army. This was a mistake. It was not the message, but the messenger. There was no way in hell that Blue was going to take an ass chewing from Suzie Brown, a woman. Blue was pissed. He could not care less if the filing of a written complaint meant that some ASG soldiers would not be deployed with the rest of the unit.

It was LTC Jim Buggy that broke the impasse. Buggy is one of the most levelheaded officers I have ever met. He always has a witty remark to break the tension and does not let too many things bother him. Buggy was the officer in charge of the section in which Blue was a member. He wanted a shot at Blue. Buggy suggested to Blue that Systick apologize to the entire Security, Plans and Operations Directorate. Blue bit and the crisis was over.[77]

Chapter VII.

"DEMOBISTAN"

After one month at Fort Dix, we started to hear rumors of units demobilizing. The Third Infantry Division had captured Baghdad and the supporters of Saddam Hussein had fled the city. President Bush declared victory in Iraq on May 1, 2003, and said that the reconstruction of Iraq would begin. In short, it appeared that some of the units placed on active duty for Operation Iraqi Freedom would not be needed.

One of the ASG's subordinate units, the 283d Personnel Services Detachment ("PSD") from Harrisburg, was told to turn in their equipment and go home.

It is quite a blow to the psyche to be ordered to demobilize. You make arrangements with your employer to be gone for a year. You tell your wife and children that you will not be with them for Thanksgiving and Christmas. Politicians and friends call you a hero. And then, the Army says, "Never mind. You are not needed here."

Soldiers react in different ways. Some are happy to go home. Others feel that they have not lived up to their own expectations of service. Some feel that they have missed their chance for glory. Most feel that they were ready and answered the call.

For the ASG, the news came in bits and pieces. The "Twins," Majors John O'Boyle and Joseph Smith, spent most of each day at the Army Reserve Intelligence Service Center ("ARISC") monitoring the SIPRNET ("Secret Internet Protocol Routed Network") for the latest developments on deployment of units. O'Boyle and Smith were generally regarded as the smartest grade O-4's in the unit.

Over time, they learned that another ASG had taken over our mission of setting up a logistics base near Baghdad. Instead of setting up an Intermediate Staging Base somewhere between the Kuwait border and Baghdad, an active duty ASG had gone straight to the capital with the Third Infantry Division. In unofficial e-mails, the 377th Theater Support Command, our higher headquarters, said we might not be needed.

By this time, morale was pretty low. In addition to the "demobe" news, we had just heard a report that Fort Dix personnel were harassing the soldiers in the 283rd PSD. The Clothing Issue Facility at Dix got upset when it thought that the PSD did not turn in all their cold weather equipment as part of their out-processing. It just so happened that the unit had shipped all of their cold weather clothing by cargo ship out of Charleston, South Carolina, for Kuwait before receiving notice of their demobilization.

Some asshole captain accused the soldiers in the PSD of stealing Gore-Tex parkas and pants. He was demanding a "health and welfare inspection" of the PSD's billeting quarters. LTC Ferdinand Janze, the Deputy Group Commander, came running into the mess hall where I was eating lunch. He told me to report immediately to the barracks of the PSD. When I got there, I found 15 NCOs from the post in formation with shouldered weapons and accompanied by the federal security police. They were ready to turn over the barracks looking for Gore-Tex issued to the PSD, which was actually on a boat heading for Southwest Asia.

As soon as the Sergeant Major in charge of the NCOs heard that an Army lawyer was present, she phoned the full bird Colonel in command of the mobilization units to come immediately. COL Pedro Velez showed up with the Post Staff Judge Advocate, LTC Richard Masterson, in tow. Velez was red hot.

He caught up with COL Wagner while both men were walking into the stairwell of the PSD barracks. A closed door inside the building separated me from my commander and client. Velez and Masterson were confronting Wagner. I could easily overhear the conversation from behind the metal door in the hallway. Screaming at the top of his lungs, Velez said to my commander, "What part of my order did this unit not understand? You have no business being here. I command this unit now, not you, and these soldiers have failed to turn in their issue."

I had heard enough. Velez was represented by Masterson as his counsel. Colonel Wagner did not have his lawyer present. I opened the stairwell door gently and peaked down the steps toward the landing where the three officers were standing. Looking at Wagner, I politely asked, "Sir, would you like me to be a part of this discussion?"

He replied politely, "No, Platte, I can handle this myself." Disappointed I was not part of the fray and feeling a little chastised, I closed the door. Somehow Wagner was able to diffuse the situation and Velez left the building. Masterson met me outside. As the NCO team ripped apart each soldier's barracks room and wall locker looking for Gore-Tex, the Post Staff Judge Advocate shook my hand and remarked, "You know that this is a legal search."

I gave a half-smile and replied, "Yeah, and Fort Dix is a great place to take a family vacation."

The soldiers of the PSD, who had been kicked in the gut with the news of demobilization, were now being humiliated by the storm troopers from the mobilization station. They stood at attention as the post NCOs rummaged through all their personal possessions. Ten officers from the ASG witnessed this needless fiasco. All were thinking that our unit would be next victim of demobilization terror.

Specialist ("SPC") Michael Deabenderfer from the ASG put a sign up on the door to his barracks room that read "DEMOBISTAN". We had learned in our country briefs that the term "stan" attached to the country names, Afghanistan,

Pakistan, Tajikistan, etc., meant "Land of the...." Afghans, Pakis, Tajiks, etc. Now it appeared that Fort Dix was the land of those undergoing a demobe. Deabenderfer and his roommates began spreading the rumor that the 213th was the next unit to demobilize.

Colonel Wagner did not want the ASG to demobe-- especially considering the alternatives. The Pennsylvania National Guard had borrowed soldiers from several units across the state to put together an "A" team for deployment with the 213th ASG. It was unlikely that this collection of talent could be put together again for another deployment within the next two years. With the way that things were going in Afghanistan, Iraq, and Kosovo, if we did not go somewhere now, then sooner or later we would be doing a rotation in a war zone.

The ASG had arrived at Fort Dix one soldier short of full strength according to our Department of the Army manning chart. Several young soldiers had given up a semester or more of college for this mobilization. It was unconscionable to demobilize after two months at Fort Dix only to be mobilized again within a year to perform a replacement rotation in some third world hot spot.

The Twins had learned at the ARISC that our higher headquarters did not need our unit in Iraq. However, the 377th Theater Support Command needed an ASG to conduct a field training exercise known as "Bright Star" for six weeks in Egypt in the fall of 2003. At the same time, the Twins uncovered a letter to Central Command from the National Guard Bureau, dated March 13, 2003, suggesting that an ASG might be able to replace a Rear Area Operations Center rotating out of Afghanistan. The issue then became whether the 213th would: (1) demobe; (2) stay on active duty at Fort Dix until September to perform the Bright Star mission and deploy from there to do a rotation in Iraq; or (3) be sent immediately to Afghanistan.

The political intrigue then began. The 377th Theater Support Command ("TSC") is an Army Reserve unit based in New Orleans, LA. The 114th ASG is a National Guard unit based in Mississippi. The Twins thought that the Southern "Old Boy" network was in play. The 377th was trying to find a way to send the 114th to Afghanistan and the 213th to Egypt. Neither the 213th nor the 114th wanted to go to Bright Star. As for the ASG, we found little honor sitting at Fort Dix for six months while waiting to deploy for a field training exercise in Egypt.

Back in 2001, the Army had told the 213th that it was scheduled for Bright Star during Fall 2003. In February 2003, however, the Army mobilized the 213th ASG for what would become Operation Iraqi Freedom. In April 2003, the Army alerted the 114th ASG for Afghanistan. About the same time, the Twins were getting unofficial guidance from the 377th that the 213th was going to demobe.

Something did not make sense. Why would the Army demobe a full strength, validated unit that had spent two months on active duty at Fort Dix while, at the same time, call up for active duty another National Guard ASG that had not spent one day at a mobilization station.

After spending two long months at Fort Dix in pre-deployment training, the 213th ASG had not gotten a demobe order from Operation Iraqi Freedom. The Twins speculated that the 377th was trying to keep the 213th on active duty until such time as the 114th could be sent to a mobilization station and validated for overseas deployment. Then, the "Northern" 213th ASG could be switched back to the field training exercise in Egypt and the "Southern" 114th ASG could march off to greater glory as part of the fourth phase of Operation Enduring Freedom in Afghanistan.

Colonel Wagner would have none of this foolishness. It meant that the 213th would spend the entire summer (March to August) at Fort Dix and then possibly go to Iraq after Egypt. He sent several e-mails to the 377th TSC asking them to "come clean" about their plans for both Area Support Groups. The higher headquarters was saying nothing. The time had come for positive action. If nothing were done, then the 213th would go to Bright Star after six months of "training" at Fort Dix and then possibly to Baghdad.

The smart people in the unit put together a plan of action. ASG Sergeant Major Terry Werley had his full time job at National Guard Bureau ("NGB"). Colonel Wagner had a West Point classmate working at Forces Command ("FORSCOM") in Georgia. FORSCOM determines what units are needed for certain assignments and NGB decides which state militias will fulfill the actual mission requirements. Wagner and Werley would call and e-mail their contacts.

The 213th already had a subordinate unit, a Military Public Affairs Detachment ("MPAD"), deployed in Afghanistan. Wagner felt certain that the MPAD could sing the praises of the ASG directly to the Commanding General of Operation Enduring Freedom. Collectively, the deployment strategy was in place.

Ultimately, what the command and staff of my unit were proposing made too much sense. The 213th ASG was already on active duty and validated for deployment. The 114th ASG was not yet on active duty and required at least three weeks at the mobilization station for validation for deployment. The 213th ASG should stay on active duty and deploy to Afghanistan in June, and the 114th ASG should stay in non-activated reserve until it was needed for Bright Star in September. The powers that be agreed. FORSCOM directed the 377th to release the 213th ASG from Operation Iraqi Freedom and re-missioned the unit to Afghanistan.

Colonel Wagner called a formation. He requested that Specialist Deabenderfer and his roommates step forward and form a line. Deabenderfer was then publicly identified as the inventor of the term "Demobistan." Colonel Wagner then ordered the Nay Sayers to assume the front leaning rest position. Twenty-five push-ups were then pumped out to the repeated cadence of "Honor First." The 213th would become part of Operation Enduring Freedom in Afghanistan. The First Defenders would join the search for Osama Bin Laden and the rest of the perpetrators of the tragedy of September 11, 2001.

Chapter VIII.

Wheels Up

A few weeks before we left Dix, what would become our higher headquarters, Combined Joint Task Force 180 ("CJTF-180"), had sent us precious little information about our mission. CJTF-180 was essentially the 18th Airborne Corps out of Fort Bragg, North Carolina, with a few Marines and Air Force personnel thrown in. We did not have a warning order, operations plan, or an operations order. CJTF-180, through its subordinate base operations command at Bagram Air Field, Task Force Dragon, simply told us we were going to take over the command of base operations at four different locations throughout Afghanistan and Uzbekistan.

While the rest of the unit went to the rifle ranges for a second time at Dix, selected members of the officer staff began mission analysis in an air-conditioned Day Room at our barracks. The Army uses an elaborate procedure to plan a mission called the Military Decision Making Process ("MDMP"). It requires the development of facts, assumptions, specified tasks, essential tasks, and courses of action ultimately resulting in a plan. Using information the Twins had pulled off the Secret Internet, the ASG spent three days in MDMP.

Task Force Dragon was for the most part an 82nd Airborne Division full bird colonel commanding a Wisconsin Army National Guard Rear Area Operations Center. The S-3 Operations officer of Task Force Dragon had sent us PowerPoint slides stating that we needed four Lieutenant

Colonels to command base operations at Bagram, Kandahar, Karshi-Khanabad ("K2"), and something called "OMC-A." Apart from Kandahar, we could not even find these places on a map. The CJTF-180 website did not even have an explanation as to what OMC-A was.

This was not a doctrinal mission for an ASG Headquarters. We are essentially managers of classes of supplies. The headquarters does not bring any personnel for actual transportation, maintenance, and engineering. Instead, the ASG is supposed to serve as a higher headquarters for battalions and companies providing these services.

Now we were being asked to divide up the 132-man organization into four parts with four separate command structures to run four base operations in a war zone. It was a challenging and unorthodox mission for the ASG staff, but every officer, with the possible exception of the Deputy Commander, Ferd Janze, was excited about the task. Janze was an infantryman who did not like the assignment and referred to it as a "SWAT" (shitters, water, and trash) mission.

The biggest problem was manning—who would go where? We had spent the last 90 days preparing to go to war as an ASG. The Lieutenant Colonels had trained the four unit sections: Support Operations Directorate; Host Nation Directorate; Security, Plans and Operations Directorate; and Judge Advocate--to work as a team. However, the mission required us to divide up our sections and send personnel to four different base operations. No Lieutenant Colonel wanted to give up any of his people.

Jim Buggy put together what he described as the "straw man" personnel chart. Using the required duty positions given to us by Task Force Dragon, Buggy had provisionally assigned every soldier in the unit to one of the four base locations. The chart was supposed to be a closely guarded secret among the Command Group and Lieutenant Colonels. However, word leaked out and there was tension. Some soldiers would not be with their friends.

The real fireworks were between Mahoney and DeMara. Dennis DeMara, who was chosen to be the K2 commander, could not even contemplate the possibility of breaking up the Twins. In his mind, he was going to fight to his last breath to keep the Twins with him. Mahoney was always diplomatic and professional, but he had the audacity to suggest what DeMara wanted was unthinkable. He remarked at a staff meeting that it might be necessary to break up the tag team to accomplish the mission. DeMara ridiculed Mahoney and scoffed at the foolishness of his ploy to break up officers that worked so well together as a team.

As we loaded our duffle bags for the final time before boarding the plane to deploy for Afghanistan, the manning issue was still not resolved. Janze, serving as chief of staff, counseled DeMara on the personal sacrifice necessary for the good of the mission. The "straw man" was put aside until we could get to theater and make a proper assessment of the personnel needs for mission accomplishment.

We gathered on the post parade field for a final ASG photograph on the day before departure from Fort Dix. In several "country briefings," our intelligence officers had told us that Afghanistan had no plumbing or sanitary sewer system. Afghans and their animals simply defecated and urinated on the ground wherever they were when they felt the urge. We were further warned about dry excrement particles circulating in the air creating a serious health hazard when they were inhaled along with the dust. So, when it came time to snap the group photograph on the grandstands at Dix, instead of saying "Cheese," the entire ASG in unison said, "Fecal Material."

The journey to Afghanistan was going to be grueling. The Council of Colonels had decided to spend their last night at Dix drinking and playing video poker in a very sleazy bar just outside the post. We missed the 10 P.M. curfew by one hour and did not get to bed until midnight. Wake-up was at 3 A.M. the next morning to clean and vacate the barracks by 5:30 A.M. The bus left the post at 6 A.M. for McGuire Air Force Base. We boarded the commercial airliner four hours later. When the pilot said the words we had been waiting to hear for 97 days, "Wheels up!", the entire plane broke out in spontaneous applause.

Members of 213th Area Support Group pack up to leave Fort Dix, New Jersey. Photograph by LTC Steven Mahoney.

On June 23, 2003, the ASG was finally on the way to its mission. We began 18 hours of air flight, traveling through Gander, Canada; Shannon, Ireland; Incirlik, Turkey; and Visbek, Kyrgyzstan.

Colonel Wagner had made the decision that Central Command's General Order No. 1 (no alcohol or sex) began in Turkey. So, the ASG made the best of its 45 minutes in Ireland. We made the security officials open up the pub and there was non-stop pouring of pints of stout. Barrett purchased four at one time and drank them before boarding.

LTC James Buggy, SGM Michael Wevodau, LTC Steven Mahoney, SPC Eric Werley, and COL Scott Wagner having one last pint at Shannon Airport, Ireland. Photograph by SGM Terrence Werley.

Little did we know what would await us in Manaus Air Field in Visbek, Kyrgystan. Manaus is a former Soviet airfield that the Department of State quickly obtained rights to following 9/11. It is where soldiers in Afghanistan go for rest and recreation. Quart bottles of beer obtained with "alcohol rations" are served in Manaus on a several hundred foot wooden platform known as the "Boardwalk."

We were dead tired after the flights and had only been on the ground for an hour when SGM Werley told Mahoney and me that we definitely had to check something out. The Dutch and Swedes were having a pool party. In a scene right out of "Apocalypse Now," these coalition troops had made a pool out of an oil bladder reinforced on the sides by sand bags. Somehow they had also gotten a Rock and Roll band to perform on a makeshift stage. The band played "Smoke on the Water" by Deep Purple while female Swedish soldiers drank beer in bikinis by the pool.

Mahoney, Werley and I just stood there in our desert camouflage uniforms watching this spectacle. One of the Danish soldiers motioned for me to come closer and offered me his hand. I was suspicious but was wrapped up in the moment and went cautiously toward the pool. At that time, two soldiers grabbed both my arms and began dragging me to the water. Fortunately, Werley and Mahoney intervened and I made the final leg of the flight to Afghanistan in a dry uniform.

Unlike the other flights, this plane trip was not commercial with stewardesses, meals, and movies. This time we were on a C-130, sitting in jump seats strapped to the sides of the airplane with our duffle bags on cargo pallets in the rear. Our destination in Afghanistan was an old Soviet airfield near the town of Bagram that had been site of the most vicious fighting between the Russians and the Afghan freedom fighters (mujahideen) in the 1980's.

Bagram Air Field ("BAF") sits in a valley 6,000 feet above sea level between mountains rising upwards to 15,000 feet. It has been described repeatedly as the most mined area in the most mined country in the world. It was frightening to learn that we were going to make a combat landing in two different airplanes at night onto the old Soviet runway in the midst of a minefield. For most, this was the first taste of combat.

Mahoney, the West Point aviator, explained the landing technique. We would fly with no running lights at a high altitude. There would be gunners on both sides of the aircraft prepared to use countermeasures if we came under attack. The pilot would then drop thousands of feet of altitude in a matter of seconds in a large semi-circular maneuver before setting down on the landing strip.

Some members of the 213th experienced just what Mahoney had described to me. I did not. My plane had mechanical problems and left five hours late out of Manaus. We landed in brilliant sunshine and were welcomed to 95-degree heat at 6

A.M. It was June 25, 2003, and our active duty combat tour had begun in country.

SSG Ritchey keeping watch over Afghanistan. Photograph by US Army Combat Camera.

One of the first persons to greet us was SGM "Big Jim" Miller of Task Force Dragon. Miller was something out of a Hollywood army movie. He had jet black hair high and tight, stood six feet two inches tall with chiseled features, spoke with a boom box voice, and could intimidate a lion. The Sergeant Major was happy to see us. After all, we were his replacements. Our arrival marked the start of Phase Four of Operation Enduring Freedom.

We soon got to know more about what would be our home for the next six months. An Afghan phenomenon known as the "one hundred and twenty days of wind" had begun in early June. Every afternoon from 4 P.M. until 8 P.M. the wind would blow, kicking up sand and dust. Visibility sometimes decreased to a few hundred feet. The 20,000-foot mountains would disappear. Soldiers would spend a good portion of each evening picking their noses to remove the "dust boogers."

In order to keep down the dust, Task Force Dragon had lined all the pathways with large stones. It was impossible to walk on these rocks without twisting an ankle. One could not get anywhere fast. We carried our duffle bags over the rocks to our tent. Even though Army Central Command ("CENTCOM") had actually written a regulation on how much space a Lieutenant Colonel is entitled to in a tent ("Sandbox Standards"), we soon realized that this "reg" was not followed in Bagram.

Mahoney, Janze, and I were all put in one tent that already was housing five field grade officers. The existing tenants had managed to spread out all over the available space, leaving our three bunks crammed between their bookcases and duffle bags along the side of the tent. There was no air conditioning and the flaps were kept closed to keep out flies. It was hot as hell.

There is no plumbing anywhere in Bagram. This meant port-a-potties for latrines. Our tent mate, COL Davis, the CJTF-180 Public Affairs Officer, told us, "Bring your own toilet paper to the shitters because they never have any. The showers are best at night when you can get warm water. Follow me if you hear an air raid siren." Actually, the shower and shaving facilities were quite nice. They were two story, high tech, and modular structures. The water recycling and heating plant was on the first floor of the large metal container, and the showers, sinks and changing areas were on the second floor.

After sleeping an entire day to recover from the ordeal of the past few days, we were ready for our in-country briefing by SGM Jim Miller and the Task Force Dragon staff. The entire ASG gathered in the dining facility on the compound. We were told that the electrical generators had broken down again and there would be no power. The briefers from the 82nd Airborne Division would not let us open the windows for fear of letting flies in the mess hall. It was not long before the 150 soldiers crammed into the small room started to cook in the intense heat.

Big Jim told us 16 coalition nations were at Bagram Air Field ("BAF"). Soldiers consume 23 gallons of water per person per day. BAF was the largest producer of electricity in Afghanistan. There was a hot air balloon with a movie camera flying over Bagram that Big Jim said, "Could see a Taliban picking his nose from the base of the mountain" some ten miles away.

The soldier population at Bagram was 83% male and 17% female. Some 1800 local nationals were employed on the airfield, all requiring soldier escorts. CJTF-180 had constructed 12 schools and dug 54 fresh water wells. Water was what the Afghan people wanted most. Bagram had 14 surrounding communities participating within its "Adopt-a-Village" program whereby the Army would supply food and clothing donated by American private citizens to the Afghan people.

A young Lieutenant gave us the unclassified security briefing. He showed us photographs of Osama Bin Laden and Mullah Omar, but there was no information on their suspected whereabouts. The Military Intelligence Officer told us that the Taliban and Al Qaeda had consolidated their remaining forces in the border regions with Pakistan. Another insurgent group, Hezb-e-Islami Gulbuddin, known as the "HIG," under the control of former Afghan Prime Minister Gulbuddin Hekmatyar, had formed an alliance with its former Taliban and Al Qaeda enemies. The HIG had begun a terrorist campaign around the Afghanistan capital of Kabul, attacking coalition soldiers and more vulnerable workers from non-governmental organizations and the United Nations. New territorial battles between Afghan warlords were taking place in the City of Mazar-e Sharif in the North.

As part of his country brief, the Lieutenant informed us that many girls had returned to school – disallowed under the Taliban - but attacks on schools and book burnings had intensified lately by some of the religious zealots intolerant of a secular education. Within the government itself, there were still power struggles between the Pashtuns led by Afghan interim

President Hamid Karzai and the Tajiks supported by warlord Muhammed Fahim Khan. Afghan police and army forces were small in numbers and limited in their ability to maintain order. Many Afghan officers had not been paid in months. Graft was simply a way of doing business in Afghanistan. Heavily armed, non-uniformed militia at remote checkpoints collected roadway "tolls" from truckers while they smoked opium, hash and marijuana.

Continuing his briefing, Big Jim Miller told us Polish, Estonians, and Slovakians were using their years of experience with their Soviet neighbors to clear the minefields surrounding the Bagram Air Field. The minefields had caused 300 casualties per month to the local people and coalition forces. The United Nations estimated that there were eleven million mines in the country covering 850 square kilometers. We were told never to venture off the black top when we left post; it was the only area where one could be sure there were no mines.

BAF was also the site of a prison for the Taliban and Al Qaeda. There was space to confine 200 persons in an old Soviet airplane hangar. The military police guarding the facility ran a flag program. One could purchase a flag at the Post Exchange and give it to the Military Police to fly for part of one day in the confinement facility. At the end of the day, one could pick up his or her ceremonial flag with a certificate that said, "This flag flew for Nine hours and Eleven minutes in the face of terrorists."

Chapter IX.

Three Days in Command

I never wanted to be in command. It was not my idea. CJTF-180 said they needed four Lieutenant Colonels to command base operations at four locations in theater. The 213th had five LTC's, but one of them, Ferd Janze, was the Deputy Commander. COL Wagner preliminarily determined on Buggy's straw man diagram that I was to command base operations at OMC-A. Judge Advocates are not normally commanders, especially in combat zones. I was thrilled with the confidence placed in my abilities by COL Wagner, but was unsure that I wanted the job.

After less than a week at Bagram, it was time for the ASG to begin the process of assuming command of base operations in Afghanistan and Uzbekistan. Three site assessment teams were formed to travel to Kabul, Kandahar, and K2 to determine the functions of and manning requirements for base operations. Since I had little technical expertise on logistics, COL Wagner decided that one of the smart Twins, O'Boyle, would come with me to OMC-A. The straw men designated for the Sergeant Major and Deputy Commander positions at that location, Terrence Werley and Major Almeida Parham, respectively, completed the site assessment team.

Map of bases operated by the 213th Area Support Group in Afghanistan and the key cities visited during tour of duty.

By now we had learned that OMC-A was based in Kabul. This location excited me. It meant the possibility to interact with embassy officials and improve my standard of living. I had visions of embassy banquets with white linens and waiters. I wanted to rub elbows with foreign diplomats as we discussed the international politics of the day.

The intelligence reports, however, about Afghanistan's capital were scary. There were many well-known incidents involving improvised explosive devices, car bombs, and rocket propelled grenades. One month earlier, a suicide taxi driver had crashed a car loaded with explosives into a bus carrying German soldiers on their way to the airport to return home to their families. Four members of this unit of the International Security Assistance Force ("ISAF") were killed and many were injured. Based upon these reports, everyone in the ASG thought that the Kabul site assessment team was heading into grave danger.

Chaplain DiBernardinis said a prayer for us after formation on the morning of our departure. "Dear Jesus, savior of the world, please be with these soldiers as they travel into harm's way. May they complete their journey and return safe to us here in Bagram."

A few minutes later, the Task Force Dragon Operations Officer, Captain Eastman, gave us a safety briefing: "Do not leave the hardball. There are mines everywhere on both sides of the road. Keep your weapons locked and loaded. There will be one M16 long rifle in each vehicle. If one vehicle breaks down or we are ambushed, don't stop for anything. Keep moving. Don't be a hero." After these briefings, I was scared to death.

I took my M9 pistol out of its shoulder holster and chambered a round. My weapon was no longer on safe. I secured my body armor to my chest and readied myself for a one-hour drive through a combat zone.

My first impression was that the roads were crap. Potholes and busted asphalt were everywhere. There were no painted lines, no street signs, no traffic control devices, and no shoulders. Driving in Afghanistan was every man to himself. Nonetheless, Eastman drove at break neck speed and we bounced up and down along the battered road.

Then, all of a sudden, we came to a "Checkpoint." I saw an Afghan in a militia uniform sitting on a lawn chair under a piece of galvanized aluminum supported by two wood poles. He had an AK-47 rifle in his hands. Captain Eastman said, "Oh, don't worry. We don't have to stop because we're coalition. He's part of the local warlord's militia. The US government is paying them to keep security in this region. He only makes the commercial "jingle" trucks stop to collect tolls for safe passage through this area. You know, local warlord extortion." I was still scared to death.

Fortunately, one of the Afghan language interpreters, Aziz, was in my Toyota Surf. Aziz had been living in Northern California since 1973 as an ex-patriot until 9/11. After the defeat of the Taliban, he had volunteered to return to Afghanistan to help rebuild his country. I was very glad he came along because I figured we were safer if a local national was in the car.

He explained to me some of the things we were seeing along the way. Aziz showed me the passage through the mountains where the mujahadeen had come to gain access to the New Bagram Road to launch attacks on the Soviets. He explained that the Soviets had built this road to permit high-speed travel and to avoid the many small villages along the old road. Nonetheless, Aziz pointed out several choke points on New Bagram Road where the Northern Alliance ambushed Soviet convoys. Destroyed Soviet tanks and personnel carriers were littered all along the roadway.

Aziz told me that the area in which we were traveling was at one time one of the most beautiful in all of Afghanistan. "Before the Taliban come to power," he said, "the Bagram Valley was all vineyards. There were grapevines throughout the valley as far as the eye could see. The Taliban burned the vineyards. They claimed that grapes were immoral under their radical form of Islam because they were used to make alcohol." "However," Aziz explained, "the real reason why the Taliban torched the vineyards was because the growth provided cover and concealment for the Northern Alliance to hide and ambush the zealots."

Actually, the trip to Kabul turned out to be great fun. After twenty minutes of talking with Aziz, I had regained my composure and became a war zone tourist. I got my first taste of what life was really like in this third world country. We saw camels and nomads. Shepherds with herds of goats crossed the road. It was definitely Old Testament.

All the people we saw along the way waved, and the Afghan kids gave us a "thumbs up". Some people lived in fortress communities made out of dried mud called "qalas". Others lived in tents and traveled from place to place to allow sheep and goats to feed in the few grassy areas near streambeds. Everyone looked parched by the sun and malnourished.

There were no incidents along the way. Captain Eastman and Aziz knew exactly where they were going. We left New

Bagram Road and went from Jalalabad Road to Massood Circle to the security gate at what Eastman called "Chick Motive". I thought we were going to OMC-A, so I asked him what was Chick Motive. He explained that he was pronouncing the acronym, "CJCMOTF", which was the Coalition Joint Civil Military Operations Task Force. O'Boyle, who often jokingly referred to himself as a "Chick Magnet," commented, "Oh great, the Chick Magnet goes to Chick Motive."

The soldiers assigned to CJCMOTF were actually in the process of leaving the compound. The President of the United States, we later learned, had made the decision to get the Provincial Reconstruction Teams ("PRT") out of the capital city and into the rural areas. CJCMOTF commanded the PRTs, and their headquarters was moving to Bagram. At the same time, the three-star general in charge of all US military personnel in Afghanistan was moving to Kabul to be in a position to put more pressure on the interim government for progress.

The name OMC-A was an acronym for the Office of Military Cooperation-Afghanistan. With CJCMOTF gone, the principal tenant at what would become known as the Kabul Compound was OMC-A. The other tenants at the compound included US Agency for International Development, Military Information Support Team, Counterintelligence, and the Military Liaison Team with ISAF.

My contact person at OMC-A was the Chief of Staff, COL Donald "Chip" Bridge. At first, he intimidated me. COL Bridge was a West Point graduate who always seemed in motion. He was a chain smoker par excellence. Even so, I quickly learned to admire and respect the Chief.

I could tell that he was a very important man in Afghanistan, and yet he made time for my site assessment team. He quickly gathered the team in a conference room in a temporary modular building known as the "Ark", which got its name because of its resemblance to Noah's Ark. COL Bridge went right to the white board with a colored marker and began to explain the role of OMC-A at the Kabul Compound.

COL Bridge told us: "Following the defeat of the Taliban and al-Qaida by the United States Air Force and the Afghan militia forces in November 2001, the leading nations of the world assembled some prominent Afghan nationals and ex-patriots in Bonn, Germany, to begin the work of rebuilding Afghanistan. The coalition, more specifically, the Afghan Reconstruction Steering Group, designated a lead nation for each of the five main focus areas of Security Sector Reform. What became known as the 'Five Pillars of Security Sector Reform' are law enforcement, counter-narcotics, judicial reform, Afghan National Army, and DDR (Disarmament, Demobilization, and Reintegration)."

"Germany has the task of training the domestic police force," Bridge said. "The United Kingdom is the lead nation in trying to bring Afghanistan's opium drug trade under control. Italy is training the Afghan judges and building the infrastructure to support them. Japan is responsible for disarming and demobilizing the militias and reintegrating the soldiers into either the Afghan National Army or the civilian populace. United States Army Major General Karl Eikenberry and the Office of Military Cooperation have the lead on building the Afghan National Army ("ANA"). The General also monitors the other pillars of Security Sector Reform for the US government."

Photograph by US Army Combat Camera.

Bridge explained that two statutes provide the legislative framework for the US Security Assistance Program that funds OMC-A. They are the Foreign Assistance Act of 1961 and the Arms Export Control Act of 1976. The Arms Export Control Act finances the Foreign Military Financing Program. This program provides congressionally appropriated grants and loans that enable eligible foreign governments to purchase US defense articles and training.

Bridge further said the temporary military compound was essentially 17 former private homes located near to the American Embassy in Kabul. Bismullah Khan, brother of Afghan Minister of Defense, Marshall Fahim Khan, had captured the houses in the upscale neighborhood when his Northern Alliance militia forces took over the capital city in late 2001. Now, Bismullah Khan and his cronies were leasing the luxury homes to the US Government for $1.3 million a year.

The Colonel then asked if we would like to go to a Fourth of July party at the American Embassy. I could not believe it. I had come from the hellhole that was Bagram to an embassy party in one day. My expectations, however, were quickly lowered. It was not the Fourth of July; it was June 28. The embassy was having a party for the lower level staff and Afghan local national servants in advance of the main party for the Ambassador and distinguished guests. The meal was hot dogs and hamburgers on an outside picnic table. White linens and waiters were nowhere to be found.

SGM Werley, COL Donald "Chip" Bridge, and author at US Embassy 4th of July Picnic in Kabul, Afghanistan. Photograph by Major John O'Boyle.

Moreover, the embassy was a wreck. I would have expected that some repairs would have been made to the American Embassy in the eighteen months we had been running the country since the defeat of the Taliban and Al Qaeda. The impact areas where rocket propelled grenades had hit the embassy building were clearly visible. The embassy had no air conditioning. The rooms in the embassy did not even have ceiling tiles in place. Exposed wires were present everywhere. Other than a banner from the New York Police Department hanging in the entranceway, there was no semblance of America anywhere. The embassy looked like just another war battered Afghan building.

Outside the embassy building were mobile home trailers. Bridge explained that these trailers were the homes of General Eikenberry and the embassy staff. The top-ranked people from the United States in Afghanistan were living in a barbed wire cage. Military Police and Afghan militia forces, not ANA, protected the compound. At the lunch, a lady was selling T-shirts that had the embassy logo on the front and a mobile home on the back. The back of the T-shirt read: "American Embassy Afghanistan—The World's Most Exclusive Gated Community."

After our embassy lunch, Colonel Bridge turned us over to Lieutenant Colonel Sean Scully, the person he had tapped as the temporary "Mayor" of OMC-A, to complete our site assessment. The team was worn out, and we decided it was time to find our lodging for the night. Scully, an Army Reservist from Kentucky, took us to the "safe houses." OMC-A had leased three houses apart from the Kabul Compound and near to the embassy as sleeping quarters for the staff. The safe houses were the nicest accommodations I had seen in Afghanistan. They featured satellite television, refrigerators, and most of all, running water with flush toilets. I knew right away that I had to find a way to stay in Kabul.

Colonel Wagner's plans to make me the first Judge Advocate commander in Afghanistan came to a crushing halt the next morning.

After breakfast, I thought it prudent to make a courtesy call to the OMC-A Staff Judge Advocate, Colonel David Gordon. I knocked on his door at the Ark and walked into his office with O'Boyle. As soon as I introduced myself as the new base commander for OMC-A, a chill filled the air. Gordon, a North Carolina Reservist who had been in theater since November 2002, stared at me and stated, "You cannot be the commander of this compound."

"Are you familiar with Policy Memorandum 02-10 of The Judge Advocate General, dated 15 July 2002?" Gordon asked me. When I answered, "No sir," the Colonel then directed my attention to his computer and punched in the JAGCNet website on the internet. Within seconds, he had the policy memorandum printed out from the top lawyer of the Department of the Army stating that Judge Advocates could not serve in command positions unless they had his approval. Gordon asked me if I had received TJAG ("The Judge Advocate General" of the US Army) approval to serve as garrison commander. I said, "No," and excused myself to send an urgent e-mail to Colonel Wagner.

Before I could react to this bombshell, Bridge caught me in the hallway of the Ark and said he wanted us to visit Task Force Phoenix and the Kabul Military Training Center ("KMTC"). He also invited us to attend the Command and General Staff meeting the next day to learn more about the mission of the office.

Captain David Dioguardi, a California Army Reservist who worked full-time as the security officer at the San Francisco American Consulate, told us to get on our body armor and prepare to travel by convoy to Phoenix and KMTC. The site assessment team then went to see the reasons why OMC-A existed. Task Force Phoenix was the base camp for the US Armed Forces training the ANA. It was a tent village similar to BAF, and I wanted no part of it.

Author at Task Force Phoenix, base camp for US Army
trainers of the Afghan National Army. Photograph by SGM
Terrence Werley.

KMTC was slightly more interesting than Phoenix only in
that it was a former Soviet school for the training of Afghan
soldiers. The Taliban and Northern Alliance had pretty much
destroyed the complex during the civil war and the United States
Air Force completed the demolition. The site assessment team
took time at KMTC to pose for pictures in front of hundreds of
abandoned Soviet tanks collected in one place and appropriately
called "The Bone Yard."

We got our first look at the ANA at KMTC. From a
distance, there seemed little discipline and negligible esprit
de corps. From closer observation, I was struck by the racial
diversity of the ANA as they walked by on their way to class.
I expected to see cleaned up mujahideen. What I actually saw
was a pageant of races from what appeared to be every part of

Asia. I saw Chinese, Caucasian, Mongolian, Arab, and Indian faces.

After returning to OMC-A, I learned that I had a secret message from Colonel Wagner. He had spoken to Colonel Robert Johnson, the CJTF-180 Staff Judge Advocate, and it would not be a problem for me to serve as the Kabul Compound commander. Colonel Johnson would recommend to the Afghanistan Theater Commander, General Vines, that TJAG approve my assumption of command at Kabul Compound. I was back in command for now. The question was, "Did I want to be?"

Sean Scully took me to meet with the outgoing CJCMOTF mayor. Major Steve Johnson was the kind of guy that knew nothing and pretended to know everything. He proceeded to tell me the entire history of the CJCMOTF compound and every aspect of his job. The mayor was responsible for laundry, electricity generators, real estate leases, meals, parking spaces, force protection, plumbing, trash, interpreters, gardening, etc... As much as I liked the idea of being in command in a war zone, I wanted no part of this job.

Back at the safe house that evening, I had one mission. I had to find a way to convince Colonel Wagner that I was not the right person for the job of base operations commander. The difficulty was finding a replacement. Mahoney would be perfect for the job. He was a West Point aviator just like Bridge. Steve loved rubbing elbows with generals and finding practical solutions to everyday problems. However, Wagner had already tapped Mahoney to assume command in Kandahar where he would be with all the Special Forces killers.

My next thought was maybe Colonel Wagner would like the job. After all, he too was a West Point aviator, and General Vines was rumored to be moving from BAF to Kabul Compound. Wagner was constantly butting heads with the O-6 Base Commander in Bagram, so Kabul might be the perfect reassignment. However, I just could not see Wagner doing what Janze had described as a "SWAT" mission.

Sean Scully did not want the job as mayor. And so, the only option left was Ferd Janze. I had to find a way to convince Colonel Wagner that he could do without his deputy. In many ways, Ferd really was the best choice for the position. As an active duty Guardsman, he had run a 1700 person military organization back in Pennsylvania as the full-time ASG Deputy Commander. LTC Janze knew how to impress senior officers and was extremely competent in all Army tasks. Ferd walked with a swagger that immediately marked him as a commander. He was my man.

Using the Military Decision Making Process, I prepared a PowerPoint presentation identifying the facts, assumptions, and specified tasks concerning base operations at Kabul Compound. I then identified five different courses of action with each of the possible field grade officers—Wagner, Janze, Mahoney, Scully, and Moring—in command. I then made sure that the advantages of selecting Janze as base commander over all the others outnumbered his disadvantages by three to one.

The next day, the site assessment team attended General Eikenberry's command and staff meeting. Each of his senior officers talked about the projects that he was presently working on to advance the ANA. When the time came for the OMC-A Staff Judge Advocate to brief General Eikenberry, Colonel Gordon said that he was speaking at a conference of Afghan lawyers and judges sponsored by the Afghan Judicial Reform Commission. Then, he had a dinner at the Italian Embassy to discuss the training of judges in Afghanistan. I knew then I wanted to stay working as a Judge Advocate and needed to find a way to work with Gordon.

About half way through the meeting, I saw Colonel Bridge hand writing a note. He then folded it in half and told the Major seated next to him to pass the message on to me. It read: "Platte—you see the complicated issues we deal with daily." Despite the pressures of running a meeting with a very demanding General Officer barking out instructions to his staff, Bridge had taken the time to give me some attention. I was convinced that OMC-A was the right place for me.

When the site assessment team got back to Bagram, Captain Barrett told me that the top Judge Advocate in theater, Colonel Robert Johnson, wanted to see me right away. I rushed over to the "Head Shed" to meet with the Colonel. I had been told the Staff Judge Advocate of CJTF-180 was a humorless military judge. His actual demeanor was equal to his reputation.

Colonel Wagner had informed me that one day earlier Johnson had given his permission for me to assume command at Kabul Compound. When I walked into his office, the judge had apparently changed his ruling. Johnson said, "I cannot recommend to the General that you serve as the base commander in Kabul. There is no need for a JAG up there, and we need you here." I was shell-shocked. I politely suggested that I needed to talk to Colonel Wagner about the situation and took my leave.

The two other site assessment teams had returned to Bagram before my team. Before I arrived, Wagner and Janze had pretty much firmed up the straw man diagram based upon what Mahoney and DeMara had reported from their visits to Kandahar and K2. They were anxious to hear my report so that they could inform the 132 ASG members where they would be going for the next six months. I presented my PowerPoint presentation.

Wagner said, "You did not pad your mattress too much. But you certainly jerry rigged your course of action advantages and disadvantages to take yourself out of a job. You did not have to do that. I have already decided to place Ferd in command at OMC-A."

What a relief. Now, I had to make sure that I could work as a Judge Advocate at the Kabul Compound. I explained to Wagner that I could perform three roles. First, I would be the Task Force Liberty Command Judge Advocate. I would serve as the personal legal advisor to COL Wagner with respect to issues that impact upon the entire "CJOA" (Coalition Joint Operations Area), i.e. Afghanistan and Uzbekistan.

Second, I could serve as the Kabul Compound Staff Judge Advocate. I would advise LTC Janze on legal issues impacting upon base operations at the compound. In this role, I would perform the same tasks as CPT Barrett did at Bagram. I could provide legal assistance services for the 300 soldiers assigned to the compound. I would be a non-voting advisor to the weekly meetings of the tenants of the compound. I would also be an advisor to the compound Joint Acquisition Review Board, the panel that reviews and approves all expenditures of government monies for the compound.

Finally, and most importantly, I could serve as Deputy Staff Judge Advocate to the Office of Military Cooperation-Afghanistan. I could assist COL David Gordon, in advising General Eikenberry on legal issues impacting upon Security Sector Reform.

Wagner bought it, and my three days in command of Kabul Compound came to an end. The Group Commander was sending me to Kabul. The straw man became the actual personnel assignment chart. The work of the ASG would begin in earnest. Now I only had to find a way to deal with Colonel Johnson.

The following day, Command Sergeant Major Wevodau called for a unit formation at 330Z (8 A.M. local time). He read off the names of everyone in the ASG and told everyone to which base that Colonel Wagner had assigned them. Captain Barrett stayed at Bagram as the base Staff Judge Advocate. Based upon his combat experience in Vietnam, Sergeant First Class Hoffman was sent to the area with the most combat soldiers, Kandahar. Specialist McFadden would remain in Bagram to assist Jack. Sergeant Cramden was assigned to K2.

I had lost my entire section. No one would accompany me to Kabul Compound. Cramden and McFadden cried in formation. McFadden wanted to be with the soldiers from her former Philadelphia unit now stationed in K2. Cramden did not want to be separated from her new "battle buddy," Staff Sergeant Dean Toretti, who would be working the base defense operations center at BAF.

Chapter X

"How Old Are You?"

Everyone gets sick in Afghanistan," said Big Jim Miller, and he was right. Some time or another all soldiers in Afghanistan are out of commission with diarrhea and an upset stomach. There is no clean water in the country. Water wells are less than fifty feet deep and the ground water is contaminated with E-coli. Afghans leave meat outside for days. Soldiers report that tapeworms found in stools after using the toilet are sometimes as much as six feet long.

During my first week at OMC-A, Colonel Gordon fell victim to the bacteria. As a result, I had an opportunity to show my value to him and the mission right away.

Gordon was reluctant to take me on at first. He had been in the Army for twenty-five years and had seen all kinds of Judge Advocates. Like every other military specialty, there were good and bad lawyers. However, Gordon's post was one that could not afford to have inferior talent. He was dealing with Afghan ministers, coalition ambassadors, and constitutional experts. Gordon did not want just any lawyer tagging along with him.

"So what do you know about comparative legal systems," the colonel asked shortly after I arrived in Kabul for the second time.

He was surprised to learn my response. "Sir, I graduated from the Woodrow Wilson School of Public and International Affairs at Princeton. My Master's Degree from the London School of Economics and Political Science was in West European government. At Vanderbilt Law School, I specialized in public international law and edited The Journal of Transnational Law." All of a sudden his interest increased.

"After graduating from law school, I worked as a law clerk to the Chief Judge of the U.S. Court of International Trade in New York City. I then got a job with the International Trade Section of the U.S. Department of Justice in Washington, D.C. I spend five and one-half years representing the Department of Commerce and International Trade Commission before the Court of International Trade." Gordon raised his eyebrows. He could tell I was not the average National Guard lawyer.

I then hit the right chord.

Attempting to redirect the focus of the conversation, I queried, "Sir, where did you go to law school?"

Gordon replied, "The University of Georgia."

"Do you happen to know a Professor Gabriel Wilner at Georgia?" I asked.

"I studied under him," said Gordon.

I volunteered, "I attended a three week course in Brussels, Belgium, on the Law and Institutions of the European Communities with Professor Wilner," hoping that I had baited the hook.

"What year?" Gordon said smiling.

"1982," I answered.

"I completed the course three years earlier in 1979," the colonel announced.

After that moment, I had no trouble with Gordon. He knew I had the qualifications and background to do the job. Plus, we had something in common. Now, I had to prove that I was more than a resume. My chance came a few days later.

Shortly after the daily Battle Update Brief at 0800 hours, July 7, Colonel Gordon came to me and said he was sick. He wanted to know if I felt capable of giving a lecture on military justice to a group of Afghan judges, prosecutors and policemen. Gordon was one speaker in a series giving lectures on comparative law to a seminar sponsored by the Afghan Judicial Reform Commission and International Peace Institute.

The purpose was to prepare the Afghan attorneys for their upcoming Loya Jirga, or constitutional convention. With little thought, I replied, "Yes sir, I can."

I had only been in Afghanistan for two weeks, and now I was going to present a speech to representatives of the country's Ministries of Interior and Justice as well as the Supreme and other appellate courts. Gordon had only given me one hour to prepare. No problem. I had been asked to make oral arguments before judges back in Pennsylvania with less preparation time. Fortunately, Gordon already had an outline in English and Dari for me to look at to see what he wanted me to talk about.

When I arrived at the Office of the Saranwali (Attorney General), I was pleased to learn that the moderator for the symposium was an American. William "Spence" Spencer was an ex-foreign service agent who was now working for a private consulting company hired by the Judicial Reform Commission to put on the seminar. He was a nervous wreck. Nothing was going right that morning. The caterer had not shown up on time, and he was running behind schedule as the participants began leaving the meeting room for morning prayer.

Spence was glad I showed up. He had feared that the military justice presentation would have to be cancelled when Gordon called in sick.

"Tell   me   a   little   about   yourself," he   said.

"Well, I'm a Philadelphia medical malpractice lawyer called up for active duty in March, and I have been in the country for two weeks. What else do you want to know?" I said half-jokingly.

"Perfect," replied Spence. "These guys need to hear from someone with practical experience. Where did you go to law school?"

"Vanderbilt, Class of 1983," I boasted.

Spence laughed and said, "Pleased to meet you. Vandy, Class of 1984. We are a long way from Nashville."

"Yeah, about half way around the world from Music City," I rejoined. "What the hell do you want me to say to these guys?"

"Speak slowly, do not use legal terms, and, by all means, be simple. They have basically no conception of justice and democratic processes," Spence explained.

"Oh boy," I said shaking my head. "I hope I don't offend anyone. I know next to nothing about the history and customs of this country."

Spence reassured me, "You'll do fine."

I presented a lecture on the U.S. military justice system to more than 100 representatives of what, in essence, was the Afghan Bar Association. I began by explaining the functions of the three branches of government and ended with the procedural steps necessary to appeal an Article 15, nonjudicial punishment. An Afghan interpreter, who I later learned worked for President Karzai, simultaneously translated every one my words to the participants who were listening on headphones.

"In the name of Almighty Allah, I am Abdul Razzouq Muhammad. Could you please explain your comment that the American military justice system is not fair," one participant asked at the conclusion of my remarks.

"Please sir, I did not mean to suggest that military courts are not fair," I answered. "What I said was that the military justice system does not guarantee a fair result. What the Army does promise is due process, which means notice of the crimes that are alleged against you and an opportunity to be heard, the right to be represented by counsel, to present evidence in your own defense, hire expert witnesses to refute the evidence of the prosecution, and cross-examine the government's witnesses." I tried to explain the basic rights of a criminal defendant, not knowing if the questioner had any clue as to what I was saying.

My suspicion was confirmed with the next question. "Does the United States Army have battlefield justice?" Fortunately, Colonel Gordon had prepared me for this aspect of the Soviet justice system still in use by the Afghan militia. When a commander satisfies himself that a soldier has committed a military crime during the time of war that is punishable by the death penalty, the commander executes the soldier on the battlefield immediately and without trial.

"No," I answered emphatically. "There are no summary executions in the United States Army." Without bothering to explain again the concept of due process, I gave the middle-aged Afghan police captain asking the question an example I thought he could understand. "The United States Army has been in Afghanistan since December 2001. Since that time, several soldiers have committed offenses that are punishable by the Uniform Code of Military Justice. However, there has not yet been a court-martial convened in Afghanistan. It takes up to six months to conduct an investigation of an alleged crime and perhaps another six months to prepare the case for trial. Soldiers have a right to a trial before any punishment is imposed upon them." The Afghan police captain just shook his head in disbelief.

I was not ready for the next one. "What is the penalty for raping someone who is not your wife," asked a seminar participant.

I did not understand the question. I looked at the interpreter and he shrugged his shoulders. I then desperately turned to Spence, who was seated next to me at the speaker's table, for guidance. He said, "Just say something. Do the best you can."

After a few moments more of reflection, it dawned on me. In this country, consensual sex with someone not your wife must be rape. How was I going to respond to this question? I decided simply to explain that adultery was not rape in America. Thankfully, no one asked a follow-up.

The next question was not any easier. "Could you please explain the intelligence courts in America?" Again, I did not know what to say. Apparently, in Afghanistan, if one disagrees with the government, he is rounded up and tried before some type of "intelligence court" for political crimes. "We do not have any intelligence courts," I replied. "Foreign spies are tried in the regular criminal courts. Government officials that disclose state secrets are subject to both jail and fines after a trial in a civilian court." I answered one more question on why the United States did not try civilians in military courts, and thankfully, Spence could see that I had had enough.

Spence called for a break and reminded everyone that it was time for prayer. I got off the podium and went outside for air. By now the temperature was over 100 degrees, and I could not stand the heat, literally or figuratively, anymore. Nonetheless, several very old-looking men wearing robes came up to me and started asking questions. I had no earthly idea what they were saying. Seeing my plight, the interpreter came over and listened for a few seconds and said, "They want to know how old you are."

Thankful for no more questions on rape, battlefield justice, and intelligence courts, I smiled and said, "That's easy. I am 46." The gray-haired and sun-withered men, whom I was sure were older than I, just shook their heads and laughed. I asked the interpreter what was so funny. He grinned and said, "This man is 38 and he is 43. They thought you were too young to be a lawyer in America."

I decided to stick around for the next speaker who just happened to be the Chief Justice of the Afghan Supreme Court, Fazi Shinwari. What an education. The Chief Justice was an eighty-year old Mullah who had received his "legal" training at a Madrasa, or religious school. He announced that the new Constitution for Afghanistan would be based on Shari'a law, the Koran. The Chief Justice then launched into an explanation of how one provision of Islamic law, requiring the hands of thieves to be cut off, was consistent with international standards for human rights.

"If I enter your home, that is not theft," explained the Chief Justice. "If I take something from your home, that is not theft. If I am found with your goods on the street, then that is not theft. I may be borrowing something from you with the intent to return it to you when I am done. If I take your goods to my property grounds, I am not guilty of theft. Only if I take your possessions into my home have I committed the crime of theft. If so, then I should have my hands cut off as is the dictate of the law."

I walked out of the symposium asking myself why I had even bothered to explain the concept of due process as it applied to an Article 15 hearing.

Chapter XI.

"They Do Not Even Know How To Use A Toilet"

The last best hope for peace in Afghanistan is the Afghan National Army or ANA. For the last 23 years, this Central Asian country has been at war. From 1979 to 1991, the mujahideen fought a war against the former Soviet Army to rid a foreign superpower from its borders. From 1992 until October 2001, the local militias fought against each other in a very bloody civil war. After the defeat of the Taliban, the militias remained in power in various regions throughout the country. At present, it is up to the International Security Assistance Force ("ISAF") and the coalition forces to keep the militias and their commanders at bay. When the peacekeepers leave, it will be the task of the ANA to preserve democracy in Afghanistan.

The idea behind the ANA is to replace the tribal and regional militias with a truly professional national army. The ANA will be composed of individuals (males) from all religions, races, tribes, and regions of Afghanistan. The ANA should provide a sense of national unity and common purpose. The ANA will return individuals to their home communities with a national perspective and a capacity for tolerance of diversity. In the summer of 2003, the ethnic composition of the ANA was 42% Tajik, 39% Pashtun, 10% Hazara, 5% Uzbek, and 4% all others. This demographic was roughly comparable to the country as a whole.

"The Afghan National Army shall be established," said Afghan President Hamid Karzai on December 2, 2002. In accordance with the agreement reached in Bonn, Germany, the ANA would consist of four major commands, would not exceed 70,000 men, would have promotion based upon individual merit, and maintain an ethnic balance. The civilian government would control the military and determine its strategic vision. This vision included a fighting force capable of securing the national government and projecting power throughout the provinces. It was not designed to repel an attack from Iran or Pakistan.

President Hamid Karzai receives the Afghan colors from a soldier from the Afghan National Army. Photograph by US Army Combat Camera.

The ANA had to be disciplined and professional, affordable and sustainable. It would cost the US government $458 million in its first year. The task of recruiting and training the ANA was that of the Afghan Ministry of Defense and OMC-A. The staff of OMC-A included members from all four services of the US military along with coalition assistance. The British and French train the officers and non-commissioned officers at the Kabul Military Training Center ("KMTC"), the old Soviet military school that was nearly leveled by the US Air Force in the war with the Taliban.

At the request of the US government, fifteen countries had donated equipment to the ANA. Most of it was used Soviet tanks and weapons abandoned by East European countries trying to get rid of their outdated inventories.

Training the ANA was anything but easy. The new government was asking these Afghan volunteers to leave their homes and villages for $50 per month and live at an old Soviet brigade base a few miles north of Kabul called Pol-e-Charkhi. Most of the recruits were illiterate and spoke different languages. American soldiers had to train the Afghans on how to use a toilet and sleep in a bed. ANA soldiers refused to wear eyeglasses because the spectacles were signs of weakness in their culture. ANA recruits frequently went AWOL for planting season and religious holidays, taking their newly issued equipment with them.

On only my second weekend with OMC-A, I went along with Major General Eikenberry on a recruiting trip for the ANA to the town of Shihbergan in Jawzan Province. My responsibility on the trip was to serve as an escort for Professor Quadir Amiryar, a member of the Afghan Judicial Reform Commission ("JRC"). Dr. Amiryar was an Afghan ex-patriot who left his native land in 1973 at the time of the "revolution" that ended the monarchy. Ever since that time, Amiryar, the former vice president of Kabul University, had been teaching international relations at George Washington University in Washington, D.C. When September 11 rocked the world, the professor volunteered to return to his homeland to work on judicial reform in Afghanistan.

Amiryar had previously served the cause of world peace. When the Soviet Union dismantled its empire and allowed its former republics to gain independence, the professor had gone to Tajikistan and Uzbekistan to author a bill of rights for those countries. Now Amiryar was earning $2000 per month on the JRC in Afghanistan. The professor is an extremely soft-spoken and gentle man. His strength of conviction and vitality defied his sixty-five years of age. It was a pleasure to be in his presence for the day.

The C-130 flight from Kabul International Airport to Mazar-e-Sharif ("MES") was grueling with the combination of heat, noise, and cramped conditions. The only interesting aspect of the air travel was the fact that I had no better accommodations than the German, British, Italian, American, and Japanese ambassadors. All of us were sitting on a jump seat strapped to the side of the propeller aircraft with plugs in our ears. General Eikenberry sat up front with the pilot as was his custom.

When we touched down in MES, one would have thought that the President of the United States was on board the C-130. Thousands of local Afghans stood on top of the control tower and along the protective fences at the airport. Twenty Toyota SUV's and Land Rovers were waiting to whisk us away. We hurriedly played "Musical Chairs" with the cars and found empty seats as security forces on the tarmac hurriedly pushed us along. I found Amiryar and the German Ambassador in my vehicle.

We then began an 85 miles per hour journey between MES and Shihbergan through the ancient "silk road" city of Balkh. Our driver, one of the governor's security guards, told us that Balkh was the oldest city in Afghanistan and was once the principal stopping place on the trade route between China and Turkey. I was impressed with the appearance of agriculture and a natural gas pipeline in this part of Afghanistan. The Soviets had built the pipeline to exploit one of the few natural resources of the country. Children and donkeys worked the fields whose primary crop was cotton. The green farmlands were a welcome change to the dust and barren clay around Kabul and Bagram.

The convoy stopped just outside Shihbergan at a cemetery. Our driver explained that the graveyard was the final resting place for over 3000 Northern Alliance militiamen who had fought against the Taliban. A group of children all colorfully dressed in robes greeted our party at the gates to the cemetery. General Eikenberry and the ambassadors listened attentively as the children sang a lovely native song.

After the singing, a young boy wearing a freshly pressed white shirt and black pants approached me. He seemed awestruck by my uniform and height. You see most American soldiers are much taller and heavier than the average Afghan. He wanted to shake my hand. I offered my hand and he said, "Howdy!"

We then jumped in the cars and once again traveled at an unsafe speed into Shihbergan. This time we were taken into what appeared to be a police compound surrounding some form of civic building. By now the temperature was over 120 degrees and my uniform was sticking to my skin under the Interceptor Body Armor.

What was worse was that I was afraid. As soon as the cars entered the compound, a local mob stormed through the gates looking for an entrance to the auditorium and the seats inside. I tried to stay with Amiryar, but he was gone. A minute later, I caught a glimpse of him tiptoeing through the muddy garden to a side entrance of the civic building. Afghan men, women, and children were all around me. If they had wanted my weapon, then there was little I could have done to stop them. I was shoulder to shoulder with the mob.

I pushed my way to the front entrance of the civic center. Amiryar had already found a seat in the second row. The local police dislodged some elder Afghans to give me a seat in the front row. I later learned that it is customary for Afghans to yield their seats to American soldiers, and it was rude for me to refuse to sit down. I was totally exhausted. Fortunately, there was a bottle of water in front of me. I had sweated out every ounce of water in my body. The heat and crowds had totally drained me of all my energy.

The only speeches I understood were those of the provincial governor and General Eikenberry. The Japanese and Italian ambassadors had not bothered to bring translators. The Governor said all the right things for his coalition audience:

(1)   The US Army had given the province security.

(2)   Afghanistan needed the ANA to create a new nation built upon the respect for human rights and the diversity of the culture.

(3)   All Afghan parents should send their sons to national service with the ANA.

Even though the German and British ambassadors had not yet spoken, the Governor then told the crowd that it was time to retreat for prayer and the meeting was adjourned.

The twenty-vehicle convoy then bounced around the streets of Shihbergan to what appeared to be a medieval fort outside of town. I later learned that this place was where the US Special Forces and CIA imprisoned the Taliban. During the interrogations that followed, American John Walker Lindh was found among the detainees.

What came next was a scene right out of a Cecile B. De Mille movie. We were driven to a hillside with tens of thousands of Afghan males standing side by side on the incline in rows. Some were wearing militia uniforms. Most were simply wearing their everyday robes, turbans, and sandals. There was no shade, and the noon sun was at its apogee. All were waiting for the governor and the local militia leader.

The crowd sat for the Governor's remarks, but sprang to their feet when the warlord, General Abdul Rashid Dostum, walked up the steps to a platform with a lectern. I have no idea what the militia commander said. Amiryar had taken a seat with the ambassadors and no one in my immediate vicinity knew Dari. However, what I saw required no translation. The militia leader apparently asked the multitude, "Who among you is ready to join the ANA" and the entire mountain moved. Ten thousand men took ten steps forward in unison. It appeared that the recruiting trip had been a success or a well-orchestrated show for the Americans.

We were next treated to lunch in the governor's palace. There was definitely a distinction between the haves and have-nots in Afghanistan. The palace grounds took up over six city blocks. White stucco walls twenty feet high rimmed the perimeter. Inside were governmental buildings and the official residence. It was the first time I had seen a swimming pool filled with water in the country. This one had an elaborate set of fountains spraying water thirty feet in the air.

I had achieved the goal I had set for myself when I left the dust and grime of Bagram—I had a table set with white linens and attended to by waiters. The food was strange to me but plentiful and, most of all, the palace had air conditioning. The British ambassador's security guard told me that the day's entree was cows' knuckles.

The governor's guests were then taken to a huge hall in the palace that was five times as long as it was wide. The dignitaries sat at one end, and sofas and chairs lined the sides. All of sudden, it appeared that the entire Shihbergan Chamber of Commerce entered the room and took seats side by side on the floor. The women went to the very back of the hall. By now, there was no floor space left anywhere in the room.

The British officer in charge of the local Provincial Reconstruction Team spoke first. For a Brit, he seemed very intimidated by the crowd. The Lieutenant Colonel stumbled through his remarks on his plan for rebuilding the civic infrastructure in the region.

After the German ambassador spoke to the assembly, a very curious thing happened. Members of the audience went to the front of the room and began speaking to the governor and his honored guests. It appeared to me that the local denizens were presenting their petitions to the governor for his decision. I asked Amiryar, who was seated next to me on the sofa, what was going on. He said, "Typical third world politics. The people are telling the governor how great he is so that the visitors will be impressed and keep him in power."

One middle aged lady not wearing a burqa or veil, however, had the courage to suggest that women should be permitted to join the ANA. I could see the local men in the audience show embarrassment at the statement and scoff at it. The governor sat expressionless. General Eikenberry decided to seize the moment. He jumped to his feet and announced that he appreciated the woman's comment. The OMC-A Chief then noted that a female pilot had flown the VIP party to MES. His enthusiasm was met with dead silence.

Chapter XII

Big Day For The Judge

"Come on and get your bulletproof vest, I want you to drive me to the Asia Foundation," said Colonel Gordon. I had no idea where we were going. There are so many nongovernmental organizations ("NGO"'s) in Afghanistan one can hardly walk down any Kabul street without running into one of them. These "Do-gooders" come from every civilized country and operate with little to no coordination with one another.

The Asia Foundation ("TAF"), Gordon explained to me, was largely funded by the US Agency for International Development ("USAID"), which, in turn, had some relation to the State Department. For reasons unknown to me, someone had given TAF the responsibility of overseeing the Constitutional Loya Jirga ("CLJ") in Afghanistan. Colonel Gordon and I were going to a weekly meeting of this NGO with other Americans to find out what was happening with the drafting of the new Afghan constitution.

On July 20, Gordon and I met the team at TAF: Michele Brant, Constitutional Loya Jirga ("CLJ")(Grand Council) Procedures; Professor Yash Pal Ghai, constitutional technical expert; Walter Odaro, data analysis; Larry Sampler, consultant; and Barbara Smith, program manager. Sitting around a tablecloth covered conference table in the rented offices of TAF, Michele Brant, a good-looking woman in her mid-thirties, explained that Afghanistan had already had an Emergency Loya Jirga ("ELJ"). This temporary assembly of Afghan delegates had resulted in a decree concerning the constitutional process. The decree identified the categories of persons and criteria necessary to be a candidate for the CLJ. The criteria included age 18, basic literacy, and Afghan citizenship.

Michele read from the decree: "Senior government officials including governors, deputy governors, district administrators, mayors, army, police and National Security Directorate personnel are not eligible to participate in the Constitutional Loya Jirga." I was shocked. How could Afghanistan have a constitutional convention without these people present? I did not know what to say. Furthermore, I did not even know whether I was permitted to say anything. *Had Colonel Gordon brought me to the meeting as a chauffeur, scribe, or participant?*

I barged right in. "Excuse me, how do the people of Afghanistan expect their leaders to support the new constitution and have some ownership of it if they are going to exclude their senior government officials from the CLJ?" I asked. Michele did not seem to mind the interruption or consider the question impudent. She responded, "The idea simply is to exclude the Commanders."

I had not been in Afghanistan for long, but I knew that the term "Commanders" was code for "Warlords." Apparently, some of the senior government officials were Warlords. Michele went on, "We do not think that we can have a convention that expresses the will of the people if the Commanders are present. The delegates will not speak their mind if their Warlord is watching over them. Believe me, the commanders will find a way to get their views known." Her explanation made sense.

Michele then told us about the composition of the delegates to the CLJ. "Women shall elect two members from every province through secret ballot. Refugees in Iran and Pakistan shall elect and introduce twenty-four members through broad consultations. Internally displaced people located in the provinces of Kandahar, Herat and Helmand shall participate in provincial gatherings and elect a total of six members. Kuchis, who are nomads, shall assemble in locations identified in consultations with their leaders and elect nine members. Hindus and Seiks shall elect three of their representatives. President Karzai will appoint 50 members of the CLJ, of whom twenty-five will be eligible women. The other twenty-five members picked by Karzai will come from among legal scholars, specialists of constitution and other experts."

Larry Sampler was the next to speak. He was impressive. Not much got past this guy. I later learned that this thin, clean cut, gentleman in his mid-thirties was an ex-Army Special Forces officer who had mixed it up in many parts of the world. Sampler, in military fashion, had developed a 5-Phase Concept of Operations. He said, "The CLJ is not an event, but a process. I would appreciate it if MG Eikenberry would educate the coalition on this point. The process will begin on 15 August with the registration of voters for the election of CLJ delegates. The election of delegates occurs between 15 September and 28 September. The actual CLJ is 29 September to 31 October."

Sampler wanted an ANA Brigade to provide back-up security to the national police and ISAF for the CLJ. He also wanted security during the voter registration process. Sampler queried whether there was an Afghan equivalent to the Posse Comitatus Act that would prohibit the use of ANA for civilian law enforcement. Gordon said, "No."

Sampler also wanted to know what the Rules of Engagement ("ROE") would be for the CLJ. He stated that the ELJ had ROE that did not allow use of force. Sampler told us the Minister of the Interior had driven his vehicles past the security guards at the ELJ because the ROE did not permit the use of lethal force to stop them. "I do not want any similar disruption of the CLJ," he stated.

Professor Yash Pal Ghai had seen the draft of the new Afghan Constitution. I did not know how to take this guy. He was from Hong Kong and looked like a combination of Chinese, Indian, and Mongol. Ghai appeared to be over 70 years old and was bald with a huge mole on the center of his head. Michele Brant introduced the Professor, stating that he had worked on several post-conflict country constitutions. She said he had just single-handedly written the new Constitution for Kenya.

Gordon asked Ghai whether the draft constitution had anything on civilian control of the military. Ghai said, "There's nothing on the military. In fact, it's not even mentioned. That is a mistake." Gordon then questioned if there was anything the Office of Military Cooperation could do to reinforce the idea of civilian control of the military in the new constitution. Ghai suggested that a White Paper be prepared for MG Eikenberry's signature on this subject within a few days.

A black man from Kenya, Walter Odaro, was the next to speak. He explained that he had led a team of twenty-five persons who consulted with Afghans inside and outside of Afghanistan concerning their views on the content of the new constitution. Beginning on June 10, 2003, the Constitutional Commission Secretariat visited eight regions within the country and refugees in Iran and Pakistan. The Commission distributed over 460,000 questionnaires to individuals and groups of persons. In addition, the Commission held 527 public consultation meetings and 361 private meetings with local leaders.

Odaro explained that he was now processing the data obtained on 50,000 completed questionnaires and 2,000-recorded interviews with the illiterate. Based upon his initial review, Odaro said the survey participants mostly wanted road construction and security. Gordon asked if there was any question on the survey concerning civilian control of the military. Odaro replied, "No."

Michele Brant then told us that the draft constitution along with the survey results was scheduled for publication on 7 September. She was very concerned that the survey results might be inconsistent with the principles set out in the draft constitution. She warned, "It will be a public relations nightmare if the survey suggests that the Holy Koran is the only law that is necessary and the constitution is not needed." Brant cautioned that the survey results be vetted for political correctness before they were released to the public. She suggested we meet again as a group within one week to take a look at the survey results.

Colonel Gordon was concerned. Afghanistan could not adopt a new constitution without any reference to the military.

Civilian control of the military was a requirement of the Bonn Accords. The ANA had to be recognized in the new constitution as the only lawful army in the country. Doing away with the militias was one of the key pillars of governmental reform. He said, "Platte, I want you to write that White Paper. I will call back to the states to the Department of the Army for help, but I bet those clowns won't come up with anything. We need to act right now."

I had my first major assignment at OMC-A. Gordon obviously trusted me or else he would not have given me such an important project. The only thing that I had written for him to date was a position paper on the proper role for lawyers in the Afghan Ministry of Defense ("MOD"). Using the US model, I had recommended a civilian lawyer to counsel the civilian Minister of Defense and an army lawyer to advise the ANA Commanding General, who would be the Chief of Staff. This paper was incorporated into a larger project to reform the MOD.

As Colonel Gordon expected, the folks in Washington would not do the paper. Instead, they sent us two thirty-page law review articles on civilian control of the military. Gordon wanted a two to four page document that Professor Ghai and the Constitution Commission would actually read and understand.

Civilian control of the military in a democracy means that tactical decisions regarding military operations in the field must serve the political and strategic goals established by the elected representatives of the people. Simply telling the Afghans that this was a great idea because it had worked for America was not good enough. I set out to research the experience of the former Soviet East European countries with civilian control of the military. As a country formerly under Soviet domination, maybe the Afghans would appreciate the lessons learned from Eastern Europe.

Just as I started to work on the White Paper, First Lieutenant Evelyn Burns entered my office at the Ark and said, "Pick a letter, any letter." She was carrying a stack of envelopes addressed to: "Any soldier in Afghanistan." I selected one from the middle of the pack and opened it. The letter was handwritten and did not contain a return address. It said:

Dear Soldier,

Thank you for trying to save our country. I'm sorry that you have to leave your family and home. I hope you come back ok. Thank you for supporting our country. You are a big lifesaver and so is everyone else out there. I hope this letter means something to you because if it doesn't then you are just wasting your time out there. If this letter doesn't mean nothing to you then nothing does. But I hope it does because you are the best. And you represent America. And I wish that you don't have to be out there and that you could be with your family. God bless America.

Sincerely, your friend,

Jasmine Alexander

The letter did mean something to me even if it came from a stranger. I was not going to waste my active duty time in Afghanistan. I believed in what I was doing and was motivated to get to work on the White Paper.

I finished the project in one week and gave it to Colonel Gordon. He liked it. He made a few changes to the introductory paragraph and said he wanted to show it to Professor Ghai before it went to General Eikenberry. "Let's make sure Ghai wants this paper in this format before we present it to the General," Gordon said.

At the next weekly meeting of the Asia Foundation, Professor Ghai was not present. In fact, Colonel Gordon and I met with Walter Odaro and a new employee named Barbara Smith. Walter explained that Professor Ghai was feverishly working on his analysis of the draft constitution and could not come to the meeting. Odaro then gave us an update on his work collating the public consultation results and said he expected to complete his survey in a week.

As Gordon and I were getting ready to leave the meeting, Larry Sampler stuck his head in the meeting room and said there was a possibility the work of TAF may be overcome by events. He had just heard a rumor that the draft constitution was going to be released in one week, two weeks ahead of schedule. Sampler said, "Brahimi," the Special Representative to Secretary General of the United Nations, "is leaving the country for awhile and "Shahrani", the Constitutional Commission Chairman, "wants to release it before the public consultation survey is published."

I asked why. Sampler said, "To make sure that there will not be any changes. He likes it just the way it is." Gordon later explained to me that Shahrani and Mullah Shinwari, the Supreme Court Chief Justice that I had heard speak at the symposium, wanted to suppress the more progressive ideas in the draft constitution which were taken from the 1964 Afghan Constitution. The Mullah and Constitutional Commission Chair wanted to make sure that the new Constitution was a failure so that the only source of law in Afghanistan would be the Koran, and with it, Islamic Shari'a law.

Sampler continued, "And you guys need to get a copy of Yash Ghai's sixty-five page treatise criticizing the new constitution. It begins with the sentence—'the draft is unworkable and cannot be implemented as it stands'-- and then goes on from there." Larry had just instilled a sense of urgency in getting my White Paper to Professor Ghai.

Within a few days, Yash placed the clarion call. He wanted Gordon and me to come to the Asia Foundation right away to discuss supplemental military provisions to give to the Afghan Constitutional Commission. COL Gordon had a few ideas. I dived right in. I suggested ten changes to the military provisions. I also suggested the creation of a civilian National Security Agency instead of a military investigation unit for political crimes.

We left TAF and then came back to their offices later in the day. At that time, Yash presented us with his revised comments that he planned to give to the Constitutional Commission. I was thrilled to learn that he had incorporated each and every one of my ten changes to the military portion of the constitution and had suggested the creation of a National Security Agency. I sent an e-mail to Colonel Wagner explaining the day's accomplishments entitled "Big Day for the Judge."

The next day, the Italian Ambassador to Afghanistan, His Excellency Domenico Giorgi, called a meeting of the Judicial Sector Consultative Group at the Italian Embassy. Mr. Bahauddin Baha, the Chairman of the Judicial Reform Commission, chaired the meeting. Participants included most of the JRC and representatives of the Supreme Court, Office of the Attorney General, Ministry of Justice, Italian Justice Project, and the governments of the US, UK, and Japan.

Ambassador Giorgi then turned the floor over to Presidente DiGennaro. The Italian government had entrusted the leadership of its judicial reform project in Afghanistan to this famous judge. DiGennaro had gained international notoriety as a Mafia prosecutor and then judge. He had developed the idea of the "Faceless Judges" in the criminal trials against the Mafia in Sicily. Judges tried cases behind curtains to hide their identity and provide for their security. For fifteen years, he had traveled from his home to the court in an armored car.

DiGennaro then presented the results of the judicial survey sponsored by the JRC. A team led by the Italian Government had investigated the status of the judiciary in the ten most important provinces. The survey found that the conditions of the provincial courts were very bad, and that the district courts were either non-existent or non-functioning. Sixty percent of the judges had just a basic university degree and twenty percent had only a high school level education. Five percent of the judges were women. There were 2,218 prosecutors, ten percent of whom were women, and less than thirty defense counsel.

Dr. Hashemzai, Secretary of the JRC and Deputy Minister of Justice, then began to criticize the priorities of the international community in the judicial sector. This Afghan ex-patriot trained at Oxford said that the JRC was not aware and did not approve of a program to compile a collection of Afghan laws by the International Development Law Organization ("IDLO") ($150,000 funded by Italy), a commercial law reform project by Bearing Point ($200,000 funded by USAID) and a Gender Impact Review of Laws by UNIFEM ($150,000 funded by Italy). He noted, in particular, that the Ministry of Justice had signed an agreement with another group to reform the commercial laws because they were not aware of the Bearing Point contract.

Dr. Hashemzai was particularly critical about the criminal procedure seminar—the one in which I had made a presentation on the US Army military justice system. "Spence Spencer's symposium was a waste of our time." He referred to the fact that the seminar had cost $120,000, and that the JRC would not have approved the seminar had they known about it.[78] He said, "Such actions must be stopped. Give us the dollars and we will bring justice to Afghanistan."

Presidente DiGennaro lost his patience. The temperamental Italian had heard enough. "How can we trust you to spend the money?" DiGennaro asked. "Your laws are a mess and your code of criminal procedure is full of contradictions. Your judges have no legal training. The Chief Judge of the Supreme Court does not know the meaning of an 'appeal' and cannot quote one article of the criminal code. Your Ministry of Justice is not even talking with your Attorney General's office. Most of this country is without any justice and no protection of human rights. Maybe, with the help of God, Afghanistan will transition into a society with justice and the rule of law. The process of judicial transition in this country will probably take a hundred years. If the coalition does not exercise some supervision of judicial reform, Afghanistan will never have the rule of law and you will continue to fight civil wars."

DiGennaro then expressed his annoyance with the JRC. He noted that the commission frequently had sponsored projects of which he, as the head of the lead nation's justice project, had no knowledge. DiGennaro stated that he was very frustrated with this situation, and asked Chairman Baha how he was supposed to coordinate the efforts for judicial reform without the cooperation of the commission.

Mr. Baha thanked DiGennaro for his efforts and asked him not to be angry.

The meeting was getting out of hand. The Ambassador called an end to the session and said the participants would return to work again tomorrow after a cooling off period.

The next day, a smaller group assembled with only the key players from each organization present. Mr. Baha commented that "DiGennaro's continued actions were not good for us," and that the Judicial Reform Commission had no information on DiGennaro's work in creating a streamlined criminal procedure code. "DiGennaro needs to propose things to the Judicial Reform Commission first. He is feeding the non-cooperation with the Supreme Court, Ministry of Justice, and Office of the Attorney General."

Dr. Hashemzai added, "Afghanistan needs the assistance of international experts. However, it is not acceptable for international actors to try to impose their legal concepts upon Afghans." He said the role of the international experts was to review the Ministry of Justice's revisions of Afghan law for compliance with international standards, and it was the role of the Judicial Reform Commission to ensure that the new laws comply with Afghan legal traditions.

Ambassador Giorgi felt the criticism of DiGennaro and the streamlined code of criminal procedure was unfair. He emphasized to the group, "To be clear, I sign the checks, not DiGennaro. I deal with the Afghan institutions, not DiGennaro." Nonetheless, he stated that that the Judicial Reform Commission needs to take into account what DiGennaro was trying to convey to them. "DiGennaro is one of the most experienced judges in the world, having been a Mafia prosecutor and President of the Italian Supreme Court. DiGennaro has great experience—I suggest you use it."

Suddenly, the cell phone of the Minister of Justice was ringing. Minister Karimi was being summoned to the Presidential Palace to meet with Hamid Karzai. He excused himself and left. Ambassador Giorgi knew the reason for the phone call to Karimi. Giorgi told the group that President Karzai had received a phone call from US Secretary of State Colin Powell that morning. The message was that the draft constitution was a sham and they had better get something workable. Continued US financial aid was contingent upon the adoption of a satisfactory constitution.

Chapter XIII.

JAG Wars

Colonel Johnson yelled at Barrett, "We got to get that Moring character up here. I don't know what the hell he is doing in Kabul, but you are swamped here. He told me before your unit left Fort Dix that I would have two JAGS in this office. Now, I have no staff and you need help. I'm going to order him up here."

Jack had given me a warning that this was coming. In several e-mails on the SIPRNET, Barrett had cautioned that Johnson was gunning for me. Jack told me that Johnson was jealous of what I was doing on Afghan reconstruction.

Johnson had come to Kabul a month earlier to meet with David Gordon to coordinate Judge Advocate activities in the theater. At that time, Gordon had explained that we were working on the military provisions of the new Afghan constitution and drafting a military justice code for the ANA. When Johnson heard this, he had remarked, "Gee, that's a dream job for judge advocates!" It was, and I was not going to let this military judge take it away from me.

The key to success in the military is finding that one commander who will listen to common sense. If a soldier is lucky, that person will be his platoon leader or company commander. However, junior officers in command are usually so concerned about appearances and their Officer Evaluation Report that they do not always do the right thing. It usually takes someone with twenty years of service and limited career expectations for the future to impose some sense of reason to military decision-making. In my case, I was very lucky to have three full-bird Colonels in my camp -- Wagner, Gordon, and Bridge.

As part of his duties as the ASG Commander, Colonel Wagner made periodic visits to all four garrisons where the 213th was providing support for base operations. In fact, CJTF-180 had cut a FRAGO (fragmentary order) at Wagner's suggestion, giving the Colonel and his newly formed six person staff the designation, Task Force Liberty, in order to supervise the standardization of the level of support services at all four bases. However, there was one problem. Wagner was junior in date of rank to the Base Commander at Bagram Air Field, Colonel Carl McNeely.

The FRAGO carved out an exception for Bagram. Wagner would be Commander of Task Force Liberty and overall commander of three of the four bases: Kabul Compound, K2, and Kandahar. However, he would have no authority at BAF. Colonel McNeely and Colonel Johnson would make sure that this was the case.

McNeely is a Kansas farm boy who has a dangerous combination of personality characteristics. He has a tremendous ego and suffers from insecurity. These traits usually blend together to make a tyrant, and McNeely was no exception. Shortly after the 213th personnel left Bagram for the three other bases in theater, McNeely called a meeting of the forty-four ASG personnel remaining at Bagram that he had inherited from Colonel Wagner and now controlled. "It is time to cut the umbilical chord," McNeely barked. "I demand absolute loyalty from you. I don't care what you did in the past or whom you reported to. You now work for me. Don't ever forget that while you work in this building."

The ASG soldiers at BAF were spooked. There was no "Army of One." It no longer was a team effort to improve the lives of soldiers serving in a war zone under incredibly austere conditions. It was simply a matter of pleasing McNeely. Colonel Wagner be damned.

While Wagner was visiting Kabul Compound, Jack Barrett sent me a memo on the SIPRNET about his supervisor's latest gambit. McNeely, with Colonel Johnson's review and approval, had ordered Barrett to prepare a legal memo divesting Wagner, the ASG and Task Force Liberty Commander, of court-martial authority over 213th personnel at Bagram. McNeely's Task Force Dragon would assume operational and disciplinary control of the ASG augmentees. It was stupid, egomaniacal, and totally unnecessary. I could not believe it.

At the same time I was fighting to continue working at OMC-A, Wagner was under attack by a devious O-6 while he was away from his duty station at BAF and visiting me in Kabul. I told Colonel Wagner about Jack's memo. I feared that my commander was going to go ballistic. He did not. In fact, he became quite solemn. He paused, shook his head, and stated, "If it were not for the O-6's, then this would not be such a bad war."

Fortunately, I did not have to give the Colonel reasons why I should remain in Kabul. Wagner took up my cause and said, "The ASG came to Operation Enduring Freedom to make the greatest contribution at the highest level. It is evident to me that that you are making that contribution here at OMC-A. There is no reason that you should not continue to serve in Kabul." I breathed a sigh of relief.

Colonel Bridge then walked into the room. Bridge and Wagner were both aviators from West Point. Despite the fact that they had completely different personalities, they had developed a trust in one another. "You hear what the JAG up at 180 wants to do with my Judge?" Wagner asked Bridge. The colonel continued, "They want to send Platte back to Bagram to help work on claims."

Bridge retorted, "That's bullshit. Have you seen the White Paper he wrote on civilian control of the military?" Wagner nodded. "What the hell do they think they are doing up in Bagram," Bridge asked rhetorically. "Do they understand the mission? They can kill all the Taliban they want in Bagram, and for everyone they kill two more will pop up. If they want lasting change in this God damn country and someday to get our butts the hell out, then they have to understand that there is a real mission here. I will write that short-sighted O-6 at Bagram and tell him Platte is staying here."

Colonel Gordon wrote the memo for Bridge. Wagner did a separate position paper on my duty station. He explained, "I did not come to Afghanistan as a commander of a group of augmentees. I came to this theater as a commander of a unit. And, I will place my Command Judge Advocate at whatever location he can best serve the mission of my unit."

Three full-bird colonels had laid it on the line for me. I was staying in Kabul. I was most grateful. A week later, I moved my office from the Ark to an old school house on the compound. Bridge sent me an e-mail wanting to know why I had moved. "Don't you love me anymore?" he wrote.

I replied, "I would run through a stone-filled Hesco barrier for you after seeing the memo you sent to Colonel Johnson."

Bridge said in response, "I did it for two reasons. One, for you, and two, for the mission."

I felt a tremendous obligation to perform.

Chapter XIV

"You Cannot Teach Old Dogs New Tricks"

Take a look at this report," Colonel Gordon said in an e-mail he sent to me on August 15, 2003. The day before, Amnesty International had published a startling expose on the judicial system in Afghanistan.[79] Among other abuses, this international human rights organization reported that a tribal elder coerced the family of a murder suspect to give two young girls, aged 8 and 15, to the family of a murder victim as compensation for the crime.

As a civilian insurance defense lawyer what struck me the most in the report was the fact that the entire country of Afghanistan had fewer than thirty criminal defense lawyers. No bar association existed, and there were no legal aid clinics for the poor. I felt like I needed to do something.

The Italian Justice Project was the offshoot of the Italian Embassy charged with Judicial Reform in Afghanistan. At a party thrown by its assistant director, Dr. Antonio Palmisano, I first met a recent graduate of Kabul University, named Muhammad Hamid Saboory. Hamid was working for IDLO, a NGO from Rome, Italy, as a translator. Somehow, Hamid had located the statutory laws of Afghanistan from 1921-2002 and translated them into English. Moreover, this 22-year old Afghan lawyer spoke just like an American.

We immediately struck up a friendship, and I asked him where he had learned his English. He stated, "During the Taliban years, there was very little to do. If you left your home you could get killed. So I stayed home all the time and watched American television shows." Hamid had never left Afghanistan, and he had learned English by watching TV during a civil war.

Colonel Gordon needed an Afghan with academic credentials to write a paper concerning the custom of compensating others for injuries caused without fault. A few weeks earlier, an Army military policeman had opened fire on a taxi full of Afghans when the taxi continued to pursue aggressively a convoy of American soldiers despite being warned away. An investigation determined that the MP had followed the Rules of Engagement, but the incident left a young Afghan captain of the ANA in the taxi with no use of his right arm.

General Eikenberry wanted to find a way to compensate the Afghan captain in accordance with Army regulations. Payment required the Judge Advocates to establish that making compensation for injuries caused without fault was a traditional custom in Afghanistan. This payment scheme was known as solatia.

With the hope of finding a knowledgeable person on Afghan customary law, I called Mr. Saboory and asked him if he knew any law professors at Kabul University. He stated that there was an English-speaking Professor on the staff of IDLO, named Wadir Safi, with whom he would be pleased to make me an appointment. The Italian Justice Project had engaged IDLO to run a training program for Afghan judges and prosecutors.

The night before the scheduled interview, I sat next to Professor Amiryar at dinner with the staff of the Italian Justice Project. Between bites of pasta, I questioned the Professor on whether he had seen the Amnesty International report. He said he had heard about the report but had not read it. I told him the report said that there was a critical need to develop independent civil and criminal defense lawyers in Afghanistan.

"Do you think that there is any merit in the idea of establishing a legal aid clinic at Kabul University?" I asked.

"I think that is a wonderful idea," replied Amiryar. "The Judicial Reform Commission has identified it as one of its goals in the Master Plan, but, to date, nothing has been done about it.

I am one of the advisors of the Ministry of Education, and I will make you an appointment to visit with the Dean."

I knew that Amiryar had been a university official twenty years ago, but I did not expect such an enthusiastic response. Having already made the appointment with Hamid, I felt that it was necessary to tell Amiryar that I was going to see Professor Wadir Safi the next day. When I mentioned the name of Safi, Amiryar had an emotional reaction. The mild-mannered Afghan bristled and said, "Why in the world would you want to speak with that Communist? He was a minister in the government after the Soviet invasion."

At IDLO the next day, I did not know what to expect in Safi. What I found was a highly educated, middle-aged professor with an open mind and a sense of humor. Safi had a doctorate in public international law and had been the former Dean of the Faculty of Law and Politics at Kabul University. He wore a coat and tie and sported a nicely trimmed beard. Safi immediately made me feel comfortable, and I soon knew we could discuss a wide variety of topics. His broken English was spiced with good humor.

Safi listened intently as I discussed the Amnesty International report's findings. The Professor agreed and told me that independent defense lawyers have never been a factor in the Afghan legal system. Safi loved my idea of establishing a legal aid clinic at Kabul University. "We must get you an appointment right away to see the Dean," he said.

Safi spent over two hours explaining the Afghan legal education program to me. He told me Afghanistan does not have a law school. Instead, it has colleges that offer a curriculum after secondary school with some training in law. Graduation from college is not a prerequisite to practicing law in Afghanistan. Religious training in the Islamic law of the Koran in schools called Madrasas is equivalent to a college degree in law.

The Professor explained that Kabul University had a four-year program in the Faculty of Law and Politics. Students within this faculty have two years of training in the arts and sciences before receiving specialized legal training. During the third year of college, the students can elect to participate in one of three departments. One department is Judicial/Procuratory, which trains future judges and prosecutors. A second department is Administrative/Diplomatic that trains future public officials and foreign service officers. The third department is called the Department of Leadership, a brand new program funded by the European Economic Community to train women lawyers only.

In order to become a judge, a graduate of Kabul University serves a one-year internship with the Afghan Supreme Court. Graduates desiring to become prosecutors have an internship with the Attorney General's Office or "Saranwali" for a year. There was no training program for defense lawyers at all.

I told Safi, "The Office of Military Cooperation is monitoring efforts by the US, coalition, and the international community in the area of judicial reform. We are not aware of any effort to train or develop defense lawyers. In my personal opinion, there will never be any semblance of the rule of law in Afghanistan until there is a properly trained and functioning defense bar."

The Professor replied, "I could not agree with you more."

"Do you think it would be possible for me to teach a course on independent lawyers at the Faculty of Law and Politics," I asked.

Safi smiled and responded, "Of course. Why not?" He did not stop for breath and immediately suggested a curriculum be developed in American constitutional law, comparative law of western nations, and criminal law. Safi further thought that I could lecture two days a week, two hours a day in two back-to-back 45-minute periods.

Just as we were finalizing our ideas for the seminar program, one of the directors of IDLO, an Egyptian judge, stormed into the meeting. "Who are you? Why are you here?" he demanded as he stared disapprovingly at my M9 pistol that I had holstered over my shoulder. As I began to explain the purpose of the meeting, he grabbed a note pad and began writing down every one of my words, repeating my words as he wrote. What followed was similar to cross-examination.

When I explained the possibility of having a legal aid clinic at Kabul University and having American Judge Advocates teach at the school, he became notably perturbed. I explained that Ricardo, the former Director of the IDLO in Afghanistan, had suggested to me the idea of Army lawyers teaching at the judicial training course sponsored by the NGO. He snapped, "Ricardo had no authority to suggest that."

When I stated that I was not looking for any support from IDLO for my initiatives, his disapproving glance told me that this qualification still did not appease him. When Professor Safi remarked that my visit had nothing to do with IDLO, even that did not quash his anger. The Egyptian excused himself and walked briskly out of the room.

As soon as he left, I felt uncomfortable and apologized to Professor Safi and Mr. Saboory if I had gotten them into any trouble with their boss. They laughed and Safi said, "You now know the trouble with IDLO." I was curious and asked him what he meant.

Professor Safi explained, "The IDLO training program is being run by very conservative Islamic Arabs from Egypt and Morocco. They do not want our judges exposed to any western ideology or statutory law. There is absolutely no way they would allow American lawyers to speak to the Islamic judges. You know they purposefully selected the seminar participants to be older men who were trained in Madrasas in Shar'ia law."

Safi told me that many, if not most, of the judges in the training program were over age 60. The Professor joked and said, "You know that old American saying, 'you cannot teach old dogs new tricks.'"

I had read in the Amnesty International report that the IDLO had refused to coordinate curriculum with the Legal Education Center, another training body, which had chosen to train younger employees of the Ministry of Justice. The IDLO had also refused to include any training on the human rights of women, claiming that it was too sensitive for their audience. Further, the IDLO made no arrangements to have any training of independent defense lawyers.

Professor Safi said, "These old judges in my training courses have no interest in learning international law and have no interest in a new constitution for Afghanistan. They think that the Koran is all we need."

Within five minutes of leaving the room, the Egyptian director of IDLO sent a messenger into the room that spoke to Safi and Saboory in Dari. They then told me in English that the director wanted to see them immediately. I sensed there was trouble and told them it was better that I leave. They told me that I should not mind the director and they encouraged me to proceed with their help with the judicial reform initiatives I had proposed at the meeting.

When I returned to OMC-A, I was full of excitement and wanted to tell Colonel Gordon about my meeting with Professor Safi immediately. He listened intently as I outlined my plans for a legal aid clinic and a seminar on the role of the independent lawyer. I also told him about my run in with the Egyptian director of the IDLO. He laughed and said, "They told me that the only open mind at IDLO was a communist, and I did not believe them."

As I left Gordon's office, I remembered what Professor Amiryar had told me a week earlier about the conservative Islamic minds controlling the Afghan Constitution and Judicial Reform Commissions. Amiryar said, "The commissioners long for the nostalgia of the past, thirty years ago, when everything was fine. The world has moved on, but Afghanistan did not. Some of the commissioners have not been involved in the law and the court system for decades. Conservatives are controlling the agenda and they will not even allow Hindus, who fought against the Russians, to have access to the public courts because they are not Muslim. The majority of the commissioners are graduates of the Madrasas, religious schools, and are not academics. Yet, they confer academic titles upon themselves. They absolutely refuse to allow the younger generation to be exposed to western ideas. "

The Yoda(from <u>Star Wars</u>)-like teacher's words continued to resonate in my mind: "The commissioners think that the international donors will be here forever and they will not be. If we Americans were not here, there would be no liberal democratic ideas in the discussions concerning reform. And, even these ideas are not enough. We need someone to advocate them and press them forward. The Northern Alliance is no better than the Taliban in terms of freedom. These warlords should never have been allowed to take over Kabul. They use religious fundamentalism to subjugate the people. If you disagree with them, you die or don't have work."

Recalling these thoughts, but determined to try to find a channel to open minds, I had both Amiryar and Professor Safi make an appointment for me to meet with the Dean of the Faculty of Law and Politics at Kabul University. The Army rule for Afghanistan was two soldiers to a vehicle, so I asked Lieutenant Victor McGee to ride with me to the college. Victor is a tall Black man with a very kind and unassuming personality. He had played football at the University of Maryland and completed two years of law school at Duquesne University in Pittsburgh. I thought he was the perfect companion to go with me to the school.

Neither of us knew the way. For that reason, we decided to pick up Professor Safi at IDLO so that he could direct us to the school. Although Colonel Gordon and I had done some traveling around Kabul to visit the ministries and NGO's, I had never been in the part of town near the university. This sector was completely in rubble.

Safi explained that the Northern Alliance led by the Great Massood had laid waste to this part of the city because it was the housing area for the civil servants of the Taliban government. It looked like pictures I had seen of Nazi Germany after World War II. Twenty months after the defeat of the Taliban, Afghans were cleaning up the remains of a city with their bare hands.

Mujahideen guarded the university. If Safi had not been with us, I do not know if they would have allowed McGee and me to enter the gate. We then entered what at one time must have been a nice residential campus. Unlike most of Kabul, the grounds had trees and some grass. However, the university buildings, built by the United States of America in 1958, were run down and in poor repair. It appeared that the university had escaped the Russian invasion and civil war, but had not been maintained for twenty-four years.

Safi told us where to park the car and said it would be safe. I was tempted to have McGee stay with the vehicle while I met with the Dean so that it would not be a candidate for a car bomb. Ultimately, McGee and I went into the school wearing our bulletproof vests and carrying our weapons. The inside of the Law and Politics building was barren. It had brick walls and cement floors with no paintings or artwork. Safi, with some pride, showed me the law library. Most Americans would have described it as a walk-in closet.

As we entered the Dean's Office, I was struck by his age. The Dean could not have been more than 32 years old. He was suffering from some skin rash and apologized for his sickly appearance. I was reluctant to shake his hand, but felt that manners dictated that I find a way to overcome the ghastly lesions that were all over his forearms. Fortunately, Professor Amiryar was already in the room and his smile gave me confidence.

Following the usual formalities and the service of a cup of green tea, I began to explain my ideas concerning a legal aid clinic and independent lawyer seminar. After the reception I had received from the director of IDLO, I did not know what to expect. Much to my surprise, the Dean, who did not speak any English, agreed with all my proposals.

I told the Dean about a meeting US Embassy officials had with Chief Justice Shinwari of the Afghan Supreme Court. When they presented their written proposals for judicial reform in Afghanistan, Shinwari said, "I do not read any documents. The only book I read is the Koran." The Dean said he did not share that view and would appreciate the opportunity to review a Dari translation of my intended curriculum. If he approved it, then I could begin my seminar on the role of the independent lawyer at the start of the second semester in September.

The defense counsel training program did not end with the seminar idea alone. The Dean further recommended the creation of a Master's Program for independent lawyers. He explained that an additional year of postgraduate training of defense lawyers would put them on an even keel with the prosecutors and judges who have a one-year internship after college.

I then had a stroke of inspiration. A few weeks earlier, my law firm Managing Partner, Mr. Starr, had sent me an e-mail stating that the firm intended to give the proceeds of the annual silent auction to the 213th Area Support Group. The intent was for these funds to be used by the soldiers to buy snacks and make T-shirts and coins. I wondered whether these same monies could not be better used to endow a chair at Kabul University for a Professor dedicated to organizing the Master's Degree Program in independent law and a legal aid clinic. After all, an Afghan full professor only made $100 per month.

Universities in Afghanistan are not familiar with the concept of an endowed chair. However, Professor Safi grinned from ear to ear when I made the suggestion and he gleefully translated my proposal into Dari for the Dean. Amiryar remarked that my law firm was very generous. I left the Dean's Office thinking that I could really make a contribution to the rule of law in Afghanistan. McGee, who had dropped out of law school, said he was reinvigorated to complete his legal education.

Chapter XV.
Abraham, Martin, and John[80]

And who, may I ask, is going to do that?" barked General Eikenberry. It was the biweekly Command and Staff Meeting. Colonel Gordon was briefing the Staff Judge Advocate slides to the Chief of OMC-A. He covered all the regular topics including constitutional reform and law of war training program for the ANA. Then for some reason, unknown to me, Gordon chose the staff meeting as his forum to tell the General for the first time about my defense counsel training initiative.

I had taken my usual place against the wall in the rear of the ARK conference room. Gordon pointed to me with pride and said, "Lieutenant Colonel Moring of the ASG is going to teach law at Kabul University." The Colonel apparently had thought that the General would be pleased to learn that his judge advocates were supporting the establishment of the Rule of Law in Afghanistan by training future defense counsel.

He had miscalculated. Eikenberry was furious. "That is way out of our lane," he instructed. "That should be done by the civilians."

"But no one in the international community is doing it," Gordon responded.

"There should be no OMC-A resources dedicated to this project. We have too many other things we need to be doing," commanded Eikenberry.

To his credit, Gordon did not throw in the towel. "Sir, may I speak to you off-line about this initiative?" pleaded the Colonel. I did not say a word. I was crushed. I had already prepared a curriculum, reading list, and Dari-translated handouts for the students. How was I going to tell the Dean of the Faculty and, more importantly, the students that the seminar would not happen? I could not wait for the staff meeting to be over after which I sulked into Gordon's office.

"Well, I guess that's the end of the defense counsel seminar," I lamented.

"Not necessarily," encouraged Gordon. "I want you to continue to prepare for your course as if nothing happened this morning."

"Sir, I thought the General was pretty clear in there. I do not want to be court-martialed."

"If anyone is going to be court-martialed, it will be me. I will provide you with cover on this." Gordon wanted the seminar to go forward. Obviously, he felt that it was quite important if he was going to risk the wrath of Eikenberry. I felt emboldened and impressed with the courage Gordon was showing on this issue.

The day the seminar was supposed to start, September 10, I got a call from Professor Wadir Safi at 8:30 A.M. "Platte, we will have to cancel the seminar today," he said. "There are security concerns."

"Do you mean cancel the whole seminar or just postpone today's class," I asked frantically.

"Oh, no," he replied, "just today." "You know that it is the second anniversary of the assassination of the Great Massood and tomorrow is September 11."

"When can we start the seminar?" I inquired.

"Next week, same time and place."

This delay was only another hurdle in the defense counsel seminar at Kabul University. The day before, Hamid Saboory at IDLO had called me to say that he could not serve as my translator. The fundamentalist Muslims running IDLO had vetoed his participation in the program. Saboory said that he did not know the reason why, but I think he did. IDLO wanted no involvement with the Western idea of counsel for the criminally accused. I would have to find another translator for my course.

The other setback came from White and Williams. Mr. Starr had told me in August that the endowed chair proposal for a Legal Aid Clinic Director would be voted on at the next meeting of the Executive Committee, which was ironically scheduled on September 11. On August 31, 2003, he had stepped down as firm Managing Partner. He was no longer in a position to influence events. The Executive Committee of my law firm denied the request to fund a $100/month Professor at Kabul University.

On September 17, the first day of class finally arrived. Dressed in civilian clothes with bulletproof vests and M9 pistols under our shirts, LT McGee and I drove into the university in our SUV. At least one hundred students, gathered outside the Law Faculty building, stared at us as we walked past. Many of them, I guess, had never seen a six foot-four African-American in their lifetime. I am not ashamed to say that I was somewhat frightened. If anyone wanted to do us harm, Vic and I were easy targets.

As we walked through the main corridor of the building, McGee and I must have looked out of place. A woman wearing a traditional Afghan scarf on her head, approached us and spoke in English. "Hi, I am Jane Montgomery from Cal Poly. Can I help you?"

"Yes, I am Platte Moring, and I am supposed to be teaching class today. Can you direct me to the Dean's Office?"

"Of course. What university are you from?"

"Princeton," I replied not wanting to reveal that I was with the Army.

"Right this way," she said, notably impressed. She took us to the Dean's Office. Professor Safi was already there with Natalie Rea from the International Legal Foundation. I had met Natalie only two weeks earlier. Someone from the Embassy found out that I was interested in defense counsel and suggested that I look her up. The International Legal Foundation was a private organization located in New York City that recruited volunteers and paid them to go to remote places of the world to serve as public defenders. Natalie wanted to see my first class.

As I walked into the lecture hall, all the students rose to their feet. They had wooden elementary school chairs with attached writing boards. The room was dark. There was no power, a frequent occurrence. I was pleased to see some women in the class. They were all seated together at the rear. I stood on a two by two foot wooden platform six inches off the floor and attached to a lectern. Professor Safi gave my introduction.

Trying to impress the students with my limited knowledge of Dari, I started counting off the three themes of my lecture in their language—"Yak, Du, Se." One male student in the back of the class quickly put me in my place before my translator, Ahmad Barkzi, could say a word. In perfect English, he shouted, "Hey, that's pretty good, sir." I soon learned that about one-quarter of the class spoke English, and I needed to be careful what I said at all times.

The Afghans were unlike American college students. First, they were older. The class age ranged from 19 to 35. Some had started their education before the civil war. Others had begun their college in Pakistan. Second, they were sober and respectful. As they entered my classroom, the students bowed to me and asked permission to enter. They stayed after class each week for up to two hours asking Vic and me questions about everything from the Christian religion to the detention of Al Qaeda at Guantanomo to Brittany Spears. I liked the fact that these academic sponges called me "Teacher."

The class continued every two weeks with different speakers I had recruited from the Army and the International Legal Foundation. Over the three-month period I had been in country, I began to understand the dynamics of international aid to Afghanistan and a sustainable future for the country. I wanted to leave my students with a message that addressed some of their concerns. And so, I gave the following lecture at one of the bimonthly seminars:

Today, we start the third phase of the Independent

Lawyer Seminar—The Independent Lawyer as Advocate for Reform. In the first two classes of this seminar, we examined the history of the independent lawyer in Afghan law. Beginning with a study of the 1964 Constitution, we learned that the statutory law of Afghanistan guarantees the right to counsel for those individuals accused of crime. More generally, the 1964 Constitution and the recently released Draft Constitution declare that liberty is the natural right of the human being and the state has the duty to respect and protect the liberty and dignity of the individual.

We next examined the Law for Organizing the Affairs of Defense Counsel. We learned that it is the duty of the Ministry of Justice to determine the qualifications of defense counsel and maintain a list of registered independent counsel. Further, it is the responsibility of the criminal court to appoint a defense counsel for those persons accused of crime that are destitute. We also learned that there are certain duties that a lawyer owes to the client and to the court, such as the duty to protect the secrets of the client.

The second phase of the Independent Lawyer Seminar introduced you to some of the basic skills of a criminal defense lawyer. We learned how to interview a client to obtain the facts necessary for his defense. We also learned how to prepare a written defense statement to explain to a Court the reasons why our client should not lose his liberty. In the most recent class, you explored methods of asking questions to witnesses of the Saranwal. We learned that by asking good questions we could determine whether the Police and Saranwal followed proper legal procedures in making an arrest and whether there is enough evidence to prove the guilt of the accused at trial.

In this final phase of the Independent Lawyer Seminar, Mr. Ken DeLuca of the International Legal Foundation of New York City and I will discuss the role of the independent lawyer as an advocate for non-violent reform. I will focus on political and social reform of the society as a whole. Mr. DeLuca will introduce you to ways in which an independent lawyer can advocate for disadvantaged individuals — the sick, the crippled, the poor, and the homeless. The seminar then will conclude with an examination on December 3.

In preparation for today's lecture, I have translated into Dari three very important documents in the history of the United States of America:

1.   The Gettysburg Address of Abraham Lincoln, 1863;

2.   The Inaugural Address of President John Kennedy, 1961; and

3.   The "I Have a Dream" Speech of Martin Luther King, 1963.

I have chosen these three writings for several purposes. First, many of you have told me that you are not lawyers because you have not gone to law school. None of these famous Americans, Lincoln, Kennedy, or King, went to law school. And yet, like all of you in this classroom, these three men were students of politics and law. With the same or less formal training in the law than you have had, these three persons were able to change the future of their country.

Second, these three men were leaders in America at the time of great conflict. Abraham Lincoln was the President of the United States during a civil war. John Kennedy was President at a time when it appeared that nuclear war was imminent with the Soviet Union.

Martin Luther King emerged as a leader in a time when America was torn apart by ethnic differences. The words of these American leaders have meaning for Afghans today as your own country tries to reconstruct itself after a twenty-three year period of civil war, Russian invasion, and racial and ethnic fighting.

My third reason for choosing these three speeches was because of the important message contained within all of them. Many of you have come to me after class asking questions about when America is going to do more to build Afghanistan. Some of you have asked when the international community is going to spend more money to build roads, schools, health clinics, and electricity plants for the Afghan people. The answer that Lincoln, Kennedy, and King would have given if they were alive today is that you, first and foremost, must help yourselves.

Let us now turn to the first speech, The Gettysburg Address, by Abraham Lincoln. Here is the historical context. It is 1863 in America. Immigrants from Germany, Italy, Ireland, and England populate the northern states. The industrial age is beginning to turn farmlands into large cities with factories and manufacturing plants.

In contrast, immigrants from England dominate the southern states. They have very large farms called plantations that grow cotton. The growing and harvesting of cotton requires a large amount of labor. The plantations use slaves brought from Africa to make them profitable to the wealthy English landowners.

Abraham Lincoln is elected President in 1860

largely by campaigning for an end to slavery. He was a man born in poverty. Lincoln never had any formal education. He learned about the law by reading every book he could find. He became a lawyer by serving as an assistant to a lawyer.

Shortly after Lincoln's election as President, the southern states declared their independence from the northern states. The southern states believed that the institution of slavery was essential to their economic well-being. The southern states thought that Lincoln's anti-slavery position threatened their way of life. They formed their own country. Lincoln did not accept their independence and a civil war began between north and south.

After three years of civil war, the South decided to fight one major battle in a northern state with the intent of forcing the North to seek a peace treaty that would allow the South to remain a separate country. The two great armies of the North and South met in the small town of Gettysburg, in the province of Pennsylvania, in July 1863. The battle lasted three days. 48,000 soldiers from the North and the South were killed or injured in the battle. The battle was the turning point in the civil war and enabled the North to defeat the South and preserve the United States as one country.

Abraham Lincoln came to Gettysburg several months after the battle to participate in a Memorial Service. He was not the main speaker that day. The main speaker spoke for almost two hours. Lincoln had written down his short speech on the back of an envelope while on a train ride from Washington, the nation's capital. At the time he addressed the crowd, the country was still involved in the civil war and he was not a very popular President even in the North.

Lincoln could have used the occasion to talk about the great victory that the North had won against the South at Gettysburg. He could have used the speech to rally the Northern troops to victory against the South. Lincoln could have used the address to criticize the institution of slavery. He did none of these.

Instead, in two minutes, he used his few well-chosen words to have his audience recall the very reason why America was created 87 years earlier. He said those first Americans sought freedom believing that all men have equal rights. Lincoln pleaded that those who died on the Gettysburg battlefield would not have given their lives without a purpose. He asked for a new beginning of freedom based upon a government, not of kings or military warriors, but of the common people working for the benefit of the common people.

Now you in this room know the horror of civil war far better than I know. Many of you probably lost parents, uncles, and other family members in the civil war. Both the United States and Afghanistan share a common history in that both countries had a civil war about racial and ethnic differences. After the civil war, both America and Afghanistan remained one nation, not two separate countries. Also, both countries needed a period of reconstruction following the civil war.

I call upon you, as did Lincoln at Gettysburg, not to allow those who died in your civil war to have lost their lives without a purpose. I further call on you, the best and brightest of Afghanistan, to the great task of rebuilding your country. To recall the words of the 1964 Constitution of Afghanistan--liberty is the natural right of every human being. That people, regardless of their race or ethnicity, are entitled to live in freedom with dignity.

We now jump ahead exactly one hundred years in American history. The year is 1963. The United States is still struggling with the problems of race and ethnicity. Despite the fact that the US Constitution and laws guarantee equal rights to all citizens, many Americans of African heritage are denied basic freedoms. Negro Americans, the grandsons and granddaughters of former slaves, are denied the right to vote. Police are beating Negroes for simply entering the same restaurants and using the same public transportation as White Americans. Some Negroes are being hung by ropes from trees without a reason and without a trial.

It is against this background that a leader emerges by the name of Martin Luther King. He is a Negro trained in religious schools. He is not a lawyer, but uses the fundamental principles set out in the United States Constitution as the legal basis for his struggle for the protection of human rights. He does not speak of violence or weapons to gain freedom and liberty for the Negro. Instead, he uses peaceful protests and marches. He encourages the Negro to take a stand and refuse to obey those rules and restrictions that are contrary to the very basic principle that all men are created equal.

Let us now look at some of his words. In the first paragraph of the speech I have translated into Dari for you, Martin Luther King says, "Now is the time to make real the promises of democracy." "Now is the time to make justice a reality for all of God's children." In other words, America must change in such a way that its actions in governing are consistent with the ideas expressed in its Constitution.

In the second paragraph, King explains how this change should take place. "In the process of gaining our rightful place we must not be guilty of wrongful deeds." "We must not allow our creative protests to degenerate into physical violence." King is not advancing war and use of guns to achieve racial justice. Instead, he is saying that the struggle for freedom must be conducted without bitterness and hatred. No one truly has freedom unless all people have freedom.

In the fourth paragraph, King, like all great leaders, reveals his vision for the future. He says, "I have a dream that one day this nation will rise up, live out the true meaning of its creed" that all men are created equal. Further, King says, that he has a dream that one day his children "will not be judged by the color of their skin but by the content of their character." In other words, he hopes that some day all people will have the opportunity to excel in life based, not on their race or ethnicity, but on the basis of their values of honor, personal courage, selfless service, and integrity.

I am certain that everyone in this room is aware of the fact that racial and ethnic prejudice exists in Afghanistan as it did, and to some extent, still does in America. Some Tajiks have negative views about Uzbeks. Uzbeks complain that there are too many Tajiks in the Ministry of Defense. Pashtun fights against Hazara. Some Tajiks complain that the President of Afghanistan is a Pashtun educated in Hindu India.

I call upon you, young and open-minded future leaders of Afghanistan, to learn from the painful lessons of

America. Hatred and bitterness is no way to achieve social and economic progress. The path to security and political freedom has its foundation in respect for the dignity of others. I encourage you to heed the words of Martin Luther King and make justice a reality for all children of Allah.

Our third and final historical document is the 1961 Inauguration Address of John Kennedy. On this occasion, the youngest President ever elected in the history of the United States, Kennedy, has replaced the oldest President ever to serve in the White House, General Eisenhower, the hero of World War II. As Kennedy says, "The torch has been passed to a new generation of Americans."

At this juncture, the United States is engaged in what the historians refer to as the "Cold War." America is espousing democracy and capitalism, and the Soviet Union is promoting communism and totalitarianism. Both nations are building nuclear weapons capable of destroying each other. Both are sending rockets into space seeking control of the skies.

In his first speech upon becoming President, Kennedy summarized the great challenges lying ahead for his country and the rest of the world. He also realized the great opportunity and responsibility that America had at that time to attempt to solve some of the world's problems.

Let us now take a closer look at the speech itself. In the first paragraph, Kennedy said, "that the rights of man come not from the generosity of the state but from the hands of God." That same idea is found in your own Constitution of 1964. Drawing upon the goals of the American Revolution, Kennedy states that the United States remains committed to human rights at home and abroad. Further, Kennedy states that America will oppose any enemy to assure the survival and success of liberty.

In the second paragraph I have translated for you, Kennedy speaks of America's commitment to the poor and oppressed of the world. He says that the United States will help these people help themselves for whatever time period is required because it is the right thing to do. In the third paragraph, Kennedy commits the United States to provide assistance to the world community through the United Nations. He describes the United Nations as the last best hope for achieving peace.

In the third paragraph, Kennedy lists the common enemies of all mankind—tyranny, poverty, disease, and war. He calls upon all of America to join with him in a historic effort to defeat these enemies. Most significantly, President Kennedy says, "In your hands, my fellow citizens, more than mine, will rest the final success or failure of our course." He then utters his most famous lines: "And so, my fellow Americans: ask not what your country can do for you—ask what you can do for your country. My fellow citizens of the world: ask not what America can do for you, but what together we can do for the freedom of man."

And so, my message to all of you today is the same as the message that John Kennedy spoke of 1961. Ask not what America can do for Afghanistan, but what Afghans and the international community working together can do for the freedom of every man, woman, and child.

There are many foreigners in Afghanistan working with pure hearts to make life better in this country. However, not everything that the international community is doing is in the long-term interest of your people. For example, Bill Gates, owner of the computer software company, Microsoft, donated thousands of wheelchairs to the handicapped people of Afghanistan this year. It was a kind gesture. Nonetheless, he single-handedly destroyed the business of the Afghan citizen who earns a living by making wheelchairs. No one would buy a wheelchair from the Afghan businessman when he could get a free wheelchair from Bill Gates. Someday the donated wheelchairs of Bill Gates will no longer be useable and there may not be an Afghan businessman prepared to make new ones. Thus, there is no progress for Afghanistan.

Foreign doctors and nurses are providing free medical care to the people of Afghanistan. This service is a much-needed and humanitarian endeavor for the short-term. At the same time, Afghans trained as doctors cannot get jobs practicing medicine. No one will pay them for their services if Afghans can get free medical treatment from foreigners. Illiterate Afghans cutting hair for American soldiers are getting paid more money than Afghans who have spent years of study in university to become a doctor. There is no incentive for a smart Afghan to become a doctor.

Many of your country's smartest people are working for foreign charities known as non-governmental organizations or NGO's. These educated Afghans serve as translators and interpreters of Dari to English. Some of you have told me that when you graduate from university, you plan to work for NGO's. Some day, the NGO's will be gone, and the jobs with NGO's will also be gone. In the meantime, no one will have developed the business skills to lead Afghanistan's economy into the future.

In summary, be mindful of the words of Lincoln, King, and Kennedy. Make sure that your fellow Afghans who died in the civil war did not perish in vain. Make certain that the human rights of all Afghans are protected and cherished. Do not become dependent on assistance from the UN and America. Be smart and do what is best for the long-term interest of Afghanistan. Use peaceful ways to protest and bring changes in society.

Afghanistan is now engaged in a process that you call a Constitutional Loya Jirga. Just this week, President Karzai released the draft of a new Constitution. In the next few months, Afghanistan will adopt a Constitution and hold democratic elections to select its national leaders. I urge you to be actively involved in these events. Do not sit back and allow the United Nations and the United States to determine your destiny. It is your future, not theirs. Seize the moment. Take charge of your own country and develop your own vision for the way ahead.

Thinking that I had just delivered the definitive speech on human rights and socioeconomic progress in Afghanistan, I stepped down from the lecture platform and awaited questions from the students. Within a matter of seconds, fifteen Afghans surrounded me apparently eager to enhance their wisdom. I was quickly put in my place.

Students at Kabul University seminar on the role of the
independent defense counsel discuss lecture after class.
Photograph by LT Victor McGee.

One of the English-speaking students seemingly
representing the group stepped forward and said, "Sir, we have
a question."

I replied, "Yes, please go ahead."

"We wanted to know if we could have a party after the
examination at the end of the seminar," he inquired.

"Well, yes, of course," I answered. "That sounds like a very
good idea," I responded enthusiastically.

Then came the blow. "And we wanted to know if the US
Embassy would pay for it."

Chapter XVI.

Security, Security, Security

S ir, I think that you had better come to the basement," said First Lieutenant Doughty, the manager of my safe house. "There has been a report of a rocket attack at ISAF."

Although I had heard of rocket attacks at Bagram and Kandahar, this was the first time that I had experienced a rocket attack in my location. Colonel Gordon had to inform me of the protocol. He had witnessed several of these attacks since coming to Kabul in November 2002.

"Get your bulletproof vest, weapon, and helmet. I will meet you in the basement," he said. It was September 11, 2003, the two-year anniversary of the attack on America, and obviously someone wanted us to remember it. Embarrassed to go downstairs in my pajamas at 10:30 P.M., I hastily put on my fatigue pants and brown T-shirt.

Doughty was already in the basement. He had the latest intelligence report. "At 2150 local, ISAF reported that one 107 rocket was fired from the mountains outside Kabul and landed in the top of a sea container at their compound," Doughty said. "When it detonated, the fragmentation injured a civilian worker. There were no other casualties."

"Thank God," said Gordon.

"Any other attacks?" asked an enlisted soldier living in the basement.

"There have been two other explosions reported, but we have no confirmation at this time," answered Doughty. "We are on high alert. Patrols have been launched in order to investigate the source of the firings. The Quick Reaction Force is deployed at Kabul Compound."

The twenty-five residents of our safe house, The Pink House, stood around looking silly in our Kevlar helmets and vests in various states of undress. Gordon locked and loaded his pistol. Finally, at 1 A.M., we received the all clear and were told to get some sleep. I could not sleep. I stayed up and watched CNN and Fox News on the satellite television in the Pink House day room. Within thirty minutes, a banner headline crossed the screen, "ISAF subject to rocket attack in Kabul, Afghanistan. Injuries unknown."

This was not the first time that the 213th ASG experienced the violence of Afghanistan. Weeks earlier, the Kabul Compound S-4, Captain Michael Frank, was in a convoy attacked with three command detonated improvised explosive devices ("IED"). Bored with the routine duties of running base operations, Frank had decided to accompany one of the engineer teams to Wardak Province where one of the Provincial Reconstruction Teams was building a school.

The convoy consisted of two Hummers and six soldiers. The Afghan Minister of Commerce was supposed to accompany the team that day, but for some unknown reason he did not show up at the departure time. Since CPT Frank was a guest on the convoy, MSG Kevin Keefe, a North Dakota National Guardsman, took the time to explain items of interest as they traveled down the road. Twenty-six kilometers outside Kabul, the team passed by disabled Russian tanks and vehicles, Taliban cemeteries, poppy fields, and irrigation ditches.

Suddenly, Keefe saw a young boy sitting on a wood frame roped bed by the edge of the road. The Sergeant had never seen this boy in this area on other trips. As Keefe was watching the child from his driver's side rear view mirror, the first IED detonated. It exploded two feet behind the rear tire and towards the shoulder of the road. Fighting off the severe ringing in his left ear, Keefe swerved towards the right and recovered to the center of the road as the second IED detonated. As he began to accelerate out of the apparent Kill Zone, a third explosion occurred.

The explosions left three craters in the paved road and another one just off the road in a bush. The trail vehicle had a mortar round in its front windshield. Thankfully, it had not exploded and no one was injured. As Keefe departed the area, he distinctly remembered seeing the young boy he had seen earlier walking away with the rope bed now on his back.

Days later, investigators determined that the attack may have been meant to send a message. The Provincial Reconstruction Teams had started paying local Afghan contractors directly for construction work instead of giving the monies to the Ministry of Commerce. And so, the Minister could not take his cut of the US dollars before giving the remaining cash to the contractors. He may have decided not to accompany the convoy team that morning for a reason.

Some of the worst fighting in Afghanistan occurred during August-September 2003. There were frequent reports that the Taliban was regrouping in the South and East along the Pakistani border. During this time period, coalition forces with some help from the ANA killed hundreds of Taliban and some Al Qaeda in the mountains outside Kandahar. The United Nations Special Representative to Afghanistan, Lakdar Brahimi, commented at a meeting of the security sector representatives, "The fighting phase is not finished. I have become more concerned in the last few weeks than I have been for a long time."

Colonel Gordon had fallen sick again, and once more I had an opportunity for a unique experience. The US Central Command Planning team was in Kabul, and they wanted to visit with Brahimi. The first stop on their agenda, however, was the Italian Justice Project. Since I was the only one at OMC-A who knew how to get there, I led the team of international field grade officers from Korea, Pakistan, Germany, Australia, France, New Zealand, and Norway to see the Italians at their compound.

I then got to accompany the delegation on their interview with Ambassador Brahimi. He had been serving as the senior

UN envoy to Afghanistan since October of 2001, with overall authority for the organization's humanitarian and political work in the country. Brahimi is a sixty-something, gray-haired Algerian with glasses. On the day of our visit, he was wearing a blue suit with a white shirt and no tie. In theory, other than President Karzai, he was supposed to be the most important man in all of Afghanistan. One week earlier, terrorists had killed Brahimi's counterpart in Iraq at the UN compound in Baghdad.[81] Security was tight.

After the usual refreshments were served in the UN conference room, the Central Command team leader from Germany requested that Brahimi speak on the Loya Jirga, national elections, and DDR. "What has been done compared to what needs to be done is very little," Brahimi responded. "The Charter given to us from the UN is very broad. And yet, the Bonn Agreement has given us specific tasks. Security will affect absolutely everything. And, the security status is not good."

Speaking on the Constitution, Brahimi said, "We are very close to getting a text which is acceptable to most. Postponing the Constitutional Loya Jirga from October until December is a setback, but should not be a detriment to the process. The next few days are critical in determining the basic institutions of the draft constitution, houses of Parliament, President or Prime Minister, et cetera."

I could not believe that I was sitting ten feet away from the point man for the UN in Afghanistan. I sipped my cup of green tea and took copious notes. I had no official reason to be in the room.

Brahimi continued, "Security problems in only one province could upset the entire process. It is no secret that the entire security of this country is in the hands of a small group of people from what you at Central Command called the 'Northern Alliance.'"

"Many people think DDR is armed soldiers forcibly removing guns from the commanders," commented Brahimi. "DDR is an agreement to surrender weapons in exchange of money and jobs. In order for that to occur, there must be reform of the Ministry of Defense. The present ministry is no more than a faction of the militia that was closest to Kabul when the US began military operations after September 11. Disarming the militia will only occur when the MOD is more representative of the entire country. Given the border situation with Pakistan now, disarming these people may actually help, rather than hinder, the Taliban. And, therefore, again, the watch word is security, security, security."

Knowing that he had a captive audience, Brahimi then turned his focus on ISAF. "We need 10,000 troops right now to expand the role of ISAF outside Kabul. We have five times the amount of peacekeepers per square mile in Bosnia and Kosovo than we do here. Killing Taliban is not the answer here. A strong central government with a National Army and Police Force is the answer. As soon as you build them, you can leave. Unless we get your help, the national elections will not take place on time next summer."

The German team leader was visibly agitated and took offense. He interrupted Brahimi and said, "Sir, do you realize the cost to the German government of ISAF? Certainly you realize that NATO has for the first time extended its area of operations outside of Europe. If ISAF was not in Kabul, the central government would not last one week." Brahimi raised his eyebrows and quickly responded, "I would consider it a very welcome development if NATO would realize that it is here for more reasons than to just chase away the baddies."

Chapter XVII.

Because They Will Not Come

Platte, see what Lynn Ridley of MPRI has done about a military justice code for the ANA," Gordon told me. "It is my understanding that he has had some initial meetings with Afghan generals as part of a working group." These instructions did not surprise me. I had known since coming to OMC-A that one of my principal duties would be to assist Gordon in writing a code of military crimes and procedures for the new Afghan National Army.

Lynn Ridley was a former army officer now working as a civilian contractor for the government with an organization known as Military Professional Retired, Inc. ("MPRI"). Somehow a group of former military officers had convinced the Department of Defense that they could provide assistance with armed forces operations worldwide as civilian consultants. These guys made about $110,00 per year and had a contract with the USG that required them to have a single room with a private bath in a safe house.

Lynn was one of the nicest guys one could ever meet. He had a gentle, grandfather-like approach. I knew that I would like working with him right away. "One of the taskers they gave me when I came to Afghanistan was to write a military justice code," said Ridley. "I am not a lawyer and do not know the first thing about military law. I am glad you are here to take this burden off my shoulders. I will introduce you to the right people at the ministries."

In my own National Guard mind, something seemed wrong. Why would the United States Government and the Department of Defense entrust such an important project as writing a military justice code for the ANA to a non-lawyer civilian contractor? Certainly there were a lot of smart people in Washington, D.C., that would be better suited to spearhead this critical assignment than a former military officer with MPRI. And now, the mission was in the hands of a part-time National Guard attorney.

I said to Ridley, "Excuse my ignorance because I am new in town, but it does not seem that we are the right people for this job." I continued, "There must be DOD civilians that specialize in writing laws and regulations at the Pentagon who would be better than you and I at writing a military justice code."

Ridley replied, "You are exactly right, Platte."

"Well, then, how come you and I have this job?" I asked.

"Because they will not come," Ridley answered. "The only reason you are here is because you were given military orders. The only reason I am here is because I need a job. No one else in his right mind would want to come to Afghanistan during a war. The US Government cannot make the smart people come here. So, you and I are stuck with this project."

Ridley then showed me his notes and the Afghan laws that he had assembled on military justice. Lynn gave me a stapled booklet with a picture of the Great Massood on the blue cover. "As best I can tell, this is the code of military crimes that they are now using at the Ministry of Defense and Supreme Court," said Ridley. "I do not have it translated and I have no idea what the damn thing says."

I immediately took the booklet to our translator, Ahmad Barkzi. OMC-A had a stable of Afghan interpreters assisting us in communicating with the government officials and translating written documents. Ahmad was a 22 year-old son of a former Afghan army colonel with a high school education. Somehow he had managed to learn to read and write English during the Taliban years. He was very smart and, had he lived anywhere in the civilized world, he would be a college graduate and making a good living.

Barkzi had trouble translating some of the words in the military crimes booklet Lynn had given me. He said that he could not translate them into English because he did not understand what the words meant in Dari. I decided to take the booklet to Hamid Saboory, my friend at IDLO. Hamid was glad to help. After quickly reviewing the text, he said, "I know why you can't translate this. "These are not Dari words, they are Tajik."

Suddenly it dawned on me. When the Soviets invaded Afghanistan, they needed a code of military justice for the Afghan army they were training. The Russians did not have a military justice code readily available in Dari or Pashtun. What they did have was a code of military crimes for the soldiers serving in their Soviet Republic of Tajikistan. Instead of translating the military code in Russian to Dari, they apparently used a code with a similar language to Dari that they already had in use. Hence, the Afghan code contained some Tajik words.

With the help of Saboory, Barkzi completed the translation of the Soviet-era code of military justice still in use by the Ministry of Defense. I told Gordon, "I cannot believe that the MOD is using a Russian code of military justice. I thought they hated the Soviets." The Colonel explained to me that most of the Generals now at the ministry were trained by the Soviets in military high schools and officer academies. "It is all that they have ever known," said Gordon.

It did not take much time to realize that this Soviet code was not suitable for the new ANA. There were forty-four punitive articles, most of which called for ten years in prison or the death penalty for the violation of some relatively minor military crimes. The existing code had no rules of evidence or procedure. There was no law for the organization of military courts.

I thought back to a question I had received at Spence Spencer's seminar on criminal law in Afghanistan. "Does the United States have a system of battlefield justice?" one seminar participant had asked me. After reading the translation of the

Soviet-era military justice code, I could see where the questioner was coming from. The code actually said that, during times of war, a Commander could render punishment on the battlefield at the time of the commission of the offense without a trial.

It was then clear to me that Colonel Gordon and I had some work to do in developing a system of military justice for the ANA. Lynn Ridley took us to the Afghan Supreme Court. It was nothing like the United States Supreme Court in Washington, D.C. The five-story building looked like it was barely able to support its own weight. It appeared to be riddled with mortar rounds and hits from rocket-propelled grenades. Inside the building, people were everywhere. Some were painting and assisting with the reconstruction of the building. Others were just lying around on the floor. We literally had to walk over people to meet with the judges in the disheveled premises.

Ridley introduced us to Lieutenant General Abdul Rafif Tahib of the Afghan Supreme Court and Major General Ahsan of the Attorney General's Office (Saranwali). Both men were wearing the tan uniform of the Northern Alliance with red epulets displaying their rank. After the perfunctory green tea and questions about our health, General Tahib, the older and more intelligent of the two men, began explaining the military legal system.

Ahmad Barkzi had some difficulty understanding and then translating legal terms of art because he was not trained in the law. Nonetheless, Ahmad was able to communicate General Tahib's instruction that both civilians and the military are subject to the jurisdiction of the military courts. Holding up the blue booklet that Barkzi had translated, he said that there is a separate criminal code applicable to offenses unique to the military. However, both civilian and military courts follow the same rules of criminal procedure.

General Tahib then described three categories of criminal punishments. They are: Kohobat--common crimes resulting in a reprimand; Jihan--more severe crimes resulting in three years detention; and Generat--capital crimes such as murder and extortion resulting in the death penalty or twenty years in confinement.

He told us there are five types of criminal intent ranked in their order of severity for punishment: (1) criminal mind due to mental disorder since birth, e.g. psychotic; (2) habitual criminal due to physical dependency, e.g. drug addict; (3) criminal act due to the passion of the circumstance, e.g. witness to rape of wife; (4) negligent criminal, e.g. automobile accident; and (5) misdirected intent, e.g. attempt to shoot animal and human is shot instead.

General Tahib then explained the criminal procedure relating to the detention of a suspect applicable to both civilian and military courts. Upon suspicion of a crime, a person will be arrested and detained for twenty-four hours. After 24 hours, the Saranwali must present some evidence of the commission of the offense to a judge. If this threshold is met, then the person may be detained for another seven days. After seven days, the Saranwali must announce his intent to proceed to trial or request a two-month extension of time to continue the investigation. After two months have passed, the Saranwali must request additional time for investigation from the second tier court judge. After six months, the person must be told whether he will be released or have his case tried.

The whole scheme sounded somewhat reasonable to me so I asked General Tahib if there was any provision in the law for a defense counsel to represent the accused soldier. He answered, "It is the responsibility of the Saranwali to ensure that the rights of the accused are protected." *Oh great, I thought.* The prosecutor is going to make sure the criminal defendant receives due process.

Tahib continued, "Minor military offenses are dealt with by the military commander in accordance with the military code. The Saranwali handle the serious military offenses." I felt that we were going to have trouble convincing this General that there was any need to reform the existing military justice code. My impression was that Tahib was generally satisfied with the present system.

A week later, Gordon and I had another meeting with an Afghan military judge. Major General Abdul Salaam Esmat, the chief military judge of the Ministry of the Interior (police), met us in his office. This ministry was in no better shape that the Supreme Court. A six-story office building had been gutted and was completely covered with dust and debris. It had no windows and no occupants. We walked behind this building and entered what appeared to be abandoned servants' quarters. After passing through an unusable bathroom in a winding maze of destruction, we finally arrived at Esmat's "chambers."

I was immediately struck by two observations. This tall, clean-shaven Afghan, had a warm smile and a judicial bearing. His office displayed a poster of the Universal Declaration of Human Rights published by the Afghan Independent Human Rights Commission. General Esmat, wearing his police uniform, greeted us with a handshake and the traditional Afghan greeting of placing his right hand over his heart and saying, "Salam Alaikhom," peace be with you.

General Esmat had met Colonel Gordon at Spence Spencer's seminar and, at that time, had requested a meeting with him to further explain Afghan military law. It was now several weeks later and the two men briefly discussed Gordon's short departure from Afghanistan in June to visit friends and family in Charlotte, North Carolina. I wanted to know a little bit about the General's background. So, when Gordon paused, I asked Esmat about his legal education and experience.

Esmat had entered the Army after graduating from military high school in 1966. After the overthrow of the Afghan King in 1973, he attended the Soviet military academy for officers in Kabul. He was a graduate of the Faculty of Law and Politics at Kabul University. Esmat had been a judge for 17 years and had been the chief judge of the Ministry of Interior for 15 years. In other words, he was a communist collaborator. However, he was quick to point out that he had no job during the Taliban years.

Much to our surprise, the General told us that Afghan military law applies not only to the army, but also to the police and the National Security Directorate. These three ministries were all considered to be part of the Afghan military establishment. The military courts have jurisdiction over police for crimes unique to the armed forces such as disobedience, dereliction of duty, selling a weapon, and abuse of official position. Civilians could be tried in military courts if they committed a crime as an employee of one of the three ministries. Any civilian accused of assaulting a police officer would be tried by courts-martial. A non-military crime involving both a policeman and a civilian could be tried in either the military courts or in the regular criminal courts dependent upon who is viewed as the more responsible party.

Esmat told us that the Afghan military court system had three levels. The Supreme Court has a deputy for military affairs who controls the final level of appeal court for officers and enlisted soldiers of all three ministries. Each of the three ministries has its own primary court or Tamis. There was one secondary court, Estanhof, common to all three ministries. The Estanhof had separate courts for officers and enlisted soldiers. If the accused or the prosecutor is dissatisfied with the result at the primary court, then either may appeal to the second level court and then, ultimately, to the Supreme Court.

The General then candidly provided us with his editorial comments on the current state of military justice in Afghanistan. "The military courts should not come under the supervision of the Supreme Court." Referring to Chief Justice Shinwari, whom I had heard speak at Spencer's symposium, Esmat said, "The Chief Justice is a mullah and does not understand military life or military law. Military judges and prosecutors have military rank and are subject to military regulations," said the MOI Chief Judge. "Their legal decisions are taken independent of commanders."

Further expressing his contempt for the civilian court system, Esmat remarked, "Military judges are better than civilian judges, because they are accustomed to military discipline and honor. There is very little difference between a civilian judge and a civilian criminal. Military judges never take bribes because that would be a dishonor to their uniform. Military judges go to the front lines and suffer the same dangers and deprivations as other soldiers."

As we ended our meeting with Esmat, he commented that it would take time for the courts of Afghanistan to adopt international standards concerning human rights. "Afghans are a different people. The international community can't expect real change overnight," he said.

The next time we met with Esmat it was several weeks later. Once again, he had called Gordon to arrange for the meeting. This showing of initiative was very unusual for Afghans. Normally, the coalition had to provide the impetus for all conferences and steps toward governmental reform in Afghanistan. We met again in Esmat's office. This time he had invited two other prominent Afghan jurists to join in the discussion. Brigadier General Abdul Najib Khawary was the Chief Judge of the Court of Military Appeals, and Brigadier General Sayed Hassan was the Chief Judge of the Military Court of the Ministry of Defense.

At the Court of Military Appeals pictured left to right: Author, Major General Abdul Salaam Esmat, Major Lance Miller, Brigadier General Abdul Najib Khawary, Colonel Gordon, and Brigadier General Sayed Hassan

General Esmat held what looked like a very old book in his left hand and told us he wanted to pattern the new military justice system for Afghanistan after the laws of 1947. Colonel Gordon and I knew about these laws because they were referenced in a 1975 publication of the UN entitled the "Compilation of the Laws of Afghanistan", but we had not been able to get a copy of the statute from any source. We asked Esmat if we could borrow the book to translate the laws into English, but he would not give it up. "This may be the only remaining copy of the law in all of Afghanistan," he said.

Esmat explained that President Karzai had recently put the military courts under the supervision of the Supreme

Court. Esmat preferred the military courts to be separate from the Supreme Court and appointed directly by the President as they were under the 1947 statute. His distrust of the mullahs running the Supreme Court was obvious.

Esmat also rejected the notion of the Ministry of Defense operating the military courts. "The warlords will not listen to the Ministry of Defense. The military courts will have no respect if they are part of that ministry. There will be too many abuses," said Esmat.

The General then looked straight at Gordon and remarked, "I am very glad that you, Colonel, have the authority to make the recommendations concerning the restructuring of the military courts." I started to squirm. We did not have the ability to get President Karzai to approve a new military court system much less the authority to even represent the position of the US government. Esmat continued, "We are not as civilized a country as the United States, and we cannot expect to have a system of military courts as developed as your country."

Gordon thought for a moment and then responded, "We can provide you with ideas, but it must be an Afghan system for the new Afghan National Army." At first, I did not know what to think. These three generals were obviously very intelligent men. *Why had they arranged for this meeting and why were they so predisposed to separate the military courts from the Supreme Court? Were they simply trying to ensure that they retained their relatively high paying jobs when the Americans got through tinkering with their court system?*

As the meeting progressed, I felt like I had answers to these questions. Unlike other Afghans, these generals knew that American involvement in restructuring the military justice system of Afghanistan was not only necessary, but also inevitable. Instead of lying in the weeds and waiting to see what would happen, these top military judges wanted to shape their destiny. They had obviously given the organization of the military courts considerable thought and their interest in reforming the system appeared genuine.

Esmat ended the meeting with the comment: "If we,

together, make a written proposal to President Karzai, then he should accept it. And, no one in the international community can criticize our efforts." I hoped he was right, but I knew that we had a lot of work to do to get to that point. The three generals and Colonel Gordon agreed that we would meet biweekly to write the new military justice code for Afghanistan.

The very next day, Gordon and I received more direction on a military justice code from the new Chief of OMC-A, Brigadier General Joseph Prasek. General Eikenberry and Colonel Bridge had left Kabul after almost a year in country. The original nine who stood up OMC-A back in October 2002 were now all gone. Prasek, the commander of the embedded US and coalition trainers of the ANA at Task Force Phoenix, would temporarily take command until such time as a new two-star general could be found for OMC-A.

BG Prasek was a short man with grey hair and aviator glasses. His sense of humor and easy-going manner would be a welcome change to the brusque and frantic style of Eikenberry. Instead of plotting a precise course for the leadership of the ANA as Eikenberry would have done, Prasek remarked at this first Command and Staff meeting: "If we make all the decisions for the ANA and do not let them make mistakes and learn from them, they will grow dependent upon us and we will never leave this country." Prasek wanted the group working on reform of the Ministry of Defense to begin allowing the newly appointed Afghan generals to chart their own course.

When it came time for Gordon to brief the new Chief, he recounted our initial contacts with the Afghan military judges. The new chief of staff, Colonel Tom Snukis, was listening intently. He was trying to get up to speed as quickly as possible. As Gordon began to detail the system of Afghan military courts as described to us by General Esmat, Prasek interrupted the presentation.

"I'm not sure I know what you're talking about Dave," said Prasek. "The only military justice I have seen in the ANA is jailing guys in latrines and taking away their pay. Just last week a battalion commander confined a first sergeant to a latrine for seven days."

Without missing a beat, Snukis added, "I bet he got his shit straightened out." It was becoming increasing clear to me that no one on the staff had any idea what Gordon and I were doing. Much less, they really did not care. Apparently, military justice was simply a big joke.

Within a few hours the mood had changed dramatically. Former US Ambassador Robert B. Oakley was in Kabul in his capacity as Director of the International Rescue Committee. Wearing a sports coat and red tie, the tall, lean man with a very long face sat in the OMC-A conference room. He had served the government in many post-conflict countries and had made himself available today to answer our questions on Afghan reconstruction.

Some of the senior officers were in awe of him. They had heard his lectures at the United States Army War College in Carlisle, Pennsylvania, and at the National Defense University in Washington, D.C. Oakley had been Ambassador to Pakistan, Zaire, and Somalia. He was the co-author of a book on the US intervention in Somalia called Operation Restore Hope and another book entitled <u>Policing the New World Disorder</u>.[82] Oakley had been the Director of the State Department Office on Terrorism.

"The fact is that the US military is running this country," Oakley stated with the authority that came from his age and resume. "People say that ISAF cannot provide security outside Kabul because they need to provide security for Kabul. I think they have it wrong. There is no security in Kabul until there is security in the provinces. The US Army must use the Provincial Reconstruction Teams as a security projection platform."

Oakley continued, "The State Department used to have a few people who understood Afghanistan. I don't know how many they have left. I hope that they have finally figured out that we are not fighting a war against terrorism. We are rebuilding Afghanistan. A little less money in Iraq is not going to make a difference. A little bit more money in Afghanistan would make a huge difference. The consequences of failure here are far more catastrophic than failure in Iraq. If things go to hell here, we will have hell to pay in Pakistan. The Army will have to take the lead. Do not wait on the Embassy. You have the resources and I think you have the smarts."

I did not know what the rest of the people in the room were thinking, but I certainly felt like I had received my marching orders.

Chapter XVIII.

"Cover Your Butt With Towel"

A Korean lady entered a small room with a table in it. She turned to me and said, "Take off all your clothes. Lie face down on table. Cover your butt with towel."

I could not believe it. Was I dreaming? I was on active duty with the U.S. Army during war times, and I was getting a massage by a very attractive Oriental woman. This was "R & R", rest and recuperation. All soldiers serving six or more months in a combat zone were entitled to three days of R & R. The Army had sent me to Doha, Qatar, and I was going to make the most of it.

There was a time when I thought it was not worth the trip. No one I knew well was going with me. The other Lieutenant Colonels said they were too busy commanding their posts to afford the time for R & R. Their devotion to duty made me feel like some kind of slacker. There was a ton of work to do on judicial and Ministry of Defense reform, but Colonel Gordon encouraged me to go.

First, I had to travel from Kabul to Bagram where I would need to spend the night. When our convoy was about ten kilometers outside the airfield, I heard an explosion on the mountainside. The postal clerk driving the SUV on the daily mail run to BAF casually remarked, "Just another day in Afghanistan. I see mine strikes all the time." As we looked out the window toward the mountains on the right, we saw a mushroom cloud of smoke and dust rising two hundred feet in the air. Apparently, some poor sheep or camel had stepped on a land mine and was sent to the happy grazing ground. The cloud was visible for about three miles.

In Bagram, First Sergeant Moyer grabbed my duffle bag and showed me to the transient tent. It was dusk and starting to get cold. I was surprised to see snow on the mountains in early October. "If you get cold, I will turn the heater on," Moyer said. "You know where to find the shitters and the shower point. Be at the APOD[83] at 800Z. You must stay there until the plane leaves, which, if you are lucky will be 1200Z. Enjoy your stay." He was awfully nice, but I hated coming to Bagram. It was the hellhole of the entire CJOA.[84]

The night in the tent was miserable. After brushing my teeth three blocks away at the shower point, I returned to a very cold ten by ten foot tent with four cots in it and two tent-mates who had apparently arrived later in the day. I had Sergeant Moyer fire up the gas heater. At the start of the evening I had two blankets and a bed spread on top of me along with my blow up bed pillow. By the next morning, I was sleeping on top of the cot and bedspread with nothing on but my underpants. The tent was a sauna. It had to approach 110 degrees in the tent, and the vent was forcing hot air in my direction like a blowtorch. I got up to use the port-a-potty one block away and turned off the heater. When I got back to the tent, my tent-mates reprimanded me for turning off the heater, saying that they were freezing.

I got to the APOD right on time, and the roll call included my name. I was manifested on a flight to Qatar. Then, the waiting game began. Sergeant Moyer had prepared me for the five-hour wait. The PX had a new Brian Haag novel in it, and this book and several cups of coffee kept me occupied while I sat on plastic chairs with twenty-two other R & R soldiers. At 5 P.M. local time, the Air Force movement control NCO announced that the flight had mechanical problems and would not be in from Qatar for another two hours.

I prepared to wait some more. Then, there came another announcement, "Flash 95, the R & R flight to Qatar, has been cancelled," the NCO said at 8 P.M. "We can get you on another flight at 2130Z."

Now it was going to be midnight before the flight left. Two people I knew from Kabul Compound said to hell with it and decided not to do R & R in Qatar. They drove back to Kabul. At 1:30 A.M. the next day, a new movement control NCO told the twenty remaining R & R soldiers who had been waiting for thirteen plus hours that there would be no flight that night.

One soldier, who was visibly very pissed off, stood up, and said, "This is bullshit. I'd rather be fighting Al Qaeda in the mountains. Some R & R, this is." Apart from the combat part, this young Army Ranger had captured my feelings exactly. It meant another night in a very hot or very cold tent and another five hour wait for a plane at the APOD. I felt guilty about all the work that needed my attention in Kabul.

About a week prior to my scheduled R & R, Colonel Wagner had told me that Colonel Johnson was once again threatening to order me to Bagram. The unit of the only Judge Advocate serving at K2 was moving to Bagram and there would be no legal support for the troops in Uzbekistan. Johnson, who was looking for any excuse to get me out of Kabul, now had a legitimate reason to transfer me. There were three other Judge Advocates in Kabul and none in K2.

Fortunately, Johnson's replacement was now on the ground, and there was some hope he would be reasonable. LTC Charles "Chuck" Pede, Staff Judge Advocate of the Tenth Mountain Division, was named Johnson's successor. Wagner had met with him on several occasions and felt that he was someone we could work with on legal issues and JAG placement. Before I had even left Kabul for R & R, Wagner had told Pede that he would send Captain Barrett to K2 if Johnson ordered an ASG lawyer to cover that garrison.

From my twenty years of legal practice, I had learned at least one thing. If you are having a difficult time with an opposing counsel whom you have never met, then make an appointment to meet with him or her. It is easy to spit venom in letters, phone calls, and e-mails with a lawyer you have never met. It is a lot more difficult to be totally hostile to someone with whom you are an acquaintance. I told Wagner that I better use my unexpected extra morning in Bagram to visit with Pede and Johnson.

I walked into the office of the top JAG in theater. Pede and Johnson knew I was coming. I was prepared for an inquisition and I got one. Even though Pede and I shared the same rank, he made it clear to me early on this day that he was the superior and I was the subordinate. Without so much as a "pleased to me you," Pede immediately used my first name and said, "Sit down, Platte." What followed was twenty minutes of cross-examination on what Colonel Gordon and I were doing in Kabul.

"Could you tell me why we need four judge advocates in Kabul?" asked Pede. Johnson, without saying a word, just stared and shook his head in agreement after each of Pede's questions.

Without pausing for a moment, I launched into a lengthy explanation of the mission of OMC-A. I wanted Pede and Johnson to understand that my presence in Kabul was essential to the continuation of the work on a military justice code for the ANA and civilian judicial reform. More importantly, I could better serve the US mission in Afghanistan by working in Kabul than by writing powers of attorney in BAF or K2. Apparently, I satisfied them, and we parted cordially. I had the good sense not to mention to them that I was about to leave on three days of R & R.

This time, the C-130 for Qatar went wheels up right on schedule. Six hours later, shortly after midnight, we were in the Persian Gulf at Camp As Sayliyah. As our R & R contingent walked down the ramp in the rear of the plane, the heat immediately struck us. It was the middle of the night in October and the temperature was 85 degrees. The land was totally flat and there was nothing but sand in the undeveloped areas.

Before we could get billeted and bed down for the night, the CJTF-180 liaison team insisted on giving us an in-briefing. We gathered in one of the many metal warehouses quickly assembled for Operation Iraqi Freedom. Fortunately, it was air-conditioned and the American Red Cross provided Gatorade and granola bars. Within a few minutes of walking around the warehouse, I realized that we were in the same building where General Franks had briefed the International Press Corps on the progress of combat operations in the spring. There were offices for all the major television networks and newspapers in the building. All were vacant now and being used for morale telephone calls for soldiers communicating with loved ones.

Some of the ASG personnel who had been on R & R before me told me about the lottery. No one was allowed off Camp As Sayliyah without an escort. We had essentially gone from one cage to another cage. This was not the Vietnam War, where R & R meant soldiers in uniform roaming free throughout the streets of Tokyo or Bangkok for three days. Force protection required all American personnel in Doha to travel in civilian clothes in small groups when outside of the wire. Only the lucky ten percent getting their identification cards picked out of a hat in the lottery would get to go on a trip outside the camp.

Fortunately, I was the only field grade officer in my R & R group. The Morale, Welfare, and Recreation officer had reserved two spots in each trip for field grade officers and the most senior enlisted soldiers. The two authorized trips were shopping in Doha Mall and water sports in the gulf. I had no interest in mall shopping in the United States much less in a foreign country. So, I put my ID card in for water sports and was selected based upon my rank to participate in this activity on Day 2 of R & R.

"Sir, you come with me," said Staff Sergeant Green, the liaison NCO. I was finding out that rank has its privileges on R & R. While the other twenty-one soldiers were piled into a bus with their duffle bags to go to billeting, I was given a private ride in a car.

Most service members coming from Iraq and Afghanistan were given lodging in ten person rooms with double bunks in an air-conditioned warehouse. SSG Green put me in a Stratex Container that resembled a mobile home with two beds, wall lockers, nightstands, and a television. Compared to the others, I was living large.

A flyer in the warehouse announced that actor Brian Dennehy, ex-Marine and star of the movie "Cocoon," was going to be signing autographs at the camp gym facility. Thinking that it might be fun to meet the movie star, I got on one of the many shuttle buses circulating around the post and went to the fitness center mid-morning of Day 1. Barrett, who had left for R&R two days earlier than I, was already there and had gotten Dennehy's autograph.

When I pulled him away from the video games, Barrett started to fill me in on the ways to have fun at R & R camp and the latest gossip. "Sir, did you hear about Bertlam?" Barrett asked.

"No," I replied. I knew that Specialist Jacqueline Bertlam was one of the enlisted soldiers serving with me at Kabul Compound. But, I had not heard anything about her activities in Qatar while on R & R.

"She's pregnant," Barrett volunteered. "Sir, you know what that means."

"Yes, unfortunately," I rejoined. "A violation of General Order No. 1 and an Article 15 or courts-martial."

"They'll never prove she got pregnant in theater," Barrett advised. "The Army docs tell me that they don't have sophisticated enough equipment to diagnose length of pregnancy."

"Well, I am on R & R. If Wagner or Janze want me, then they know where to find me," I said, trying to distance myself from this potential firestorm.

"Hey, sir, do you want a massage?" said Barrett, trying to move the conversation away from a subject that he knew I did not want to deal with at that moment. "I signed up for a massage two days ago and I have no interest in it now. You should do it. Appointments are hard to get here."

The next thing I knew I was lying face down on a table with a towel on my butt, and a Korean lady was walking on my back. She then sat down on my rear end straddling me like she would ride a horse while working on my back. Within thirty minutes, she had given me a head to toe massage. I could not believe that the Army was supporting this "morale" activity. In my 46 years, I had never had a massage, and I left the day spa feeling great.

After getting my Dennehy autograph, I felt that it was necessary to go to church after indulging in such selfish pleasure. There was no Chaplain at Kabul Compound so I had not attended services since Fort Dix. From my e-mails to home, I had learned that the children were having a very difficult year at school. Past friends had joined new cliques. Social opportunities were limited. Few people were calling to check in on my family. I wanted to pray for the safety and happiness of Susan and my family.

The US Central Command press briefing room now served as the post chapel. While listening to a Master Sergeant deliver a perfectly awful sermon, I thought about the irony of the House of the Lord on Camp As Sayliyah once being used as a citadel of war.

On the way out of church, I stopped at the R & R help desk in the same area where we had received the in-briefing the night before. Something from the PowerPoint presentation had stuck in my mind. I asked the enlisted soldier manning the help desk if there was a golf course nearby. The Specialist gave me the name of a retired Lieutenant Colonel working at the headquarters building that played golf. Armed with this information, I was on a mission.

LTC James Woods (retired) is a handsome man in his mid-fifties. Although he did not care to talk about it, he had served in Vietnam, Central America, and Africa performing special operations with the Army. He now worked for a defense contractor similar to MPRI, called Alion. Woods selected his assignments so that he could be near a hostile fire zone. I found him in Central Command headquarters preparing intelligence reports for the commander, General Abizaid.

"I understand you are the man to see if I want to play golf," I stated hopefully.

"That's right," Woods said. "Can't play today. Already got a match. Playing nine holes with the ladies tomorrow night. Can't give that up. How about Tuesday?"

I could not believe it. I was going to get to play golf in Doha, Qatar. "That's great," I said. "Is the golf course one of those I hear about in Saudi Arabia that is all sand and you have to carry a piece of plastic turf around to hit your ball on?"

"Are you kidding?" replied Woods. "The Doha Golf Course is where the European Professional Golfer's Association plays the Qatar Masters. It is a championship course. It's a little pricey, in fact." I did not care what it cost. This was great.

Day 2 was water sports. As the only officer and only person over age thirty, I felt a little uncomfortable as I boarded the shuttle bus for Doha that morning. These guys had just come out of the nightmare in Iraq and were having the time of their young lives. Most of the soldiers on this all-male trip were hung over from the night before. We were entitled to buy only three beers per person per day on R&R. However, these infantrymen had obviously traded in the black market located behind the "Top Off Club" and purchased additional beer coupons at premium prices. They all fell asleep on the thirty-minute ride to the boat dock.

Having only consumed one Foster's Lager the night before, I stayed awake and took in the scenery outside the wire. I knew right away I was no longer in Afghanistan. The people here had money and lots of it. Qatar has more natural gas than almost anywhere else in the world and this natural resource provided a very high standard of living for the Qataris. All roads looked like they were freshly paved. The streets were filled with beautiful homes occupying a whole city block and resembling Mediterranean castles with ten-foot perimeter walls. The center city surrounded a semi-circular bay of water called the Corniche. A tall hotel resembling a huge pyramid stood adjacent to the oceanfront. Everything was neat, orderly, clean and modern.

I had some reservations about getting on the boat intended to take us out to sea for our water sports. It stood two stories high and had a completely rusted hull. The keel was made out of wood and operated by hand. The boat resembled a Chinese Junk and looked like it had been built in the Forties. The Qataris, consistent with their Islamic heritage, do not favor partially nude bodies romping around their beaches. And so, we had to take the rusty scupper to a sand island some thirty minutes away from the city. After pulling a motorboat, two jet skis, and a hot dog shaped inflatable raft along the way, we dropped anchor.

Somehow I was one of the first in line to ride the hot dog. This thing was about ten feet long and two feet wide. A rope attached the hot dog raft to the powerboat. We had no instructions or safety briefing. Our three Qatari guides did not speak English. They were also apparently cultural renegades because they wore Speedo swimsuits and were totally wild. One guide dived thirty feet from the top of the second deck of the tour boat, almost landing on a jet ski. Then he proceeded to show off for the Americans, driving the Jet Ski at top speed, spinning, and coming within one foot of the tour boat.

The motorboat operator went from floating still in the water to top speed dragging the hot dog. Within the first fifty feet, I realized I was in trouble. My forty-six year old body had no business being on this fast food float. I was sitting with my feet forward and flipped right off the rear of the float. After being fished out of the Persian Gulf, I remounted—this time like a jockey in a horse race. To avoid further embarrassment, I hung on for dear life and let the maniac boat driver pull us around for fifteen minutes. My thighs and arms were stretched in ways I had never imagined. I needed another massage.

Having had enough of this, I volunteered to be the spotter for the motorboat driver. It was obvious to me that he did not care if people fell off the raft. He was determined to propel that boat through the water at top speed and litter Americans throughout the gulf as he went. I kept watch for my fellow soldiers.

The next hot dog crew consisted of two inner city African-Americans and an Okie white boy. They at least had the benefit of watching my mistakes so they could be better prepared to ride the raft. Nonetheless, within the first quarter-mile at high speed, the two Black guys were jettisoned. The life jackets given to us by the guides had broken straps and plastic buckles. While falling off the hot dog, one soldier lost his life jacket. I immediately yelled, "STOP" to the boat driver. We slowed down and circled back toward the two overboard men. One of the fellows in the water pointed at his buddy and started screaming, "He cannot swim." I looked in the direction of this infantryman without a life jacket and saw that he was panicked and flailing his arms.

My immediate instinct was to dive in after him. However, my Boy Scout training came to the forefront. "REACH, ROW, THROW, GO." I quickly looked around the boat. Of course, the damn Qataris did not have a life buoy or rescue pole on board. If I jumped in after the guy, he would quickly pull me under in an effort to hold himself up to get air. I was not going in unless I had to. I motioned to the Qatari driver to pull the boat up next to the drowning soldier. Holding to the boat rail with one hand, I reached down into the water to the soldier who was coughing and gasping for air.

He grabbed my arm with both hands. This guy must have been able to do fifty pull-ups in physical training or had assumed super human strength in the heat of the moment. He lifted his entire body up and almost entirely out of the water by pulling on my arm and then my neck. While my waist was being squeezed into the boat rail, the driver, thankfully, came over and helped me get the soldier the rest of the way out of the sea and into the boat. My comrade in arms spent the next ten minutes belching water.

When I got back to Camp, I needed a drink. The line to buy beer coupons at the Top Off Club was a hundred soldiers long. Since I had not communicated with Susan in three days, I decided to go back to the in-processing warehouse and use the telephones to call home. Every one of the twenty phones had a caller and there was a waiting list of fifty names to use them. Frustrated again, I thought about using the Internet. Within twenty minutes, a terminal became available and I got on-line. After sending Susan and the children a lengthy e-mail recounting the day's adventures, I read my e-mail.

LTC Janze had sent me a message to call him immediately. Where was I going to get a phone? I went to the "help" desk and they would not help. The fact that I was a Lieutenant Colonel and this was official business meant nothing. The phone had to remain available to receive incoming calls. My frustration was building.

I decided to go to the Central Command headquarters building. They had a twenty-four hour operations center. The young female private first class on duty was very gracious and let me use the phone. I called Janze. "We have a soldier with a medical problem," he said. "I need for you to be my commander's representative in Qatar."

"Are we talking about Bertlam?" I asked.

"Yes," replied Janze.

"Depending on when she got pregnant, we may have a military justice issue," I suggested. "Does Wagner want to prosecute?"

"I don't know."

"Well, if she is less than three months pregnant, she had sex in theater and it is a violation of General Order No. 1. If Wagner wants to prosecute, I'm the prosecutor. I don't think that I am the best person to provide comfort to her."

"Just see how she is doing, okay?" the Kabul Compound commander asked, exasperated by my apparent lack of cooperation. "Go see the doctor. She needs someone there to express concern for her," Janze pleaded.

The medical clinic was closed for the day. I would have to see the doctor tomorrow. Day 3 was golf day. I had to get business done in the morning. Moreover, if Wagner wanted to prosecute, then it looked like I was to remain in Qatar for a few days.

After breakfast, I went straight to the medical clinic. As soon as I mentioned that I was there to see the doctor about a pregnant soldier in my command, the female receptionist said, "Oh, you must be here to see about Jackson."

Apparently, Camp As Sayliyah was having a bad week with pregnant R & R soldiers. "No," I said. "I am here to see about Bertlam."

"Are you her commander?" the clerk asked.

"No, I am an officer in her chain of command."

She then brought me in to the office of Captain James Jones. I quickly scanned the certificates and diplomas on the wall. He was the highest-ranking medical person at the clinic and he was not a doctor. Central Command had a physician's assistant running its medical clinic.

Captain Jones said, "She's seven weeks pregnant by ultrasound. She cannot return to Afghanistan. She cannot wear body armor due to her condition and there is insufficient pre-natal care in theater to tend to her needs. CFLCC[85] policy states that she must be transported back to the States within seven days."

"Can I see her medical records?" I inquired.

"No. Privacy issues prohibit disclosure. There may be things in those medical records which the command has no need to know," replied Jones.

"Such as?"

"Well I am not talking about any soldier in particular. But, frequently medical records can reveal drug use and prior pregnancies."

"What if my commander wants to make this a military justice issue?"

"I can give you a letter. In fact, I have to give you a letter stating the length of her pregnancy and getting your consent to transport her home."

I thanked the doctor and left his office, knowing that I would need to find a Judge Advocate office. I called SSG Green and asked him if there was a Staff Judge Advocate on post. He said no, but there is a paralegal, Sergeant Terrence Barnes. I could not believe it. Here I was at the forward headquarters of US Army Central Command and they did not have a doctor or a lawyer on post.

SSG Green took me to the office of SGT Barnes. This paralegal had a bigger and nicer office than either Colonel Gordon or Colonel Johnson. Brand new building, air conditioning, Internet connectivity, wooden desk, easy chair, and sofa. "I need you to help me with a violation of General Order No. 1," I told Barnes.

"What is it, alcohol or drugs?" questioned Barnes.

"Neither. Sex while on deployment," I answered.

"That's not a violation of CENTCOM General Order No. 1," said Barnes.

"I'm sure it is. You got a copy of General Order No. 1? Let's look it up."

Barnes was right. There was nothing in the CENTCOM order prohibiting sex. I then asked Barnes to look at General Order No. 1 for CJTF-180 in Afghanistan. Once again, no reference to sex.

"I know that I am not making this up," I said. Barnes suggested that we call the Military Justice Judge Advocate in Kuwait. He got the same answer. There was no prohibition against sex in the Iraq-Afghanistan theatre of operations. "Let me call the lawyer up in Bagram," I said incredulously.

Lieutenant Walt Pollard answered the phone in Colonel Johnson's office. He got on the CJTF-180 website and looked for General Order No. 1. Finding nothing, he told me he would look at the policy memos for Bagram Airfield. Sure enough, there was a sentence prohibiting sex between persons who were not married to each other. The question now became whether Bertlam had become impregnated at BAF or Kabul.

"Let me check with Colonel Johnson on this," said Pollard. "Generally, the command guidance has been not to prosecute pregnant females. It generates bad press for the military." I thanked the Lieutenant and hung up.

"I need to call Colonel Wagner now," I told Barnes. "We need to get some guidance as to what to do with this mess."

Colonel Johnson had made a decision early in Operation Enduring Freedom not to conduct any courts-martial in Afghanistan. Instead, soldiers would receive an Article 15 non-judicial punishment or, if the offense warranted a harsher punishment, a courts-martial back in the United States. Wagner felt that this policy had led to lawlessness at Bagram. Soldiers were using alcohol and drugs with relative impunity. Colonel Wagner wanted to send a strong message to the soldiers in his command.

I directed Barnes to prepare the Article 15 and ran out of his office to change clothes for golf. There was no way I was going to miss my tee time with Mr. Woods. Carrying my clubs, I walked right past General Abizaid's office in my golf attire. After I had made my appointment with Woods for golf, two junior enlisted guys had also found the former Lieutenant Colonel. We now had a foursome. Woods got an off-post pass for three of us and we were off to Doha Golf Club.

The leading natural gas company in Qatar had built this course apparently to please foreign customers. There was no way it could make any money. The Course Superintendent paid $100,000 a month just to irrigate the fairways and greens, and there was no one on them. In addition to the championship links, there was a nine-hole course completely under the lights. The lighting system allowed golfers to enjoy play at night when it was cooler to avoid the daytime 120-degree temperatures.

I had borrowed clubs from the camp R & R office. They looked pretty good. I got metal woods with graphite shafts made by Top-Flite. It did not cost me a dime. On the first tee, I hit the ball solidly on the sweet spot of the clubface of the driver. The club head left the shaft and went further than the ball. After one shot, my driver was unplayable. We picked up the separated club head fifty yards down the middle of the fairway.

The golf course was magnificent. Situated adjacent to the Persian Gulf, the views from the fairways reminded me of Pebble Beach. Somehow the course superintendent found a way to grow grass on sand. From tee to green the Bermuda grass was a brilliant hunter green. I played badly, lost five balls, and did not care. I was on the golf course. Life was good.

After golf, Woods picked up his girl friend of the week and took us all out to dinner. The enlisted guys from Iraq were dying for steak, so, we found a Bennigan's in a section of Doha called "Cholesterol Corner", aptly named for its proliferation of American fast food establishments. In a restaurant with seating for 250 persons, there were only the five of us along with two sheiks wearing full robe and turban.

No one working in the restaurant appeared to have come from an Arab country. The greeter, waitresses, and cooks were Indian, Philippino, and Greek. Woods explained that most Qataris do not work. They live off their investments in oil and gas. Qataris receive free education and medical care from the government. Manual laborers and skilled professionals are imported from foreign countries on limited two-year visas. One must be born in Qatar or marry a Qatari male to become a citizen.

Bertlam's Article 15 gave me two extra days in Qatar. I never left post again. After spending the mornings in Barnes' office processing the non-judicial punishment, I relaxed in the afternoons at the outdoor swimming pool directly behind CENTCOM headquarters. I was easily the oldest person at the pool and the only one seen reading the <u>Wall Street Journal</u>.

Chapter XIX.

Tashkent

It was my second trip to Karshi-Khanabad, Uzbekistan, better known to the US Army as "K2". The ASG had held a Commander's Conference here in August, but I had never left the installation. Some of the soldiers and airmen on this post thought America's war on terrorism started at K2. In fact, it had started in the hijacked airplane over Somerset County, Pennsylvania, when the civilian passengers decided to take control of the commercial airliner and prevent the terrorists from making it a weapon of mass destruction. Nonetheless, the military effort against the Taliban and Al Qaeda was launched from K2.

Shortly after 9/11, the governments of the United States and Uzbekistan entered into an agreement whereby the host nation allowed US forces to occupy a former Soviet airfield at K2. Just walking around the compound made me feel like I was on the set of a movie from the Cold War era. There are seven huge mounds arrayed in a semi-circle referred to as hardened aircraft shelters. In these forty-foot high structures with gigantic metal doors, the Soviets had housed their fighter jets, called MIGs. These shelters could withstand any form of bombardment or aerial attack.

Unlike BAF, the land surrounding the airfield at K2 was flat. Even though K2 was two hours flying time north of Bagram, the temperature was a lot warmer due to the lower elevation at about 2,000 feet above sea level. Another difference from Bagram was the presence of female local nationals on the compound. BAF was the largest employer of Afghans in that country, but all the "Haji's",[86] as we called the local laborers, were male. Some of the local women on K2 were striking Orientals.

The improvements to K2 by the US military made it look more like an American Air Force Base. The ASG Airfield Commander, LTC DeMara, called it the "Poconos", referring to the region of Pennsylvania which he called home. Unlike Bagram, everything here was clean, orderly, and up to date. The soldiers and airmen lived in hardstand air-conditioned buildings called Sea Huts with running water that one could actually drink and hot showers. Given the fact that there was no security threat to the compound, it was hard to see why the personnel stationed at K2 were drawing combat and hostile fire pay.

Never in my lifetime had I thought that one day I would be in the Soviet Union, much less on a former Russian air base. Having spent most of my military career in the National Guard preparing for a Soviet attack of Western Europe, it was eerie to be here. This feeling was reinforced my second day in K2 when the New York Times reported, "Russian Official Cautions U.S. on Use of Central Asian Bases." Apparently, this intermediate staging base in a former Soviet Republic, which served as the refueling and logistics hub for the American attack on Afghanistan, was causing some discomfort for the Russian Defense Minister.

The future use of K2 was one of the reasons that DeMara had asked me to come to his airfield. Dennis had a number of issues with the Government of Uzbekistan concerning the operation of the base that he wanted to bring to the attention of the US Ambassador. Along with a translator and a couple of mail carriers, DeMara and I were making a trip to Tashkent, the capital and fourth largest city in the former Soviet Union.

We were only one mile past the compound gates when we came to a checkpoint manned by the Uzbek military. They motioned for us to stop. Apparently, they had not read, could not read, or had not been told about the US-Uzbek Status of Forces Agreement that allowed American armed forces free passage throughout the country. The checkpoint guard, who could not have been older than 17 years, wanted to inspect the mailbags the couriers were taking to the US Embassy personnel in Tashkent.

Our Russian interpreter, Scott Lipjack, a good-looking former US serviceman, would have none of this. He started yelling at the Uzbek. Scott later told me that this is the normal way of communicating with government officials. The guard continued to insist upon examining the mail. Knowing that we were late for our plane and Uzbek police do not carry guns, Lipjack stepped on the accelerator of the van and got us through the checkpoint and on our way to the airport.

I was afraid to get on the twin-engine propeller airplane. The commercial airliner looked like it was built in the 1950s and only occasionally maintained thereafter.[87] The runway had cracked tarmac with vegetation growing through it. Then, I experienced culture shock. The airlines had a stewardess in a 1960's style uniform with a mini-skirt and bobby-pinned pillbox hat. After seeing nothing but blue head to toe Birkas in Afghanistan, this was a sight to behold. A beautiful Oriental woman speaking Russian was showing me to my seat.

DeMara had given me a tour book[88] in English to read on the plane. I learned that the geographical area that is now Uzbekistan came under the control of Russia in 1882, and its first Governor General was Konstantin Kaufmann. After the Communist Revolution, Lenin had made Josef Stalin the Commissar of Nationalities. Stalin divided the Russian controlled land mass called Turkestan into four new republics based upon their predominant ethnic heritage—Uzbekistan, Turkmenistan, Kazakhstan, and Krgyzstan.

Unfortunately for the Russians and for present day Afghans, the ethnic groups were not all contained within the territorial borders of these republics or even within the Soviet Union in general. Half of the Uzbek ethnic population remained in Afghanistan. The Uzbeks remained more loyal to their ethnic group than to their new nation. This Diaspora frustrated Stalin's grand policy of divide and rule.

After taking one look at the Stewardess, it was hard for me to believe that Uzbekistan was an Islamic state. The Uzbeks look Chinese, speak Russian, and are Muslims. According to my tour book, Genghis Khan in 1227 divided his realm between his four sons and most of present day Uzbekistan came under the control of his second son Chagati Khan. This son begat Uzbek Khan, who gave the country its present name, and who also converted it to Islam.

When we touched down in Tashkent, it was difficult to comprehend that we were only a few hundred miles north of Kabul. Here was a modern Islamic city. Unlike Qatar, everything had not been built in the past five years. Tashkent had well-preserved and maintained mosques and government buildings. Beautiful fountains spraying water a hundred feet into the air were scattered throughout the city. There were no donkeys, camels or goats in the streets. Tashkent had an underground storm and wastewater sewer system. Most strikingly, this city had grass and tall oak and sycamore trees providing shade and cool comfort.

The Embassy had a car waiting and took us to our meeting with the State Department officials. The Charge d'Affairs, David Appleton, a very amiable, bespectacled, gray-haired gentleman, led us to his office. Dennis and I were wearing jeans and sports shirts as we met the Acting Ambassador. He treated us like combat heroes, extending every courtesy.

DeMara got right to the issues. K2 was not getting enough diesel fuel from the Uzbeks. The Ministry of Defense kept promising to supply more liters, but the shipments had not been forthcoming. If the problem were not rectified shortly, K2 would not be able to operate its generators to supply electricity to the compound. Appleton promised to address the issue immediately.

Uzbek Customs Officials were stopping shipments of American food and water at the Russian border. Disregarding the Status of Forces Agreement that provided for free movement of US military equipment and supplies, the border agents were demanding payment of taxes, i.e., bribes, for the goods to pass through the checkpoint. When the transporters refused to pay the bribes, the Customs officials were breaking the seals on the containers of food and water. As a consequence, the Army food inspectors in Bagram could not rule out tampering and had to destroy tens of thousands of dollars of government food intended for soldiers.

After the Ambassador stated that he would take up that issue with the Ministry of Interior, I wanted his thoughts on the New York Times article about the future of K2. "Sir, can the Russians put enough influence on the Uzbeks to make us leave K2?" I asked.

The Ambassador replied, "That is very unlikely." He then went on to explain that the present President of Uzbekistan, Islam Karimov, was the former first Secretary of the Communist Party of the Soviet Union. I thought right away that this past life would make the President favorable to the Russians. Appleton quickly vanquished this belief with more facts.

"Prior to 9/11," the acting Ambassador said, "Uzbekistan faced a serious threat from Islamic fundamentalists." I learned that the IMU, Islamic Movement of Uzbekistan, was a terrorist network supported by the Taliban and Al Qaeda seeking to create one Pan-Islamic state in Central Asia. Russia provided little assistance to Karimov in combating these terrorists, and they seriously undermined the credibility of his government. "The United States after September 11 defeated the Taliban and Al Qaeda and thereby defeated the IMU," he continued. "9/11 was a blessing for Karimov. It redefined his role as a leader of Central Asia and an ally of the United States."

I wanted to stay and talk politics with the Embassy political and economic officers, but DeMara had heard enough. He wanted to leave and go shopping. The mail clerks, Master Sergeant Peters and Specialist Timothy McLaughlin, had already checked into the Intercontinental Hotel and were down on "Broadway," the open-air market of Tashkent. Our interpreter, Lipjack, had collected his Uzbek girlfriend from the coffee shop where she was working. The two of them were waiting for us when Dennis and I entered the hotel lobby.

This girl immediately struck me. She was tall, blond, and thin. Tatiana was wearing skin-tight jeans and a T-shirt two sizes too small. On the front of the T-shirt, it read in English, "Ooh, Do you like what you see?" And, on the back, it said, "It would be my pleasure to serve you." Dennis and I thought we had died and gone to Uzbek heaven. We were spending the night at a five star hotel and were going to enjoy the company of this incredibly sexy young woman for an afternoon and night on the town in Tashkent.

Lieutenant Colonel Dennis DeMara, Tatania, and author at the Intercontinental Hotel in Tashkent, Uzbekistan. Photograph by Scott Lipjack.

Tatiana got us a taxi within seconds. No less than three cars stopped to pick her up. Lipjack, DeMara, and I stood ten feet away obscured by the bushes as she worked her magic. We all crammed into the mini-car. Our destination was Broadway near Amir Timur Square. In many ways, the history of this public park told the story of Uzbekistan. At various times in the last two hundred years, the park has had a different central statue that served as the national symbol of the era.

A statute of the first Russian Governor General of the territory, Konstantin Kaufmann, had stood in the park for over fifty years. Then, Josef Stalin replaced Kaufmann as the park statue in 1947. When Stalin grew in increasing disfavor, the Uzbeks took his statue down and erected a new one of Karl Marx in 1968. After Uzbekistan declared its independence from Russia in 1991, the Uzbeks decided to claim Tamerlane as the national hero and put up a statue to him.

I was curious about this Tamerlane fellow so I consulted the tour book. In 1370, Amir Timur was dubbed "Conqueror of the World." His empire extended from Moscow to Delhi to Damascus and his capital city was Samarkand in what is now Uzbekistan. It was the greatest amount of land area ever controlled by a single ruler in the history of mankind. As a consequence of arrow wounds to the right leg, he became known as "Timur the Lame" or in the anglicized version, "Tamerlane." Despite the fact that he had killed over seventeen million people and used Christian knights' heads as cannonballs, the Uzbeks had somehow reinvented him as the patriarch of their country. The actual creator of Uzbekistan, Stalin, had become Tamerlane and Tamerlane had become an Uzbek.

Within a few feet of Tamerlane, Dennis, Scott, Tatiana, and I ran into the postal guys who were all panicked and in a frenzy. McLaughlin, an Army Reservist from Massachusetts, was wearing a sleeveless muscle shirt, shorts, and a Boston Red Sox baseball cap. Even in a liberated Muslim country like Uzbekistan, he did not fit in with the rest of the shoppers on Broadway. Peters was dressed more conservatively, but his height, over six feet tall, gave him away as an American.

"You would not believe what happened to us," said McLaughlin in his Boston accent. "We just got shook down by the damn Uzbek cops." The Ambassador had told us that the Uzbekistan had rampant corruption and over 8,000 political prisoners, but none of us believed what we were hearing. "Some old policeman asked us to show him our passports. We told him we were in the American military and we did not carry passports. This apparently pissed him off so he took us to the police station. He said he had to 'register' us. We did not know what to do. We figured if we said 'no' or ran, half the Uzbek police force would chase us through Tashkent."

"How the hell did you get out of it?" I asked.

"By buying two bottles of vodka from a local restaurant," Peters answered. Lipjack was furious. As our Russian interpreter, he also took on the role of protector of American soldiers. He had been to Tashkent before and knew his way around town a little bit.

"Those bastards," Lipjack said. "Did you get their badge numbers? Do you know what they look like?"

Tatiana was getting upset. She started speaking Russian frantically to Scott. I asked Lipjack to translate. He told me that Tatiana was afraid of the police. She thought if we made too much of a stink about the incident that the cops would come down hard on her. After all, she was a single Uzbek woman with four Americans. When we considered her feelings, we decided to forget about the incident for now and go shopping.

The Embassy Administrative Officer, Mr. Bohne, and his wife, Primrose, took us all out for dinner. Once again, like Mr. Woods, here were overseas Americans treating servicemen with kindness. I was most appreciative and asked to go to a traditional Uzbek restaurant. Bohne said he would take us to where the visiting congressman and state department officials went to eat in Tashkent.

"Caravans" was located in an alley. It was open-air eatery and the night was chilly. The waitress wore a full-length wool robe and passed out matching ones to Tatiana and Primrose. When McLaughlin and Peters recounted their day's adventure with the Uzbek police, Bohne was perturbed. He wanted to report the incident immediately to the Embassy Regional Security Officer. "The Uzbeks have replaced Cold War vigilance for their security with blatant profiteering," said Bohne.

The main dish on the menu was a traditional Uzbek meal called a Monty. DeMara selected the Monty and the waitress said it was likely that he could not eat it all. Acting on this advice, Dennis ordered a half Monty. He finished it and complained that he was still hungry. "You should have done the Full Monty," I said.

The next morning, DeMara and I decided to relax by the indoor pool in the Intercontinental and have coffee. After a huge breakfast and a massage (my second in as many weeks), we headed back to Broadway for my shopping. Wearing the same clothes as yesterday, Tatiana went with us. Lipjack had obviously had a very nice evening.

After more meetings at the Embassy, we boarded the plane and flew back to Karshi. The postal guys, DeMara, Lipjack and I were the only Americans on the flight. The Embassy had given us two bags of their mail in sealed and locked diplomatic pouches for transport. At the terminal, the Uzbeks quickly claimed their luggage and left the airport. We waited thirty minutes for the mail. The place was deserted except for a few Uzbek police in their green uniforms and French Foreign Legion style hats.

Lipjack knew it was a problem. In Russian, he asked a policeman standing nearby when we would get our diplomatic pouches. He said he did not know. They were being checked. I did not know postal regulations, but I did know that diplomatic pouches are given free passage without inspection in every civilized country in the world. DeMara was pissed.

Dennis told me to stand by our luggage, and he, Lipjack, and the postal clerks went after the mailbags. They exited the terminal and started walking back toward the plane on the tarmac. Three Uzbek policemen stopped the soldiers and told them to come back into the terminal. Seeing the diplomatic pouches sitting on the runway, DeMara and the postal guys went running after them while Lipjack screamed at the police in Russian. The K2 commander and his troops retrieved the mailbags, reversed direction, and stormed through the terminal en masse. DeMara turned to me and yelled, "Platte, let's get the hell out of here." We ran to our van, fired up the engine, and sped away.

Chapter XX.

9/11 Commission

I had barely gotten off the C-130 returning from R&R in Qatar when I ran into Colonel Wagner. "Judge," he said, "Have you heard about your new assignment?"

"No, sir," I replied.

"Colonel Pede wants you to be the escort officer for the 9/11 Commission," he explained.

"You're kidding," I stated quizzically. "I thought the congressional committee had already issued its report. Is this the Presidential Commission?"

"I don't know. I am on my way to the Command Group meeting. Why don't you come along with me and we will find out."

The General Staff of CJTF-180 was located catty-corner from the ASG's base operations building on BAF. It was the same rat-infested Soviet-era building in which I had had my prior confrontations with Colonel Johnson. Apparently, my decision to meet with Pede before leaving for R&R had paid dividends. He was now in charge of the Judge Advocates in theater, and he was giving me a very important assignment.

Colonel Wagner and I walked into a small fifteen by twenty foot room with no windows and a twelve-foot ceiling. In it were a small table and a television stand and an array of twenty-five chairs. I had previously met Brigadier General Bagby, the Chief of Staff, but I had never seen the combat commander of all coalition forces in Afghanistan. When Major General Lloyd J.

Austin walked into the meeting of the Command Group, I was immediately struck by the fact that he was an African-American. The two leading Generals of CJTF-180, Austin and Bagby, were Black. I mused to myself, *The Army was way ahead of the rest of American society in promoting persons based upon the content of their character.*

All of the subordinate commanders in the room gave a report on the significant activities of their respective units. When the time came for Wagner, he had me stand up and introduced me as the JAG officer who would accompany the 9/11 Commission on its visit to Afghanistan. General Austin, who had his back to me as he was seated at the table, strained his neck and took a long look, saying nothing. General Bagby said, "Good morning, Colonel Moring. Will you be available to discuss the itinerary for the commission sometime this week?"

"Yes, sir," I replied. "Whenever it is convenient for you."

General Austin then turned to his Protocol Officer and asked, "Who are these guys and what do they want from us?"

Captain Patrick McDarby looked shell-shocked and answered, "I don't know, sir."

"Well, are they Senators, Congressman, some staffers or what," demanded Austin.

"I don't know, sir," replied McDarby meekly.

General Bagby, in an obvious effort to resurrect his staff member, said, "Sir, we are now in the process of getting details on the visit."

Right then I knew that I was in trouble. No one seemed to have a clue as to the purpose or composition of the 9/11 Commission. Fortunately, General Austin decided to move on to the next subject, and we were all off the hook for now. As the meeting adjourned, Wagner and I asked Pede to provide any additional information he had on the VIP visit. He said for me to read my e-mails and look at the website for the 9/11 Commission. I told Pede that I had a trip planned for Tashkent to visit with the K2 Commander and the US Ambassador and wanted to know if I should still make the journey. Pede said for me to go, and he would monitor the goings on of the 9/11 Commission from BAF.

I only returned to Kabul for one night. My R&R trip to Qatar, intended to be four days, ended up being eight. I needed to check in with Colonel Gordon, read my e-mails, and get clean laundry and civilian clothes for my trip to Uzbekistan. Back at my Kabul Compound computer, my web research revealed that Congress had passed a statute creating the National Commission on Terrorist Attacks Upon the United States (commonly known as the "9/11 Commission"). The purpose of the commission was to examine and report upon the facts and causes relating to the terrorist attacks of September 11, 2001. And then, give the President and Congress its findings and recommendations for corrective measures to be taken to prevent acts of terrorism.

The website had biographies of the commission members. It was a virtual who's who of the last thirty years of American history. Richard Ben-Veniste had been the Chief Prosecutor of Watergate. The commission vice chair, Lee Hamilton, was the congressman who had headed the investigation of the Iran-Contra scandal. Fred Fielding had been President Reagan's White House Counsel and John Lehman was the former Secretary of the Navy. *Certainly, I thought, I am not going to be responsible for showing all these bigwigs around Afghanistan.*

Back in Bagram, I went immediately to Colonel Wagner's office. He did not have any further information on the 9/11 Commission visit. I then went to see Captain McDarby. He said, "All I have is the State Department cable, which I am sure you have by now."

"No," I stated. "I haven't seen it. What does it say?"

"Four commission staffers and a White House counsel will be here 20 October," replied McDarby.

On the plane to Tashkent, I read the State Department cable, website information, and printed e-mails from Colonel Pede. I learned that the Legal Counsel to the Joint Chiefs of Staff ("JCS") had tasked Pede with identifying a JAG officer to be present at all military briefings of the 9/11 Commission. More specifically, JCS Legal wanted a senior Judge Advocate to make sure that the staffers did not get answers to questions concerning current operations, unit locations, and troop strengths. These topics were off limits to the 9/11 Commission.

I sensed that I would be in the middle of a conflict. From the commission's first and second interim reports posted on the website, I learned that the 9/11 investigators were dissatisfied with the level of cooperation they were receiving from the Executive Department with respect to its briefing and document requests. Members of both parties were accusing the White House of stonewalling the 9/11 Commission by blocking its demands for documents.[89] Further, the <u>Wall Street Journal</u> had just published an article stating that the Commission had issued its first subpoena for records to warn government agencies that it demanded complete cooperation.[90] I knew then that this assignment was not going to be like defending a deposition in a medical malpractice lawsuit.

After returning to Afghanistan from Uzbekistan, I sought out Major Fred Fillers, the officer in charge of the Kabul Joint Visitors' Bureau. Fred had no knowledge of my involvement with the 9/11 Commission, but told me that there was a meeting later that day at the US Embassy to plan for the arrival of the delegation. As I entered the conference room at the Embassy, the Army officer responsible for coordinating all political-military operations, Lieutenant Colonel Tucker Mansager, looked at me and said, "Hey, Platte. What are you doing here?"

This was not good. It appeared that no one had visibility concerning my role as the escort officer for the 9/11 Commission. The Embassy Control Officer, Machut Shishak, distributed a Draft Schedule for the 9/11 Commission visit to Afghanistan. The schedule listed every person from the Department of State and Department of Defense involved in the VIP visit. My name was not listed. I had to explain to the entire Country Team at the Embassy that I was the DoD agency representative. No one seemed to understand my role.

The next day, after joining the daily convoy from Kabul to BAF, I went immediately to Captain Barrett's office and got on his computer. I considered this assignment a potentially dangerous mission. There was no better target of terrorists for symbolic value than to seek out and kill the 9/11 Commission. I wrote an email to my children:

> Leigh and Will:
>
> I have been given a very important job. The Army has requested that I serve as the escort officer for the President's special commission investigating the terrorist attacks of September 11, 2001, at the World Trade Center in New York and at the Pentagon in Washington, D.C. The reason that I am here in Afghanistan and not home with you is because of these terrible events. You should take pride in the fact that your father is part of the team conducting the investigation to make sure that such attacks never happen again.
>
> Love, Dad

Since I was not leaving to meet the commission in Kandahar until the next morning, I thought it timely to visit the enemy agents that had caused the tragedy of September 11, 2001. I spent the afternoon taking a tour of the "PUC" Facility at BAF. The ASG Command Sergeant Major, Michael Wevodau, arranged for me to see the PUCs, the Taliban and Al Qaeda "Persons Under Confinement." On the way in, he suggested the name of the prison be changed to "Fugitives Under Confinement." Wevodau said it would make a better acronym.

Before entering the old aircraft hangar serving as a jail, the MP Commander made me sign a statement that I would never reveal the methods of interrogation and conditions of confinement contained therein. And so, I never will. Nonetheless, I got to stare into the faces of the terrorists who had supported the 9/11 attacks on America. Much to my surprise, I felt no hate in my heart and I saw no hate in their faces.

Later that night, I reported my experience in the PUC facility to Susan in an e-mail. She sent me an instant message in return. Susan wrote, "I don't care if you saw no hate in their faces. After what happened in New York, I think they all should die."

In the morning, I took an eight-seat C-12 from Bagram to Kandahar. It was my intent to arrive hours ahead of the Commission so that I could brief the military officers on the ground about the nature and scope of the visit. The itinerary showed that the 9/11 Commission had dinner and bed down after arrival from Pakistan later that day. Then, the meetings for the next morning were with the provincial governor and city chief of police. At noon, the delegation would board a C-130 and fly to Kabul.

After only a few minutes on ground in Kandahar, I realized that the schedule was meaningless. At the VIP visit planning meeting, the Kandahar JVB informed me that neither the governor nor chief of police would be in town the next day because they had gone to Kabul for a meeting. I immediately suggested that we substitute local Afghan officials living in country on September 11, 2001, as interviewees. The Commander of the First Brigade of the 10th Mountain Division, Colonel William Garrett, graciously volunteered to give a briefing to the 9/11 staff on the mission of his unit.

As we prepared for the briefing, I repeated my guidance from Pede and told the Colonel that current ops were off limits. "That's not what I heard from 180," said Garrett. He authoritatively stated that he had received contrary information from CJTF180 on the permissible lines of inquiry for the Commission and would call BG Bagby for clarification.

Now, I was in a dilemma. *Why did Garrett have different instructions than those given to me? Do I dare let the Colonel do his own thing in contravention of my marching orders? Wouldn't Lieutenant Colonel Pede want a head's up that Bagby was likely to walk into his office after talking to Garrett and want to know what the First Brigade Commander could say to the Commission?* I told Garrett that I would seek further clarification from Pede.

The first person off the aircraft was the Executive Director of the 9/11 Commission. In preparation for the VIP visit, I had read the biographies of the staff members published on the Internet. Dr. Philip Zelikow was the Director of the Miller Center of Public Affairs and Professor of History at the University of Virginia. Two other 9/11 staff members and a White House counsel accompanied him. As Zelikow bounded toward me with an abundance of energy, I observed an individual that was obviously full of himself. I extended my hand and he said, "I am Philip Zelikow."

"Please to meet you, Phil," I replied without thinking. From the scowl on his face, I knew that I had made a big mistake. I should have known better. *Why couldn't I have said, "Dr. Zelikow," "Professor Zelikow," or even simply "Philip."* No, I used the familiar "Phil." He was not pleased with me from the first hello.

The plane was a little late so I had to make special arrangements with the cooks, Brown and Root Services, to hold the Commission's meals. At dinner, I showed Dr. Zelikow the proposed schedule. "There's nothing scheduled for tonight," he barked at me.

"Sir," I said, "we figured you would be tired from traveling and would simply want to bed down for the night."

"Let me make one thing perfectly clear to you from the outset," he announced, staring piercingly into my face. "We are here to work. We will work 24 hours a day if necessary. This schedule is totally unsatisfactory. I sent a specific request to OSD[91] identifying exactly what we wanted to see in Kandahar. This schedule includes none of the places I want to visit and none of the people I want to see. CENTCOM just told me that the visit to Salerno[92] was cancelled without even consulting me."

What was I going to say? I did not arrange the schedule. I did not even know who did. "Sir, the Salerno trip was turned off at a level way above my pay grade," I offered.

"Well, I demand to see the base commander this evening," the arrogant professor ordered.

"I will see if I can arrange a meeting and I will knock on your door later this evening." Now I had to find Colonel Garrett and determine whether he was willing to meet Philip. It was already 8:00 P.M. Earlier in the day, I had received an e-mail from Pede about the permissible scope of inquiry by the Commission. "We should avoid discussions of current operations other than generalities," Pede advised. "No need for units, plans, locations, results to be discussed."

Colonel Garrett was still hard at work in his office. I let him know that Zelikow demanded to see him. I also reiterated the guidance that I had received from Pede, his own Staff Judge Advocate. "That's not what General Bagby told me in our telephone conversation," said Garrett. *Just great, I fretted. More conflict.* "Bring him here. I will talk to him," the Colonel instructed.

Zelikow gave Garrett the same tongue lashing that he gave me. Neither the full bird Colonel's rank or warrior status meant anything to this UVA Ph.D. Philip started spouting out the code names of places and missions that I could only imagine that he had read in some Top Secret CIA report on pre-9/11 Afghanistan. He demanded to be taken by helicopter to former Al Qaeda training camps and the home of Mullah Omar. Colonel Garrett was incredibly gracious and said that he would make the necessary arrangements.

Kandahar was the former nerve center of the Taliban and home of its former spiritual leader, Mullah Omar. Twenty months after the US Air Force had laid waste to Al Qaeda and these religious zealots, this region was still the most dangerous in all of Afghanistan. Just a few weeks earlier, terrorists had killed several police and some volunteer workers in the province. And yet, here I was riding in a helicopter at 0800 hours at approximately 200 feet above hostile territory. Colonel Garrett had machine gunners locked and loaded on both sides of the bird as we sped through mountain passes.

About thirty minutes outside of Kandahar, Garrett looked at Zelikow and pointed down toward a valley. There were not enough headsets for everyone on the flight, so I had made sure that the Executive Director had one. The noise of the helo blades beating above made talking to each other impossible without a connection to the devices. I could see Garrett's lips moving deliberately, but I could not make out any of the words.

Outside the window, I saw a rectangular camp with clay walls. There were a few buildings inside the compound. Most were in rubble. No one was in sight on the ground. We circled around the area three times at a lower altitude. From the trip briefing, I knew that we were above an Al Qaeda training camp. The US Army had made sure that these terrorists would never have sanctuary here again.

The pilot then changed directions and took the chopper away from the place only known by a secret code name. Within a few minutes, we were over what looked like a movie star's house in the mountains outside Los Angeles. Garrett motioned for the bird to land. On the ground, he explained to us that we were at the home of Mullah Omar, present day leader of the Taliban and confidante of Osama Bin Laden.

For some reason, I had thought that Omar lived in the city of Kandahar in a modest home suitable for a religious leader. Instead, he had chosen one of the most picturesque places in all of Afghanistan to build his estate. There were no other houses for miles. The ranch was nestled in a valley with mountains on three sides. A 3,000-foot formation resembling "Pride Rock" from the Disney movie "Lion King" towered above the Mullah's property.

The compound was a collection of white stucco buildings surrounding the strangest looking water fountain I had ever seen. Painted aquamarine with fish, seaweed, and land creatures interspersed among what appeared to be hills and rivers, Omar's water monument was hideous. Thankfully, the US Air Force had made sure that it would never work again.

A middle-aged man in civilian clothes greeted the VIP party. He immediately engaged in a conversation with the two silent members of the Commission staff. I asked a non-uniformed person carrying an assault rifle, "Who is that guy?"

The young African-American whom I assumed was some type of Special Forces soldier replied, "Oh, he's OGA."

"What the hell is that?" I asked.

"Other Government Agency." Enough stated—read CIA. No wonder he got the two quiet members talking. Michael Hurley was a Senior Counsel with the CIA who served as Director of Operations in Afghanistan shortly after 9/11. He had red hair, a ruddy complexion, and high-pitched voice. The Irishman always looked like he had just crawled out of a sleeping bag. The other CIA agent, Kevin Scheid, was the Deputy Director of Central Intelligence for Community Management. His job was to make sure that all the government intelligence agencies were talking to each other. Scheid was tall, polite, cerebral, and somewhat scary in that one never knew what he was thinking.

The OGA guy gave us a tour of the Mullah Omar compound that was now serving as a US Army forward operating base. Pointing to places where bomb damage was evident, he said, "As soon as the Air Force knocked out the radar on Kandahar Airfield, the Mullah knew that he was under attack. Supposedly, he fled this area by car toward Pakistan." From the roof of the tallest remaining building on the ranch, we could see collapsed structures. However, I was taken by the fact that most of the place was still standing. I would have thought that we would have reduced this Bin Laden-Mullah Omar meeting site to dust.

"Watch out for snakes," said the OGA man as we walked toward a thousand foot high mound just outside the walls of the compound. "There is no known antidote for their bites." *Wonderful, I thought.* He took us through a long tunnel to an underground cave. It had three entrances at the North, South, and West compass directions of the small mountain all at ground level. "As you can see," explained OGA, "the Mullah was expecting an attack from above." The cave had electricity, bedrooms, and a kitchen. "There is room here for Omar and his family to live quite well for some time." Conjuring up images of Harrison Ford in "Raiders of the Lost Ark", I kept thinking about the snakes and was glad to get out of there.

Garrett said it was time to leave. We thanked OGA for the tour and boarded the helicopter for Kandahar Air Field. Zelikow was smiling. He had gotten to see the secret places he had read about in the CIA reports. Garrett had saved the day and now was going to give his briefing on the 1st Brigade, Light Infantry. Five minutes into the briefing in the conference room, I was frustrated. My mission was to screen questions about current operations, unit names, locations, and troop strengths. The Colonel gave the Commission all that information in a full color Microsoft PowerPoint presentation.

Garrett then took the delegation to the lobby of the old Kandahar airport terminal. He explained that the US government had built this airport in the 1950's before the advent of jet engines to serve as a refueling place for propeller planes on route to India. Twenty-two Afghans greeted us. Some were wearing western-style business suits and others were dressed in turbans and robes. Most of the men were over fifty years old. Garrett told us that these men had lived in Kandahar during the Taliban and Al Qaeda years.

Zelikow introduced the commission staff members and instructed the assembly that he was there to learn from them. One Afghan after another told a similar story. When the mujahideen drove the Russians out of Afghanistan with American help, the US and Europe turned their back on the Afghan people. The Taliban exploited religion, illiteracy, and famine with help from Al Qaeda and opium drug traffic. Within a few years, Bin Laden and his Arab brethren controlled all of southern Afghanistan. Prominent Afghans from the northern part of the country had tried to warn Americans at international conferences, but no one was listening.

After thanking the leaders of Kandahar for sharing their thoughts and observations, the delegation boarded a C-130 and flew to Kabul. At the US Embassy, the Commission met with the group of DoD and State Department experts known as the "country team." During the briefing, the Embassy Political Officer, Jeff Hawkins, referenced the upcoming Loya Jirga.

"What's a Loya Jirga?" asked Zelikow. Deep inside, I was smiling. The Executive Director did not know everything about Afghanistan. Hawkins then explained what I already knew. The Loya Jirga was a traditional national assembly of Afghans. In December, Afghanistan would have a constitutional convention to adopt a charter for self-governance.

Glancing at me as I was about to enter his office, David Sedney, Chargé d'Affairs and acting US Ambassador, said, "You can't go in there." While the delegation was getting their rooms for the night, White House Counsel Dylan Cors and I were scheduled to have a preparation session with Sedney and Combined Forces Commander, three-star select, General David Barno. Now, Sedney, a fellow Princetonian, was telling me I could not go into his office for the meeting. Privately, I was pissed. *When is the Embassy going to get the message that I am the DoD representative? I thought to myself.* Fortunately, Cors was on board and he explained to the Chargé that I had a legitimate reason to be in his office with the General.

Barno and Sedney listened intently as Cors and I explained what had happened so far with the Commission and what the two of them could expect from Zelikow and the CIA boys. However, nothing we said could have prepared them for what followed. The Executive Director entered the General's office at the Embassy with a head of steam.

"The schedule for tomorrow at Bagram is totally unacceptable," fumed Zelikow. He demanded to meet with MG Austin to get a countrywide assessment of the current threat and military strategy, to receive a briefing from the Special Forces Commander concerning current operations, and to meet with Defense Intelligence Agency officers operating prior to 9/11 in Afghanistan. I could not believe that this UVA professor was giving orders to a three-star general.

Unshaken, Barno said he would see what could be arranged for BAF and would look into scheduling a Commission observation of an ANA live fire exercise for Wednesday evening.

The General knew that there would be no training on Friday, the originally scheduled ANA visitation day, because it was the Muslim Sabbath.

The 9/11 group was slotted to go right from the Barno briefing to dinner and an Embassy reception with prominent people from the diplomatic community. Of course, the Embassy had left me off the invitation list. As it turned out, I could not have gone anyway. The Zelikow diatribe in the General's office necessitated that I make frantic phone calls to coordinate a new agenda for the next day. Barno had promised Zelikow that he would have an amended typewritten itinerary for Bagram by the end of that night's reception.

BG Bagby greeted the 9/11 staffers as they jumped out of the helicopter onto the tarmac at Bagram Airfield. Before getting on the chopper, I felt I needed to call Pede and warn him about Zelikow. Among other things, I told him that Philip was a horse's ass. When I got off the phone, I was not pleased with myself. Maybe I should not have said such uncomplimentary things about the Executive Director of a Presidential Commission. A few hours later, I was glad that I had said every word.

"The 9/11 Commission is the largest investigation into the structure of the US government in history," puffed Zelikow as he addressed MG Austin in his office. "It is even bigger than the investigation that followed Pearl Harbor." Without pausing to draw a breath, Philip stared at Austin and sternly inquired, "The visit to Forward Operating Base Salerno was turned off without consulting me, and I want to know why. We made our intent clear to OSD (Office of the Secretary of Defense), and I cannot comprehend why this instruction was not followed."

Even though Austin had the benefit of the warning that I had given to Pede before the encounter, I had to admire the General. He stayed calm and said, "There is no evil intent here. There is nothing going on at Salerno." Zelikow then started asking questions about US Army plans to counter the Al Qaeda threat in Pakistan. Austin tried to divert the conversation to another topic, mentioning that the coalition had successfully denied sanctuary for the terrorists in Afghanistan. Unwavering,

Philip continued to press for information about the terrorist tactics in Pakistan. He said, "I assume that Eisenhower wanted to know a little information about the German Army before he engaged the allies in an attack."

Pede was squirming in his chair. The harangue continued. Zelikow spouted, "We have been at this for two years now. We are not at the embryo stage. I thought that you might be a little more informed than the readers of the Washington Post." Once again, Austin deflected the frontal assault. Without any ire, he quickly noted that newspaper stories are often incorrect. He gave a specific example of a US Army investigation revealing that press reports of the Taliban killing a hundred persons and burning buildings in southeastern Afghanistan had no basis in fact. Ultimately, Austin explained that a Trilateral Commission had been set up consisting of Afghans, Pakis and Coalition to address the threat in Pakistan.

General Austin had next arranged for the 9/11 delegation to meet with soldiers who had recently seen combat. These 10th Mountain infantrymen were impressive. They were mostly from New York and were anxious to inflict casualties on Al Qaeda and the Taliban. Their only complaint was that they were not allowed to seek out and destroy the enemy. Instead, they were manning defensive positions on the Pakistani border.

One Sergeant described the terrorists as cowards. "They are afraid to engage. They do not try to take ground. Instead, they fire rockets from two kilometers away and run." Zelikow and the CIA guys seemed genuinely moved by their testimonies, and for the first time during their visit showed some respect to those in uniform fighting the war on terrorism.

When we left Bagram by helicopter, I figured the worst was over. All we had left was the ANA briefing at Task Force Phoenix and the night live fire exercise at the ranges. Jeff Hawkins met us at Kabul International Airport, and his security detail whisked us away down Jalalabad Road. Colonel Mark Milley, 10th Mountain Division, 2nd Brigade Commander, met us at the entrance to the camp of the embedded trainers of the ANA.

The hard-charging Ranger was all smiles for the delegation. He showed them the PX, soldier recreation facilities, and gym.

Milley then ushered us into a plywood building with a makeshift conference table and chairs. As he began his briefing on the plans for training and equipping the ANA, Hawkins got a call on his cell phone and left the room. It was now after dark. Hawkins returned to his chair and said, "The trip to the live fire exercise is cancelled due to security reasons." I quickly glanced over to Zelikow to gauge his reaction. He looked like a volcano waiting to erupt.

"Can you give us an explanation as to why the trip was turned off?" I asked Hawkins trying to upstage the attack I knew was coming from Philip.

"There was a Lieutenant Colonel shot twice last week on the same road that we were scheduled to travel on to get to the exercise area," answered Hawkins. "The Embassy cannot guarantee the security of our guests."

Zelikow turned to Milley and questioned, "How does your unit intend to go out to the ranges tonight?"

"In SUV's wearing body armor," Milley responded.

Apparently trying to show how tough he was, the Executive Director stated, "The Commission will accept the same risk as the 10th Mountain Division."

I rolled my eyeballs and wondered to myself, *does this idiot have any idea of the publicity that the Taliban and anti-coalition militia would receive if they killed the staff of the 9/11 Commission on their fact-finding tour of Afghanistan?*

After the briefing was over, I immediately walked over to Zelikow. "I just wanted you to know that this trip was cancelled by the State Department, not the Department of Defense," I volunteered.

Philip sneered and retorted, "I thought we all worked for the same government. FIX IT!"

Milley was unflappable. He calmly told me, "Let them go to dinner. We have an hour to work this issue." Hawkins called his Regional Security Officer and put him on the phone with Milley. The infantry Colonel knew his area of operations better than the Embassy security guru, and somehow found a way to get the trip to the live fire exercise turned back on.

Zelikow, who had no military experience, was eating up all this HOOAH stuff. Scheid did not even get out of the car at the range. Hurley looked like he was dead tired. Milley told everyone watching the live fire exercise to put on his or her interceptor body armor and Kevlar helmets. Everyone quickly did as instructed except for Philip. His helmet would not fit. Apparently, his head was too big.

I was relieved to have a day off from the Commission. There were no military officials scheduled on the itinerary for the third day of the delegation's visit to Afghanistan. I had only one more activity with the group the following day, a second interview with General Barno.

Zelikow began the meeting by thanking Barno for his cooperation in rearranging the schedule at Bagram. He did not mention my name and did not even throw me a bone. Philip said the Commission had obtained the information it needed. However, he still had a few questions. The Executive Director spent the first ten minutes telling Barno his understanding of the General's own battlefield. Philip then proclaimed the global war on terrorism a transnational problem. He wanted to know why the coalition did not take the fight across the border to Pakistan.

As smart as Zelikow obviously was, I could not believe he was suggesting uniformed troops invade Pakistan. After all, didn't he realize that the Pakis had nukes. The president of Pakistan was barely maintaining control of his own government. The majority Muslim fundamentalists in Pakistan cheered the events of 9/11 and would love any excuse to attack India over the Kashmir issue.

General Barno fielded the question with more patience and skill than I could have had in his shoes. He told Philip that the coalition would act as a bulwark against the Taliban and Al Qaeda in Afghanistan. The US government would continue to pressure the Pakistan government on the terrorist presence in that country. Over time, the coalition would disarm the warlords, and the ANA would provide security for their own country. Mercifully, the interview and the 9/11 visit were over.

A week later, General Barno sent an e-mail to his Chief of Staff and "OMC-A All Users." He wrote, "The 9/11 Commission received the best support on this visit of any experience they ever had anywhere." There was no mention of the name of the escort officer and DOD representative.

Chapter XXI.

The Streamlined Code

S ir, I think we have a crisis," I told Colonel Gordon. "The Italians have published their streamlined code of criminal procedure and the Judicial Reform Commission is about to reject it. On top of that," I continued, "Professor Amiryar has resigned from the commission. He thinks his credibility has been undermined. This could be the beginning of the end of judicial reform in Afghanistan."

Gordon replied, "Calm down, Platte."

Once a week since July, Gordon had chaired a meeting of the international actors on the Rule of Law. At that time, General Eikenberry felt strongly that the Italians were not moving fast enough on judicial reform. He had asked the Colonel to develop a strategy to jump-start the Italian Justice Project. The plan Gordon developed was to shame the Italians into action. Gordon would invite the members of the international community working on police academies, courthouse renovation, prison construction, and judicial instruction into one room. When the leaders of the Justice Project heard about all the progress the other nations were making in the area of judicial reform, then maybe they would start to do something.

The Gardez Rule of Law Project was an initiative to bring justice to the provinces of Afghanistan, beginning with four courts in the cities of Gardez, Kandahar, Mazar-e Sharif, and Bamian. It included all the persons in the coalition working on the Rule of Law in Afghanistan. USAID's Democracy Officer,

Ana Klenicki, was providing the funding for courthouse renovation. The US Embassy's director of International Narcotics and Law Enforcement ("INL"), Ken Thomas, was building police academies. The Asia Foundation, shoring up the Judicial Reform Commission ("JRC"), was responsible for a public awareness campaign concerning the project. The United Nations Development Program ("UNDP") was supposed to erect a prison in Gardez. And, the Italian Justice Project, led by Presidente DiGennaro, was to contribute a streamlined code of criminal procedure.

At an October meeting of the Gardez Rule of Law Project, Presidente DiGennaro announced that he had almost finished the streamlined code, a task he had started in April. Ana Klenicki, a crotchety, sixty-plus year old Argentinean turned American, asked DiGennaro, "When will the US government have a chance to look at it?"

Dr. Antonio Palmisano, an anthropology professor at the University of Trieste and second in command at the Italian Justice Project, quickly replied, "When it is done."

Ana was visibly perturbed. She stared down Palmisano and inquired, "Don't you want our input?"

The Professor answered, "You will get it when it is done."

I was the next American to draw the ire of the Italians. Colonel Gordon, trying to break the tension, turned to me and said, "Platte, why don't you tell the group the progress you are making in getting defense counsel for Gardez." For some unknown reason, the Italians had not contemplated criminal defense counsel as part of judicial reform for Afghanistan. IDLO was not training defense counsel and the Italian Justice Project was only planning on providing instruction to judges and prosecutors.

"I have made contact with an organization known as the International Legal Foundation," I began. "They are a New York City-based private organization that fosters the rule of law by establishing legal aid clinics in post-conflict countries. They have opened the first legal aid clinic in Afghanistan here in Kabul. The ILF is willing to supply us with a defense counsel for Gardez," I concluded with pride, thinking that I had made a real contribution to the project.

DiGennaro started to boil. "Why do we need defense counsel?" he demanded to know. Without waiting for me to answer, he shouted, "This country has never had defense counsel. Why do they need them now?"

I could not believe what I was hearing. Here was one of the worlds' most well-known and respected jurists, and he was questioning me on the need for defense lawyers. Showing deference to the Italian Supreme Court President, I responded, "Sir, certainly you are not suggesting that defense counsel have no role in re-establishing the rule of law in Afghanistan."

Realizing that he could not answer my question affirmatively and apparently ashamed of the fact that the Italians had not come up with the idea of defense counsel first, he retorted, "Your idea is a Soviet one. We cannot force criminals to have a defense counsel." I lost it. I no longer cared who DiGennaro was. I had seen these lawyer tricks back in Philadelphia. When one knows that he is on the end of a losing argument, then change the subject. I went on the offensive.

"The 1964 Constitution guarantees a person accused of a crime the right to counsel. I think that we can all agree on that," I said. "We are not forcing Afghans to have a public defender. I am simply suggesting that any judicial reform project must have an adversarial system in which the accused has the right to question the prosecution's case with the assistance of defense counsel."

DiGennaro was not used to losing arguments, especially with American lawyers. "Afghanistan cannot pay for defense lawyers, and no one should be required to use a lawyer selected for him by the state," he said. "Are you suggesting we adopt a Soviet system here?"

"Of course not," I barked. "Are we communicating here? No one is suggesting that criminally accused must be represented by defense lawyers selected by the central government. All I am saying is that the criminally accused should have the right to counsel."

Colonel Gordon had heard enough. He adroitly diffused the situation by moving on to a different topic "Can we now talk about who is going to build the prison?" he said.

During the first week in November, the Italian Justice Project forwarded its streamlined code of criminal procedure to the Judicial Reform Commission for review and approval. Apparently, DiGennaro was arrogant enough to think that his name being associated with the proposed code would win it instant sanction.

JRC Chairman Bahauddin Baha had other ideas. He accepted the streamlined code for review by the full commission, but made it clear that he opposed it. First, he did not trust the Justice Project's translation of the code from Italian to English to Dari. He had it independently translated. Then, he said the code was contrary to Afghan legal traditions and an unnecessary interim law that would confuse judges and prosecutors. Finally, he claimed that the Commission had no role in the drafting of the code. Baha was blowing smoke.

In fact, Professor Quadir Amiryar was a member of the JRC and one of six Afghans who sat on a committee at the Italian Justice Project to help draft the proposed law. The other Afghan representatives came from the Ministry of Justice, Supreme Court, and Attorney General's Office. All committee members had agreed to the text of the DiGennaro code.

While the streamlined code was in the hands of the JRC awaiting its formal position on the suitability for Afghanistan, Colonel Gordon was packing to go home. He had spent almost one year in theater. The Army had decided his next assignment would be Baghdad, Iraq. I was sorry to see him go. We had developed a bond based upon professional respect and personal friendship. Although he had reluctantly given me a job at OMC-A, he now was my biggest supporter and let me go anywhere in his place. There was no guarantee that his replacement would give me such responsibility and freedom.

"Hi, I'm John Mantooth," said the almost sixty-year old Colonel from Oklahoma. "I am going to be the Staff Judge Advocate for OMC-A, and Combined Forces Command, and the United States Ambassador. I was personally picked by the Judge Advocate General of the US Army for this job."

We met in the School House where the 213th ASG had its offices for base operations in Kabul. After only thirty minutes on the compound, he was getting his photograph taken for an identification card. He had not even been to his quarters. He was on the ground and in charge.

I introduced myself. He said, "I have heard a lot of good things about you from Colonel Pede and Colonel Gordon. I know that we will be good friends." I thought that was pretty presumptuous. But, at the time, I gave him the benefit of the doubt, figuring that he was just trying to be nice.

He continued, "I know that you have an extensive background in international law." Seeing no right shoulder combat patch on his uniform, I doubted Mantooth had ever been on active duty or in a war zone. "I want you to know that I have a lot of experience myself," he proclaimed. "I have been practicing law for thirty-four years, and I have been a city judge in Purcell, Oklahoma, for twenty-five years. And, I studied Central Asia in college." I started wondering to myself, *"And, exactly how many years ago was that?"* Turns out, Mantooth, like me, had never been on active duty before. Unlike me, he had volunteered for this assignment.

Colonel Tom Snukis from Reading, Pennsylvania, was the new Chief of Staff, having replaced Colonel Bridge, who rotated back to the States. Bridge's prediction had come true. President Bush had moved the Three-Star Commander of the Afghanistan Theater from Bagram to Kabul. Further, the newly created organization, Combined Force Command-Central Asia ("CFC-CA"), was now in charge. Colonel Snukis took an immediate liking to the people from the ASG because we were all from near his hometown. I had done a few projects for him after Bridge left, and he knew what I could do.

On the way to chow one day in early November, Snukis, a big Bull Dog of a man with a crew cut, stopped me. "Hey, this Mantooth guy is a bit of a loose cannon," instructed Snukis.

"I'm counting on you to keep him under control. He can be the judge of CFC, and you can cover down on OMC-A."

"Sir," I answered, "He's not looking at it that way. He says he is the Staff Judge Advocate for the Ambassador, CFC-CA, and OMC-A. I have been told that I am his deputy."

"Hang in there," said Snukis.

I suggested to Mantooth that we needed to go see Baha. The fate of the Gardez Rule of Law Project was in the balance. The JRC was opposing the streamlined code of the Italians. And, the lead nation on judicial reform in Afghanistan was refusing to do anything to advance the Rule of Law until President Karzai signed a decree making the code law. Further, I had heard a rumor from Ana Klenicki that the Italians were pressuring Karzai to shut down the JRC.

Mantooth locked and loaded his M9 pistol and held it at the ready in his hand as we got into the "JAG Mobile," a red Toyota Surf. He had not been outside the compound in the city of Kabul. As always, I kept my piece in the holster with no round chambered and the weapon on safe. The building being used by the JRC was in the middle of a busy market, and there was no place to park. We drove onto the sidewalk and got out of the vehicle. I raced inside the building to find a JRC employee to sit in the car. I did not want Mantooth's first full day in theater to be ruined with an improvised explosive device.

The purpose of the JRC was to coordinate judicial reform in Afghanistan by bringing together three feuding ministries— Supreme Court, Attorney General's Office, and Ministry of Justice. Chairman Baha was another American citizen working on reconstruction who was an Afghan ex-patriot. Before 9/11, he had been working as an Imam in a mosque in Mission Viejo, California. Now, he was the chief advisor to President Karzai on judicial reform.

Baha greeted us warmly and asked us to sit down. In broken English, he said, "I would offer you some tea, but it is Ramadan and we are fasting."

"That is okay," said Mantooth. "We are here to talk about

the Italian Streamlined Code. Did you know that the Italians are trying to terminate the Judicial Reform Commission?"

Baha, a gray-haired man in his late sixties with glasses, wearing a suit and tie, looked shocked. He replied softly, "Who told you this?"

I was flabbergasted. We had just learned from USAID in strictest confidence that there was an effort to dismantle the JRC, and now Mantooth was blurting it out to the man most affected by the back room maneuvering. I thought Baha was going to cry. He said, "Who would do such a thing?"

"Sir," I said trying to work damage control, "let me try to explain the situation from the Italian perspective. The Italian Justice Project believes that it had assembled a working group with representation from all three justice ministries and the JRC. The Italians felt that approval of the streamlined code by the working group was also approval by the represented agencies. DiGennaro and his staff are now very surprised to learn that the JRC opposes their plan for judicial reform of the criminal procedure code."

"Let me explain to you about Professor Amiryar, the so-called JRC representative on this committee," instructed Baha. "Amiryar has never been a judge in Afghanistan. He has never practiced law in this country. He is not even a lawyer. What does he know about criminal law, I ask you?"

Without directly responding to the question, I explained that the United States had a strong interest in preserving the JRC. The Italians viewed the JRC as an obstacle to their plan for judicial reform. Moreover, the entire Rule of Law Committee at the United Nations was composed of Italians. Mr. Brahimi, the UN Special Representative, had placed a letter on President Karzai's desk at the behest of the Italians, asking for the dissolution of the JRC.

"Well, what do you recommend that I do?" questioned Baha.

"You must find a way to compromise," I stated.

"I would not be serving the people of Afghanistan if

I accepted the Italian criminal procedure code," Baha said rubbing his eyes. "That code is contrary to the legal traditions of Islam and Afghanistan. It calls for one judge on a court, instead of three. It would only apply to certain parts of the country. It is an unnecessary temporary law that will confuse Afghan judges and prosecutors. I cannot accept it. Here is a copy of the letter that I sent to the Italian Ambassador opposing the adoption of the code."

This was a battle that would have to be fought on another day. We exchanged further pleasantries, promised to keep him informed of all developments, and took our leave. There were about twenty children surrounding our car when we left the building. The JRC employee was still sitting in the JAG Mobile. Every kid wanted a handout. I just hoped no one had been paid to put a bomb on the car.

"We need to speak to the Ambassador," I said to Mantooth as we drove the car back to the compound. "This issue has now gotten well over our heads, and it appears that the whole process of judicial reform is going to stop in its tracks until the Afghans and Italians resolve this streamlined code issue one way or another." Mantooth agreed, and we called Ana Klenicki to arrange a meeting with the Deputy Chief of Mission, Mr. Sedney.

Two days later, Sedney called Mantooth, Klenicki, Ken Thomas, and me into his office at the embassy. On this occasion, Sedney was more gracious than he had been when I had previously entered this room with General Barno and the 9/11 Commission. In fact, he remembered me and called me by my first name. "I understand we have a problem with the Italians," he said. "How can I help?"

Ana Klenicki just wanted to talk about the status of the JRC. USAID had a stake in the continuation of the Commission. By Presidential Decree, Karzai had established the JRC. When the UN reneged on its promise to provide a support staff for the Commission, USAID, through its contractor, The Asia Foundation, had provided the necessary personnel. The end of the JRC meant pink slips for a lot of government contractors.

Sedney then asked, "What does this streamlined code have to do with all of this?"

Mantooth replied, "Sir, we believe the code takes away human rights."

"How so?" queried Sedney.

"I will let Colonel Moring answer your question. He has done all the research," said Mantooth punting the difficult question to me. I was pleased to have the floor. I then proceeded to tell the acting Ambassador all the reasons why the streamlined code was inconsistent with the 1974 Afghan criminal procedure law. Additionally, I explained why the US Government should oppose the Italian proposal.

"Sir, the streamlined code is the work of a former Mafia Prosecutor who thinks the best model for criminal justice reform in Afghanistan is an inquisitorial system. President DiGennaro would empower Judicial Police, acting on their own initiative, to enter homes, seize personal property, and make arrests. The actions of these Judicial Police would only be subject to review by the Prosecutor after thirty days. No judge would review the propriety of the investigative techniques of the Judicial Police until trial."

At this point, Ken Thomas, the tall thin police coordinator with INL, jumped in. "I saw the Italians try this same stunt in Bosnia. They somehow got the lead on judicial reform there and created the Judicial Police. It was an unmitigated disaster. There were a lot of doors being kicked down in Bosnia supposedly in the interest of justice."

Sedney then looked at me. "Platte, what do you think we need to do?"

"Sir," I answered, "the Italians have agreed to meet with us this week to discuss our problems with the streamlined code. I have prepared a six-page memo outlining our concerns with their proposal by topic and paragraph number. My memo, I understand, has been faxed to Rome to be read by Presidente DiGennaro. I suggest we meet with them. Let's see if we can find away to get them to change the most heinous sections of the code and make the rest of it consistent with Afghan law."

Sedney then surveyed the room and asked, "Can we all agree to that?"

"Platte has my complete confidence," Thomas said.

"And mine," Klenicki rejoined.

"Well, keep me posted," Sedney instructed.

Antonio Palmisano and Vincenzo Lattanzi of the Italian Justice Project agreed to meet with Mantooth and me before DiGennaro came back to Kabul from Rome. We all hoped that we could reach a compromise with our cooler heads without the hot-tempered Presidente present. Antonio and Vincenzo listened intently as I went through the streamlined code from start to finish, identifying the provisions that were inconsistent with Afghan law and unacceptable to the United States. Once I showed them the actual articles from the 1974 Afghan law on criminal procedure which were at odds with the DiGennaro code, they appeared convinced that some modification was in order. They promised to fax my eight pages of comments with citations from Afghan law to Rome for the Presidente's review.

"Platte, can we get together a few minutes before the Gardez meeting?" Palmisano asked me in a cell phone call three days later.

"Sure, Antonio," I answered. "What's up?"

"We have heard back from the Presidente," he replied.

After Mantooth and I arrived at the Italian Justice Project for the weekly Gardez committee meeting, Palmisano motioned for me alone to enter his office. "Platte, we have a problem," he said. I nodded, expecting what was to follow. "The Presidente has reviewed your paper. He is offended. He cannot understand how you would suggest he has written something that violates human rights. Presidente DiGennaro has rejected all of your changes. Here are his written comments to your paper."

We might as well have cancelled the meeting of the Gardez Rule of Law Project. It appeared we had reached an impasse. I certainly had no desire to talk about courthouse plans and prison construction under the circumstances. The Italians were not going ahead with judicial reform without the streamlined code, and the US Government could not accept it as presently written. After the short session, I was feeling defeated. "I will read the Presidente's comments on my paper, and maybe we can talk again," I said to Palmisano as we left his office.

Back at Kabul Compound, I began to pour over El Presidente's diatribe on my objections to the streamlined code. It was hard to believe that it was written by a lawyer. The document contained more invective than it did reason. There was only one citation to a written law. When I looked up the referenced article from the 1974 Afghan criminal procedure code, I discovered that DiGennaro had misquoted the section and discussed it out of context. I was angry.

My cell phone rang. It was Guiseppe Fedele, the Second Secretary of the Italian Embassy. "Platte," he said, "Could you come over to the embassy sometime tomorrow to talk? We need to discuss the Presidente's comments to your paper. We have a final version of our comments that we would like to review with you."

"What time would you like us to come?" I answered politely. "I am just now working on a written response to Presidente DiGennaro's comments to my suggestions on the streamlined code."

Mantooth and I went to the Italian Embassy the next morning at 8:30 A.M. I had spent most of the night before polishing my rebuttal to the DiGennaro hate mail. I was loaded for bear. Fedele welcomed us to his office on the second floor of the embassy. As usual the Afghan power system had failed, and his office was without heat and freezing. There was no coffee, and Fedele said he only had a few minutes before he would have to go to his next meeting.

The Second Secretary asked if we had a chance to review the paper prepared by Presidente DiGennaro. Mantooth shook his head vertically in acknowledgement. "You know that DiGennaro is one of the world's leading experts on human rights," Fedele stated. "He would never author any document contrary to international standards."

"The issue is not international standards," I replied. "The issue is compliance with the traditions of Afghan law. No one asked Italy to write a criminal procedure code for Afghanistan. That was the charter of the Judicial Reform Commission. According to the Bonn Agreement, any new laws for Afghanistan are supposed to be drafted in accordance with Islamic principles, traditional Afghan law, and international human rights standards. The streamlined code is simply DiGennaro's attempt to impose his prosecution-oriented view of justice upon Afghanistan. It is not acceptable to the United States as written."

I was on the warpath. Mantooth just sat there in silence, wondering what I might say next. "Italy is the lead nation on judicial reform in Afghanistan. The United States is very interested in seeing that Italy continues in that role. We are ready to support you. We want you to shine. We have suggested a few modifications to make it acceptable to the Judicial Reform Commission. However, this streamlined code will be opposed by us unless you are willing to compromise."

"It is unclear when the right to counsel attaches in this code," I continued. "At present, there is no Judicial Police in Afghanistan. DiGennaro would create a special police force to act 'on their own initiative' and 'to do whatever justice requires.' After a trial in which the accused was found not guilty, DiGennaro would permit a second trial at the request of the prosecutor in which new evidence could be offered and the accused charged with a different crime. These provisions are contrary to the 1974 Afghan criminal procedure law."

Fedele seemed shocked by this onslaught by a Philadelphia trial lawyer. I assume that he was not used to such plain speaking in diplomatic circles. He had no substantive response. The Second Secretary ended the conversation where he had started. "I am certain that the Presidente would not have written a criminal procedure code contrary to human rights," he reiterated. "Presidente DiGennaro has considered your comments, and the Government of Italy cannot accept your modifications."

"Guiseppe, I do not know where we go from here," I rejoined. "The United States cannot recommend the streamlined code to President Karzai as written. Without the support of our government, the streamlined code is dead, and the role of Italy as the lead nation on judicial reform is in question. Colonel Mantooth and I have a meeting with our Ambassador at 3:00 P.M. today. We will report Italy's unwillingness to compromise and seek his guidance."

I had just given the final examination to my students in the Defense Counsel Seminar at Kabul University. It was a wonderful event. Twenty-four students had been waiting for me outside on the steps of the building housing the Faculty of Law and Politics as I pulled up in the JAG mobile. At first, I thought the exam had scared away the rest of my class. By 1:00 P.M., however, most of the kids were in their seats. Seventy-one students sat for the exam. They wanted to talk to me afterwards about the questions. I had to go. The US embassy was on the other side of Kabul, and I did not want to be late for my meeting with the acting Ambassador. We waved good-bye to the kids. My force protection for the day, Captain Shane Paul, and I drove away with me at the wheel.

As we waited in traffic, my cell phone began to ring. There was no way I could dodge taxis, apple carts, and women in Birkas and answer the phone. I passed the cell phone to Shane. Guiseppe Fedele thought he was talking with me. He told Shane that he had talked with Rome and Presidente DiGennaro. They were willing to discuss modifications to the streamlined code. Fedele told Captain Paul that DiGennaro would meet us at the Italian Justice Project the next morning at 9 A.M.

Women in birkas gather in the marketplace in Kabul to shop for food for the evening meal. Photograph by US Army Combat Camera.

I was late getting to the embassy. Mr. Sedney was already meeting with Ken Thomas, Ana Klenicki, Mantooth, and Jack Bell. Mr. Bell had just arrived in Kabul to take over as the Executive Director of the Afghan Reconstruction Group. Mantooth had already reported the intransigence of the Italians, and they were discussing the future of judicial reform in light of the impasse on the streamlined code. I waited for the right moment to tell the group about the phone call I had just received from Fedele.

Mr. Sedney instructed the group that Italy must be preserved as the lead nation on judicial reform. President Bush had personally asked the Italian Prime Minister that Italy assume this role. Sedney wanted the assembled group to propose courses of action. He started to suggest that the new US Ambassador would have to arrange a meeting with the

Italian Ambassador or have the issue referred to Washington for resolution. At that time, I entered the dialogue.

"Sir, I apologize for being late to the meeting. I was caught in traffic on my way back from Kabul University. In the car, I got a phone call from the Second Secretary of the Italian Embassy. He requested that Colonel Mantooth and I come to the Italian Justice Project tomorrow for a meeting with Presidente DiGennaro. He wants to reach a compromise on the streamlined code."

"Well, it seems that Platte has given us our answer," said Sedney. "Good luck with Presidente DiGennaro."

"Yeah," said Ken Thomas. "I would love to be a fly on the wall for that meeting. Be sure to wear your bulletproof vest."

After spending most of the rest of the day and night re-reading the 1974 Afghan criminal procedure code, I was ready to confront the leadership of the Italian Justice Project. Presidente DiGennaro, Vincenzo Lattanzi, Dr. Palmisano, and Fedele met us at the door of their compound. Mantooth had a child-like excitement as he met the Italian Chief Justice figure for the first time. I was just hoping the day would not turn into a shouting match.

For early December in Afghanistan, it was unusually mild. The temperature inside the Justice Project, however, was about to get warmer. As expected, DiGennaro took the lead. "Platte, I have read your memo. I guess from what you have written that you know little about me. Let me tell you a few things. I was a Mafia Prosecutor in Sicily for ten years. On three occasions, I was sentenced to death—by the Fascists, the Nazis, and the Red Brigade. I was the principal architect of the new penal and penitentiary legislation in Italy. I reformed the criminal justice systems in Albania and Kosovo. I have served both the United Nations and the European Commission as an officer and advisor on human rights..."

His introduction continued for twenty minutes. It was obvious where this was leading. DiGennaro wanted me to roll over simply because he was an international legal superstar. I was not going to do it. I had a mandate from the US Embassy to negotiate a compromise with DiGennaro, and I was determined to make it happen. I smiled and nodded politely as he continued to detail his resume.

"There is no law in this country," DiGennaro continued. "Maybe there never will be. The judges have no legal training. The courthouses are destroyed. The Chief Justice of the Supreme Court is a Mullah. Afghanistan needs a legal system that can address these problems. I know you do not like my inquisitorial approach to judicial reform, but these people cannot have any other system."

For some reason, Mantooth felt compelled to review his resume in response. I chose to remain silent. By my way of thinking, my insignificant qualifications to be in the same room with DiGennaro talking about the fine points of comparative law were not worth mentioning and arguably laughable. Nonetheless, Mantooth told DiGennaro about his thirty-five years of legal practice and twenty years as a municipal court judge in Purcell, Oklahoma, trying traffic accident cases.

It took some time for DiGennaro to realize that we were not going to be intimidated and we meant business. As we applied more pressure, he began to back down. I would like to think that it was my analysis of Afghan law in comparison to the streamlined code that persuaded the Presidente of the wisdom of my arguments. But, I was not that naïve. He had obviously been told by Rome to find a way to get American support for the code.

The dynamic of the debate was interesting. Palmisano and Lattanzi were not lawyers. They viewed the eight-hour dialogue as simply an exercise of convincing the Americans to go along with DiGennaro's view of judicial reform. These two academics had no time for the subtleties of comparative law. They saw no reason to make the proposed criminal procedure code consistent with the draft Afghan Constitution or existing statutory law. At one point, Palmisano remarked, "Now, Platte, you know the Afghans are not going to follow the law anyway. We are just creating rules of a game that will never be played."

Throughout the course of the debate, I gained respect for DiGennaro. He was not simply defending a point of view as an American lawyer would do in motions court. The Justice genuinely wanted to understand the reasons for our objections to the streamlined code. He asked us to identify by article number our support for the argument that the proposed criminal procedure code was not consistent with Afghan law. Presidente DiGennaro considered the merits of our position like a fair and impartial judge. He probed and pondered. Ultimately, DiGennaro caved on almost every one of the American objections to the substance of his streamlined code.

Pictured left to right: Author, Vincenzo Lattanzi, Presidente DiGennaro, Afghan interpreter, Enayata Qasimi, and COL Mantooth at the Italian Justice Project working on the streamlined code. Photograph by LTC Kyle Goerke.

Before I accepted the plaudits of the US embassy for extracting the concessions from the Italians and preserving

Italy's role as the lead nation on judicial sector reform, I knew there was a lot of work still to do. The streamlined code was not yet law. Since DiGennaro had not gotten along well with the Afghan ministries, it would be up to Mantooth and me to sell the draft law to the leaders of the transitional government.

I knew the Italian approach of walking the streamlined code into President Karzai's office for signature was a no-go. We would need to build consensus for the criminal procedure code by shopping it around the ministries. The first stop was a return trip to Chairman Baha of the Judicial Reform Commission. Since Ana Klenicki of USAID had previously gotten a commitment from Baha to be flexible in his consideration of the streamlined code, she accompanied Mantooth and me to the meeting.

This time he was not ready to face the USG alone. Baha had invited Dr. Hashemzai, his Secretariat and the Deputy Minister of Justice, to sit in on the meeting and shore up his defenses. The Oxford-educated professor had full command of the English language. He was wearing a tailor-made and well-pressed suit with tie for the interview.

Mantooth made the pitch. "We have revised the streamlined code. It is now the Interim Criminal Procedure for Courts. It is consistent with Afghan statutory law and international human rights. Colonel Moring will explain to you all the technical amendments in great detail. The code has the approval of the American and Italian governments. We would now like for you to get on this train with us and ride it all the way to Gardez, our first courthouse."

Hashemzai was balking. "We would be happy to review your proposal and see what articles can be incorporated into the draft criminal procedure code that the Judicial Reform Commission is working on," he said.

Klenicki never minced words. Her age and experience as a democracy officer gave her more leeway with the Afghans than her more disciplined military counterparts. "You must stop working on your own draft law," she said. "This code is the only criminal procedure code. Certainly, you must see that. Listen to what Colonel Moring has to say."

After I had explained how Mantooth and I along with the Italian Justice Project had revised the streamlined code to address the concerns of the JRC, Hashemzai was still not satisfied. "There is absolutely no way you can reduce the five hundred articles of the existing law into ninety-eight articles," he insisted. "The criminal procedure law enacted in 1974 has worked well for us and there is no reason to change it."

It was hard for me to suppress my laughter, but I remained expressionless. Most of the judges and prosecutors in Afghanistan had never seen a statutory law. The Russians and the Taliban certainly did not apply the 1974 law to criminal investigations and trials. The twenty-three years of war since 1979 were not a strong endorsement for the 1974 law's contribution to the rule of law in Afghanistan.

"Dr. Hashemzai, the whole idea behind the streamlined code," I rejoined, "was to make criminal procedure easier to teach and simpler to apply in practice. In just ninety-eight articles, the code lays out all the steps of criminal investigation, trial, and appeal in a way that is entirely consistent with the 1974 law and international human rights standards. The international community urges you to give it your thoughtful consideration."

Klenicki, Mantooth, and I left the JRC discouraged. Although we had not expected to get the commission's stamp of approval on this visit, we certainly thought that they would be pleased that we had hammered DiGennaro into submission. Fortunately, I had arranged in advance for a dinner that evening with Professor Amiryar to talk strategy. I needed guidance on what to do next. The Italians had staked their credibility in the streamlined code, and our judicial reform initiatives could not get started until the proposed law became a Presidential Decree.

We met in the mess hall on Kabul Compound. I had wanted to treat Amiryar to a nice dinner at the Iranian restaurant near our safe house, but Colonel Snukis denied our request. The start of the Constitutional Loya Jirga had placed everyone on a high state of alert. No one at CFC-CA or OMC-A could have a meeting off the compound at night. Terrorists had set off an explosion at the Intercontinental Hotel, and three rockets had been launched in the Kabul area at the start of the constitutional convention.

"Do not worry about the JRC," said Amiryar. "They are powerless. Karzai has no respect for Baha and has roundly criticized the JRC for inaction. You must go to the Minister of Justice, Karimi, and get his approval for the streamlined code. If Karimi says yes to the code, Karzai will sign it into law."

"But sir," I interjected, "we have already spoken with Karimi's deputy minister, Hashemzai, on the code. He said the Ministry of Justice would never accept the Italian proposal."

"Hashemzai is an opportunist," Amiryar replied, lowering his already soft voice. "He wants the JRC and the Italian Justice Project to go away so that he can be Karzai's personal advisor on judicial reform. Go to see Karimi." With Yoda's advice, Mantooth and I knew where to go next.

Minister Abdul Rahim Karimi had invited television cameramen and photographers to the start of our meeting with him. It soon became apparent that this gentleman had a big ego and needed to be stroked. "I am a personal friend of General Eikenberry," the Justice Minister said in Dari. "He frequently invited me to accompany him on ANA recruiting trips because of my outstanding speaking ability." Apparently, his Excellency had not kept up with current events. General Eikenberry had left theater in September, and his replacement, Air Force Major General Craig Weston, had been on ground for a month.

Karimi sat on a large couch by himself while his personal assistant and interpreter, Mr. Mansoori, sat in a chair close by. The minister was a short, stout man, with jet-black hair and beard. He was wearing a three-piece suit with tie. Mantooth and I were pleased to learn that he was aware of the streamlined code. However, he had another agenda.

"President Karzai has recently signed a decree putting my ministry in charge of the registration of new political parties," Karimi announced. "I will not register any political party that has guns. When the warlords learn that I have denied them status as a political party, then they will come for me. You must provide security for me and my ministry."

Colonel Mantooth and I were beginning to learn that wearing a military uniform and walking into an interview with an Afghan official apparently elevated us to the status of US Ambassador in the eyes of these people. Any request for assistance from the US Government was fair game. We had absolutely no responsibility for the physical security of the ministers of the transitional government. And yet, we were being tasked to develop this minister's defense plan against the warlords.

I tried to get the conversation back to the streamlined code. "Your Excellency, do you believe that the Ministry of Justice can act quickly on the draft criminal procedure code after it is received from the JRC?" This question apparently lit a fuse with Karimi.

"The JRC goes away when the Loya Jirga concludes in eight days," he proclaimed. "They have done nothing. Hashemzai has been telling lies about me. He tells everyone that I have no time to discuss judicial reform. My door is always open. You will find no one more reform-minded than me in all of Afghanistan. Do not worry about the JRC. I will convene representatives of the Supreme Court and Attorney General and get approval for the criminal procedure code."

Having succeeded so far, I decided to bring up another issue. I wanted his buy in on defense counsel for our model courthouse program. I had hoped to use a non-governmental organization, the International Legal Foundation, to recruit and train criminal defense lawyers. However, I had just learned from its Executive Director, Natalie Rea, that they could not perform this function. There simply were not any experienced independent lawyers in all of Afghanistan for her to recruit and train.

If there were to be defense lawyers as part of the legal team for the Four Courts Initiative, then they would have to come from my defense counsel class. Apart from the fact that these college graduates were not lawyers and had no experience or training, some of them were not even the statutorily required age of twenty-five. Under Afghan law, the Minister of Justice had to certify all defense counsel. Much to my surprise, Karimi immediately blessed the idea of using my students as defense counsel in the new criminal courts of Afghanistan.

Mantooth and I left the Ministry feeling sky high. Karimi had just endorsed the streamlined code and the defense counsel initiative. There was only one stop left—The Supreme Court. We were going from the most reform-minded minister to the least. Just one month earlier, Chief Justice Shinwari had condemned to hell a twenty-five year-old Pashtun who was the first woman in thirty-one years to compete in a beauty contest as "Miss Afghanistan." Shinwari called the woman's wearing of a red-hot bikini in the beauty pageant "totally un-Islamic" and against "tradition, human honor and dignity."

Author, LTG Tahib, Chief Justice Shinwari, and COL Mantooth at the Afghan Supreme Court.

The meeting with Shinwari came about unexpectedly. Mantooth was not with me. He had another mission. General Prasek's personal security detachment traveling in a SUV had collided with another vehicle, causing it to run over and kill an Afghan on a bicycle on October 31, 2003. Following Afghan custom, Colonel Mantooth, on behalf of the Army, had taken a sheep, a bag of rice, and a liter of cooking oil to the family of the dead cyclist. I had gone without him to the weekly meeting with the Afghan judges who were working on a military justice code for the ANA. One hour into the meeting, much to my surprise, General Tahib, the military judge on the Supreme Court, told me the Chief Justice wanted to see me.

General Tahib pointed to my Interceptor Body Army and said something in Dari. My interpreter told me to wear my bulletproof vest because we were going to travel with an Afghan militia convoy to the home of the Chief Justice. I climbed into a SUV and immediately began racing through the streets of Kabul at a high rate of speed. Tahib stopped the car in a crowded market area adorned with slaughtered sheep hanging on meat hooks. Kids suddenly surrounded the SUV and stared at me. Armed gunmen then ushered me down a narrow corridor to the rear of a private home.

I found Chief Justice Shinwari lying on a blanket on a raised patio surrounded by other mullahs who were sitting in a circle. He had recently broken his leg. As I leaned over to give the customary Afghan greeting to the mullah, I surveyed the scene. There were men wearing traditional clothes and carrying AK-47s on the front, back and roof of the house.

I was scared. No one from the compound had authorized this trip or knew where I was. My M9 pistol was no defense to this collection of armed fundamentalist warriors. I tried to remain calm as Shinwari's servants served Chai tea and we exchanged pleasantries. My translator, Parwaiz Barkzai, assisted me in the conversation with the Chief Justice.

We first talked about the grand opening of the newly paved Ring Road between Kabul and Kandahar. I told him about the model courthouse program for the four provinces and the interim criminal procedure code. Shinwari seemed mildly interested. What he really wanted to know was why I had come to his country. When I said I was in Afghanistan to do "Allah's will," Shinwari seemed particularly pleased with me.

At the next meeting of the military justice working group, General Tahib told me that I had done well with the Chief Justice. The night after the interview, Afghan radio broadcast that a US Army Colonel had met with Shinwari. Tahib said, "Your visit with the Chief Justice has solved all our political problems." I had no idea what he meant by that and did not think it was my business to seek clarification.

"Sir, I need you to come to the General's office right away," said First Lieutenant Todd Doughty, General Weston's aide. Mantooth had just gotten back to Kabul Compound after his meeting with the relatives of the deceased Afghan. I had returned from my meeting with the Afghan judges at the Supreme Court. We went immediately to Weston's office at the Rose House.

"Thanks for coming," said the General. "Here is the situation. The Italian Ambassador has requested a meeting with our new Ambassador on judicial sector reform. I want you two to prepare a briefing for Ambassador Khalizad so that he knows something about the subject before he meets with the Italians. Are there any problems with the Italians that I should know about?"

Before I could speak, Mantooth answered. I was a little miffed. A week earlier, the OMC-A Chief of Staff had told me that I was going to be the Acting Staff Judge Advocate for General Weston, quashing Mantooth's plans of being the head lawyer for two generals and the ambassador. The chiefs of staff of CFC-CA and OMC-A had seen the wisdom of having separate legal advisors for General Barno and General Weston. Now, Mantooth was addressing my client, the general.

"I have patched up all the problems that existed in the past between the judge advocates at OMC-A and Presidente DiGennaro," volunteered Mantooth. I am certain that I raised my eyebrows. It was one thing for a senior officer to take precedence over a junior officer in speaking with a General Officer. It was quite another thing for Mantooth to suggest that Colonel Gordon and I had a bad relationship with the Italians and that he had miraculously cured it.

"We continue to enjoy a good relationship with the Italian Justice Project," I insisted, finishing the thought for Mantooth. "Sir, I fully expect that Ambassador Giorgi will only have positive reports about the cooperation between DiGennaro and the American judge advocates.

"Well that's good to hear," replied General Weston. "Have a briefing ready for me to review in two days. I need to have more visibility on what the two of you are doing."

Ambassador Zalmay Khalizad had just arrived in Afghanistan. The United States had been without an ambassador for almost five months. He had no previous experience as a diplomat, but had achieved success as a businessman. Khalizad was a take-charge kind of guy.

There was no discussion between Mantooth and me as to who was going to do the actual briefing for the Ambassador. The day before the embassy briefing I had done a rehearsal of the Microsoft PowerPoint presentation on judicial reform for General Weston. It was a good warm-up, and Weston approved the content. It made good sense that I be the one to brief the Ambassador. Weston, General Prasek, Mr. Sedney, and Ana Klenicki were all in attendance in the ambassador's office at the embassy.

Khalizad asked thoughtful questions. He also wanted expedited timelines on judicial reform. Preservation of the JRC was a priority for him. I asked for the Ambassador's help in getting the streamlined code approved by the Afghan judicial ministries and onto President Karzai's desk for entry into a Decree. Khalizad said he would speak to Karzai the next day.

I was thrilled with my briefing to the United States Ambassador to Afghanistan. However, Ana Klenicki was upset with me. "You army lawyers make it sound like only you are responsible for judicial reform in Afghanistan," she scolded. "If the Director of USAID had attended that meeting, he would be very upset. It is AID that is paying for judicial reform in Afghanistan."

"I am very sorry, Ana." I explained, "When I used 'we' I meant the 'USG'—AID, INL, OMC-A, and the embassy." She accepted my apology. Only later did it occur to me that I had not given Ana's efforts enough credit and may have weakened her standing with the new ambassador.

A week later, it was Christmas Eve, and Klenicki called me on the phone. "Mr. Sedney wants us to go over to the Italian Embassy and meet with Ambassador Giorgi this afternoon," she instructed. "We are supposed to give the Italian Ambassador some ideas on restructuring the Judicial Reform Commission." I hurriedly created a briefing with five courses of action for the future of the JRC. At 1630 hours, Mantooth, Klenicki, and I met with Giorgi for almost two hours. Ten hours later, on Christmas morning, a rocket hit the Italian compound, destroying a wall but causing no injuries.

Chapter XXII.

Push Back

I think I got bad news," said Sergeant Major Werley. "Rumsfeld is holding a press conference tomorrow, and he is expected to announce that everyone in Afghanistan in OEF4 will have 270 days of boots on the ground. I cannot believe it! Thirty days from going home, and now we are extended another ninety days. This fucking sucks."

Janze and I looked at Werley with stunned disbelief. Werley had spent most of the week on the SIPRNET searching for the Alert Order for our replacement unit. He knew that for our unit to go home at the end of 179 days, or by December 26, 2003, the follow-on ASG would have to go to the mobilization station by November 1. It was now November 17, and the 33rd ASG from Illinois had not received an alert order.

Two weeks earlier, I had gone to Bagram to participate in a video telephone conference. Modern technology allowed a soldier to see his family on television and at the same time talk with them. The unit Family Support Group was having a Halloween Party back in Allentown at the armory for soldiers' spouses and children. Thirty-six soldiers waited for up to three hours to say hello to mom or the wife and kids for just three minutes on TV. There were smiles on the way in to the VTC room and tears on the way out. Leigh and Will spent the entire three minutes fighting over who would put his or her face closest to the camera.

Since Colonel Wagner and I were the most senior soldiers, we had allowed all the other personnel to go ahead of us in the VTC line. The long wait gave us time to chat. I wanted to know if he had heard any news about our redeployment. Wagner assured me that everything was on track, and we could expect to leave theater no later than December 26. "That's our story," he proclaimed, "and we are sticking to it."

Not satisfied with that answer, I asked Wagner if he had taken any steps to confirm our departure plans with the Department of Army or Forces Command. He said he had sent an e-mail to the Colonel at National Guard Bureau in charge of operations. The focus of the message was that extended deployments of Reserve and National Guard soldiers in Iraq and Afghanistan were having a detrimental impact on recruiting and retention.

This was not good enough for me. I knew that the 33rd ASG had not been alerted, and I wanted a written order stating that I was going home. "Sir," I pleaded, "I think you need to be as pro-active about our redeployment as you were about our deployment. If we just wait around and hope that the Army will do something, then we are likely to get screwed. According to Sergeant Major Werley, the National Guard Bureau does not even have us listed as one of its deployed units. Somehow, we are completely off the radar screen."

The Colonel told me that his West Point classmate who had helped us get deployed to Afghanistan had since moved on to another position. In short, he had lost his leverage inside the Pentagon. Trying to appease me, he advised, "I will speak to the people here at CJTF-180 and follow-up."

As far as Afghanistan was concerned, the November 20 press conference of the Secretary of Defense received little fanfare. The main story coming out of the briefing was that 45,000 National Guard and Reserve soldiers would be called up in February for Operation Iraqi Freedom. The fact that over 10,000 soldiers serving in the fourth phase of Operation Enduring Freedom were extended from 179 days to 270 days never made the headlines. The 213th ASG had gone from

"Demobistan" to Afghanistan to "Extendostan." Our departure date was now pushed back to March 26.

I had no idea how I was going to break the news to Susan. She had tentatively made vacation plans for the last week in December on the small chance that I would be released before New Year's Day. The kids had an extra long school holiday because Christmas and New Year's Day fell on a Thursday. I had hoped to use some of this time to be with the children before school resumed on January 4. Now, it would be lucky if we were home for Easter.

Susan took the bad news well. Her strength and courage surprised me. Her unwavering support sustained me. Leigh was disappointed, but pressed on. On the other hand, William was very sad because I was gone and would be gone longer. The school administration was offering little support, and some older students were mistreating him. He became very depressed and refused to go to school. Susan needed help with him. I was not there to reassure Will or assist his mother. I felt devastated. It was the lowest point of the entire deployment. I contemplated asking Wagner for emergency leave. Janze said he would recommend it to the Colonel.

Will stayed home from school for four days. Leigh wrote me an e-mail crying out for help, begging me to come home. It was awful. I spoke with Susan several times on the phone. I sent a frantic e-mail to the Middle School Director asking for assistance for my son. I questioned whether I had put my own desire to serve my country over the responsibilities to my family.

If it did not take at least four days to travel from Afghanistan to Allentown, then I probably would have gone home. My family needed me, and I was not there. Somehow Susan got through it. I am not sure how other than through her sheer strength of character. I knew that I had married a very good woman.

As it turned out, those four days were some of the busiest I spent at Kabul Compound. Negotiating the revisions to the streamlined code had meant hours in meetings at the US and Italian Embassies. I spent even more time in preparation.

Apparently, all my time with the Italian Justice Project had earned me the confidence of Ambassador Giorgi. A few days after Christmas, he invited me to an international conference at his residence on extending judicial reform to the provinces. Colonel Mantooth and I were among the first to arrive. Along with Robert Wilson of USAID, we were the only Americans invited to the meeting. The rest of the participants were from the United Nations.

Ambassador Giorgi was the first to speak. He announced that Italy wanted to develop a provincial justice strategy. Giorgi reported that the Italian Justice Project had completed the renamed "Interim Criminal Procedure Code for Courts" and that the Ministry of Justice was presently in the process of reviewing it. The Italian Justice Project would like to begin the training of the trainers, the "Mobile Court Team," on January 24, 2004.

The Ambassador asked the guidance from the representatives of the international community present as to whether the Mobile Court Team should personally assume the duties of the incumbent judges, prosecutors, and police in the provinces or simply act as mentors. Further, he requested guidance as to how long the team should be deployed in any one place. Finally, he requested recommendations as to which provinces the team should deploy.

I had some definite ideas in answer to the questions posed by the Ambassador but thought it better politics to defer to Mr. Wilson as the senior representative of the US at the meeting. Margareta Wahlstrom, a tall, slender, over-55 Swede, sat opposite the Ambassador at the conference table. As Chief of Staff of the United Nations Assistance Mission for Afghanistan ("UNAMA"), she did not hesitate to speak for her organization. This obviously strong-willed woman either did not understand the questions or deliberately avoided providing any answers.

"There are serious security problems in Gardez," Wahlstrom said sternly. She had obviously read my minutes from the Gardez Rule of Law Project meetings and knew that Italy intended to send the Mobile Court Team to the City of

Gardez first. Redirecting her eyes toward Mantooth and me, the only persons in uniform, she continued, "A provincial security task force must be deployed to Gardez before we can even begin to start thinking about operating a court system in the province. Additionally, there must be police on the ground to demonstrate the central government's commitment to that region."

The UN was always talking about security. UNAMA despised the US military for invading Iraq without the specific authorization of the United Nations. It seemed that they enjoyed lambasting the US Army for failing to prevent every terrorist act in Afghanistan and Iraq. Even though the United Nations had had a presence in Afghanistan for scores of years before 9/11, somehow, in her view, the inability of American and coalition armed forces to maintain security was the major obstacle to Afghan reconstruction.

Ever since I first stepped foot in country, I had been given the cold shoulder by the UN. Shortly after my arrival in Kabul, Dr. Palmisano of the Italian Justice Project had invited Colonel Gordon and me over to his residence for a pasta supper. Gordon thought it advisable to wear civilian clothes to the dinner. I borrowed his sport coat and trousers and wore a shoulder holster for my M9. There must have been over ten UNAMA people in attendance at the party. As soon as I introduced myself as a US Army Lieutenant Colonel, they immediately found someone else in the room to talk to.

Back in September, Wahlstrom had somehow found out that Colonel Gordon was making real progress toward establishing a courthouse in Gardez without the "assistance" of UNAMA. Right away, she sent a note to Gordon requesting that the next Rule of Law Project meeting be held at her compound. Respecting the need to maintain good diplomatic relations, Gordon accepted her invitation and moved the weekly gathering to UNAMA.

As Gordon and I entered the UNAMA compound, we immediately realized that something was different. With the rest of the City of Kabul buried in debris, the UNAMA compound was in pristine condition. It had either brand new or recently refurbished buildings with fully functioning air conditioning systems. Surrounding the offices were well-maintained gardens with roses and many varieties of flowering plants. There were water fountains, shade trees, green grass, concrete sidewalks, and wooden swings. The parking lot contained fifteen brand new Toyota Land Cruisers, each outfitted with a $20,000 antenna. Compared to Kabul Compound, we thought we had arrived at the Versailles Palace.

Much to the chagrin of Gordon, who had chaired the Gardez meetings since July, Wahlstrom took the seat at the head of the conference table. There was no doubt that she was in charge. It appeared that she had invited every UN worker in Gardez to the meeting. Some thirty people stood along the walls of the assembly room. She then announced that UNAMA was assuming control of judicial reform in Afghanistan.

The Colonel was pissed. He had seen what the UN had done with other reconstruction projects during his year in Afghanistan. UNAMA took a very long term view. They had been in Afghanistan for over forty years and they planned to be in the country for at least the next fifty years. There was no sense of urgency. Instead, there was a lot of bureaucratic feathering of the nest.

Gordon and I decided to get direction from a US policymaker. If UNAMA were going to take over the Gardez Rule of Law Project, then it would only occur with the express consent of the Democracy Officer at the Embassy. We immediately scheduled a meeting with Ana Klenicki. She was upset about the situation as we were.

"David," she said, "You know you have my complete confidence. If UNAMA gets involved in this project, they will end it. My grandchildren may come to Afghanistan some day, and the UN would still be discussing the location of the first courthouse. Please continue to do what you are doing. I will support you."

Now, at the meeting with the Italian Ambassador, it appeared UNAMA was about to disrupt DiGennnaro's plan for bringing justice to the provinces. Wahlstrom told Giorgi, "Any justice reform will require a multi-year commitment. UNAMA is looking at plan that seeks funds over a twenty-five year period." I took off my glasses and started rubbing my eyes, hoping that this bad dream would go away. I wanted to scream.

"The Government of Afghanistan must take the lead role," Wahlstrom insisted. "Justice must be coordinated with all governance projects to be undertaken in the provinces. Let's determine where the synergies are. We are more strategical than tactical. Deployment of mobile court teams should not begin until there is an overall strategy for management training and civil service reform, including higher salaries for government workers. I suggest we create a steering committee including UNAMA, coalition representatives, and international donors. UNAMA will soon produce a report outlining an overall strategy for provincial security, governance and reconstruction."

I was glad to see that Ambassador Giorgi was as perturbed by this bureaucratic and non-responsive answer to his detailed questions as I was. He stared at Wahlstrom and commented, "If security is the priority, then the rule of law will have to wait. If governance is the priority, then the rule of law must be an essential and immediate component. The Rule of Law needs more emphasis than it has had in the past. I hope that you will be flexible so that we can find some common ground." He then suggested the convening of a judicial reform conference in the Northern provinces in which the key political, judicial, and law enforcement officials would participate.

Once again, Wahlstrom did not respond to the Ambassador's proposal. Instead, she stated that the rule of law would necessarily follow as a long-term result of the UNAMA plan for security, governance, and reconstruction.

"And exactly how long do we have to wait for this plan?" questioned Giorgi. Wahlstrom did not know the answer. She squirmed in her seat and looked to her colleagues for direction. Finally, Marco Toscano-Rivalta, UNAMA Rule of Law Officer, suggested we could expect to see the report in approximately ten days.

Mr. Wilson from USAID tried to play the peacemaker. He stated that the development of new courthouses in the provinces should be linked with the deployment of provincial reconstruction teams to provide security. He maintained that it should be easier to bring judicial sector reform to the northern and western provinces. Since Wilson represented the embassy position, Mantooth and I remained silent. After all, we were not supposed to be the policymakers. I passed a handwritten note to the Colonel—"UN position: delay, delay, delay."

On the way out of the Ambassador's residence, I was disgusted. As we opened the doors to the JAG mobile, I looked at Mantooth and said, "You and I want to do a job here and go home. The UN wants to make judicial reform in Afghanistan a career. I don't know how we can work with these people." As soon as we got back to Kabul Compound, I wrote a situation report for General Weston. I made the following assessment:

1. UNAMA refuses to recognize the strategy of the Italian Justice Project and USG for judicial sector reform.

2. UNAMA is extremely reluctant to coordinate its activities with anyone other than the Afghan government unless the international actors play by the UN rules and timetables.

I recommended that the Italians and USG move ahead with judicial sector reform without UNAMA.

The next day, I got a phone call from an elderly lady with a Swedish accent. She sounded very upset and remonstrated, "Colonel Moring, I just read your memo and I an extremely angry with you." I thought to myself, *Oh, my God, how did Wahlstrom get a copy of my e-mail? I only sent it to the General and the political-military advisor. I have just created an international incident.*

I replied, "Is this Ms. Wahlstrom?"

"Why, of course. Who else would be calling you? I am very offended by your statements here in this memo about me not answering the questions of the Ambassador. How could you say such a thing?"

"May I ask who gave you a copy of the memo?"

"Why, my good friend Adrian Waddell, the English Lieutenant Colonel, who is the OMC-A political-military advisor."

Now I knew I was in trouble. I had sent Adrian a copy of the memo. *I wondered how he could be so disloyal to the coalition and send Wahlstrom my report?*

I guess by now Adrian had had enough fun. Reverting to his British accent, Waddell said, "Wake up, Platte. It's Adrian." The two other officers with him were howling with laughter in the background.

I had little time to recover from being the butt end of this April Fool's joke. Much to my surprise, the Minister of Justice had acted quickly following our interview with him. Karimi had scheduled a meeting for that same afternoon for representatives of the Afghan judicial ministries on the streamlined code. Colonel Mantooth and I took a taxi to the conference. We were escorted into a large ballroom with sofas and coffee table arranged in a huge square. There was no heat, as usual, so I kept on my DCU Field Jacket.

The delegates began to arrive slowly. The Chief Prosecutor of the Attorney General, the Assistant Chief Justice of the Supreme Court, and the Director of Legislation of the Ministry of Justice. All told there were twenty-five Afghans sitting in the ballroom with Mantooth, Guiseppe Fedele of Italy, and me.

Before the start of the meeting, I asked Fedele for a sidebar outside the hearing of the Afghans. "Guiseppe, what is the purpose of this gathering?" I inquired.

"The Minister of Justice is ready to approve the Interim Criminal Procedure Code and simply wants approval of this group before referring it to President Karzai," he replied.

"That's great news," I said excitedly. "What can we do in this meeting to support you?"

"Oh, I don't expect that you will have to do anything. Just

answer their questions about the revisions to the code if they have any."

Minister Karimi's Director of Legislation addressed the legal assembly first. He explained that the Minister of Justice was in the process of reviewing the Interim Criminal Procedure Code for substance and its conformity to Afghan legal traditions. Karimi wanted to make sure that the Afghan judicial ministries supported the code before sending it to the Council of Ministers for final action and implementation by Presidential Decree.

The Chief Prosecutor immediately took the floor and began speaking in Dari. Mantooth and I had to wait for the English translation. "This draft law is totally unnecessary," he declared. "We have no need for an emergency law. We have laws that have served Afghanistan well for the last thirty-five years. We know these laws. We have judges and prosecutors in every province trained in these laws. This new code is confusing to us and is not based upon Afghan traditions."

Fedele was dead wrong. This was not going to be a confirmation ceremony for the streamlined code. It was an ambush and massacre. By the time the Afghans had finished speaking, twenty-four of their numbers opposed the interim code. Few had actually read it. It did not matter. They had made up their minds in advance.

The ministry representatives thought that the JRC would give them cover on their position. "We should not discuss this draft law until the Judicial Reform Commission has had a chance to give its opinion," said the Assistant Chief Justice. I was ready for this argument.

"The JRC has already approved the code," I announced to the group. "Just yesterday, I received a letter from Chairman Baha stating his consent for the adoption of the code as an interim law. In any event, according to Mr. Karimi, the JRC terminates its existence upon the enactment of the new Constitution in a few days. It is up to you to decide the future of this draft law. You should know that international donor support for judicial infrastructure rebuilding is tied directly to this code."

I had convinced no one. Fedele spoke next. He wanted to emphasize that the streamlined code now on the table for discussion was the new and improved Italian-American version. "The Government of Italy has worked very hard with the American military lawyers to make this criminal procedure law better than the one that was originally drafted by Presidente DiGennaro. The Interim Code is now completely consistent with Afghan laws and international human rights standards," he maintained. "We are prepared to train your judges and prosecutors on the new code."

I had to laugh inside by the irony of the situation. Just three weeks earlier, Fedele had stared Mantooth and me in the face and said that Italy would make no changes to the streamlined code. He had insisted that the code as originally drafted by DiGennaro was in conformity with Afghan law. Now, he was arguing that the American lawyers had taken the necessary steps to make it compatible with Afghan legal traditions. It did not matter. They were not buying Fedele's pitch either.

Mantooth took the last shot. He gave a very eloquent and organized argument summarizing all the reasons why the ministry officials should recommend the adoption of the streamlined code. On the way back to Kabul Compound in the taxi, I commented, "Sir, I now know why you are a trial lawyer. That was an excellent closing argument. We may lose the case, but you gave it our best effort."

Chapter XXXIII.

CLJ

I f you can come now," said David Hoffman, USAID Democracy Officer, "then I can get you into the closing ceremony of the CLJ." Mantooth and I had been meeting with Ken Thomas at the embassy on the new counter-narcotics strategy for Afghanistan. Hoffman had interrupted the meeting to tell us that he could get us into Constitutional Loya Jirga.

By this time, General Prasek had decided that I would become the Acting Staff Judge Advocate of OMC-A and Colonel Mantooth would serve as the top lawyer for Combined Forces Command. The news was broken to Mantooth in a very unceremonious fashion. While setting up the name cards on the conference table for the weekly staff meeting at OMC-A, a junior officer told Mantooth that he would have no seat at the table. Further, he said there was no reason why Mantooth should come to the daily morning briefings.

"And exactly who made that decision?" demanded Mantooth.

"The Chief of Staff," came the reply.

"Well, we will certainly see about this," muttered the Colonel. I could never understand why Mantooth was so upset about this reassignment. Sure, he had come to Afghanistan thinking that he was going to replace Colonel Gordon as the Staff Judge Advocate of OMC-A. However, in the meantime, the Army had stood up a new command for all of Afghanistan, Uzbekistan, Tajikistan, and Pakistan. It seemed logical to me that the senior Judge Advocate would take over the top JAG position at the higher headquarters. Nonetheless, Mantooth wanted both jobs. His fate, however, had been sealed a few days earlier.

OMC-A Acting Chief, General Prasek, had given a clear order that he wanted a Commander's Inquiry conducted concerning the motor vehicle fatality that had occurred on Halloween involving his Personal Security Detachment. A Commander's Inquiry involves less paperwork and is less thorough than a formal investigation under Army Regulation ("AR") 15-6. Despite Prasek's unambiguous direction, Mantooth made an office call with the CFC Commander, General Barno, and raised the issue of the October 31 traffic accident. At Mantooth's suggestion, Barno overruled Prasek and ordered a formal investigation under AR 15-6 of the accident.

When Prasek found out about Mantooth's maneuver, he was livid and stormed into the office of CFC Chief of Staff Snukis to vent his anger. Mantooth never had a chance of becoming SJA for Prasek after this episode. To me, it only made sense for each general to have his own legal advisor. As a result, I became the acting Staff Judge Advocate of OMC-A.

Things got worse for Mantooth that afternoon. He had called a staff meeting of all the Judge Advocates on Kabul Compound to discuss the establishment of a single "law firm" on post. Recently arrived Oklahoma National Guard Lieutenant Colonel Kyle Goerke and two lawyers from the Netherlands, Lieutenant Colonel Hans Wiersma and Captain Eric Pouw, attended the session along with me. Just as we started our discussion of the decision made earlier in the day about my new placement, Richard Berthon entered the room.

"Sorry, I'm late," he said. The British civilian nattily dressed in a sport coat, slacks, button down shirt and Oxford tie sat down at the conference table. He continued, "I just got back from a meeting at the Ministry of Defense. What have I missed?"

I could literally see the blood rising in Mantooth's neck and head. He stared down Berthon and said, "You were not invited to this meeting. I am going to have to ask you to leave. This is a meeting of the judge advocates on my staff. You are not a lawyer."

Berthon had recently been appointed as assistant director of MOD/GS Reform. His mission was to provide teaching, coaching, and mentoring for the Afghans recently appointed by President Karzai to run the Ministry of Defense ("MOD") and General Staff ("GS") of the ANA. Richard was a tall, handsome man whose strength of personality was only overmatched by his arrogance. The Dutch lawyers seemed enamored with him. They wanted to work with Richard.

"I am most certainly not leaving," barked Berthon. "You cannot hold a meeting with my staff without me being present."

"Well, then I'm leaving," shouted Mantooth. "I do not know how you can be so rude. This is my staff, and I can meet with them without you being present anytime I feel like. I have been told your status with the British Government is equivalent to that of a full bird Colonel, but I am not going to stand for this."

"You think I am being rude?" questioned Berthon. "It seems to me that you would have had the common courtesy to inform me in advance that you were having a meeting with my staff. I am just now hearing about this conference. Colonel Goerke, Colonel Wiersma, and Captain Pouw work for me. If you want to meet with my people, then you should ask me for permission."

I felt very uncomfortable. I had no dog in this fight. Colonel Gordon had told me that the Dutch lawyers were coming to help us write a law of war training program for the ANA. Now, it seemed like they were part of MOD/GS Reform. All I knew was that I was the top lawyer in OMC-A, and I had no staff. Gordon and I had made a good team. Civilian and military justice reform would be difficult with no help from other attorneys. The meeting abruptly adjourned with no discussion as to how the lawyers on the compound would work together, if at all, to accomplish the mission.

My job description at OMC-A did not include counter-narcotics policy. However, as the top lawyer at CFC, Mantooth's portfolio included national policy on drugs and crime. He asked me to attend a meeting with Ken Thomas at the embassy on narcotics interdiction. Mantooth seemed annoyed when David Hoffman entered the room during the meeting. The Colonel was unaware that I had earlier asked Dr. Hoffman if he could get Mantooth and me into the CLJ.

"We will have to leave in five minutes in order to get there in time to hear Karzai speak," said Hoffman.

Mantooth had a million excuses. "We are in our uniforms, and we do not have time to change into our civilian clothes. What vehicle will we take? What will we do with our weapons? What about dinner?"

"Sir, I really want to go," I insisted. "This is a once in a lifetime type situation. We have a chance to see history being made. I have been involved in this constitutional process since June, and I would like to see its conclusion."

It had been over a month since I had last attended the weekly meeting of the American contingent in Afghanistan planning the Constitutional Loya Jirga. Back in August, Larry Sampler had advised the working group organized by the Embassy that the CLJ was not an event, but a process. Throughout the fall, Sampler's crew had been running voter registration and delegate elections in eight regions of the country. By September 2003, the process was way behind schedule, and UNAMA made the decision to push back the CLJ from October until December.

Gordon and I were concerned about only one thing: civilian control of the military. Professor Amiryar had told us that the White Paper I had prepared had been circulated among the members of the Constitutional Commission and to Ambassador Brahimi. By September 8, Lynn Tracy, the Embassy Political/Economic Counselor, told us that the draft Constitution was near completion and civilian control of the military was not a disputed issue.

At the September 22 weekly meeting, Sampler told the CLJ working group that a private consulting firm had begun the rehabilitation of the old Soviet Polytechnical College, which would be the site of the convention compound. Michelle Brant from the Asia Foundation announced that the Constitutional Commission had completed its work, and the official draft would be distributed after Karzai returned from the UN General Assembly meeting in October. Brant said the CLJ had a budget of $11 million.

Walter Odaro had finally finished his survey for the Asia Foundation on what the Afghan people wanted to see in their new Constitution. He stated that President Karzai wanted the survey results released to the public. The survey would say all the right things. The Afghan people wanted to preserve the sacred role of Islam, provide for gender equality within the confines of the Koran, develop a constitution acceptable to the international community, and maintain local traditions and languages.

By mid-October, fierce factional fighting between Warlords Dostum and Atta interrupted voter registration meetings in Balkh. Fortunately, the Afghan government and the international community brokered a ceasefire between the two militias, and the CLJ process continued without incident. Because many of the voters were illiterate, candidates for delegate were designated by a symbol (star, heart, moon, arrow, etc.), and electors cast their ballot by drawing the symbol on a piece of paper.

"They call me alarmist," said Sampler at the October 27 weekly meeting. "But we don't yet have any rules of order for the conduct of the CLJ." He was visibly upset. Michele Brant had been given the task of writing the rules of procedure for the CLJ nine weeks earlier, and she had not yet completed her work. Sampler continued, "You just can't throw rules of procedure together in a month and expect to train people to follow them in a few days. The CLJ will be an unmitigated disaster unless Karzai appoints a chairman and the chairman has some rules."

Apart from Sampler's ravings on rules, I learned that President Karzai had rejected the Constitutional Commission's draft calling for a Prime Minister as head of the National Assembly and returned the draft constitution to the commission for additional rewriting. Sampler said that Constitutional Commission Chairman, Niamatullah Shaharani threatened to resign from his post as a result of the elimination of the position of Prime Minister.

After a late night session involving negotiations between Karzai and David Sedney, the Draft Constitution was officially approved and presented to the public at a ceremony at the Presidential Palace on November 3, 2003. I first learned of the ceremony after the fact by watching taped coverage of the event on the Armed Forces Radio and Television Service. When I finally got a hold of the Constitution later that night by means of an attachment to an e-mail from David Hoffman, I quickly read through the document to locate the military provisions. I was pleased to see that the drafters had provided for civilian control of the military.

Ken Thomas convinced Mantooth to go to the closing ceremony of the CLJ. Hoffman called the Regional Security Officer at the Embassy to arrange for an armored car. It was dark. The streets of Kabul had a soldier from the ANA with an AK-47 on every corner. As we approached the Soviet Polytechnic, the number of security personnel increased. Since the vehicle had diplomatic license plates, we breezed past all three checkpoints.

It was now January 4, 2004, and the CLJ had lasted 22 days. Hoffman was pleased because his office had only budgeted monies for this amount of days and he would not have to go looking for emergency supplemental funds. As Mantooth and I passed through the metal detectors and received our VIP badges, we immediately felt out of place. Apart from a handful of ANA wearing their green berets and camouflage uniforms, no coalition military personnel or US soldiers were anywhere in sight. Mantooth and I were the only Americans in uniform at the closing ceremony of the CLJ.

We quickly took a seat in the back of the assembly room. Most of the delegates and visitors were in the turbans and gowns of their native dress. There were very few suits and ties. The CLJ was being held in a tent in a valley next to the Intercontinental Hotel in Kabul. The tent was designed by the

Germans for October Fest and transported to Afghanistan after that celebration. It was outfitted with a heating and ventilation system. The tent was decorated with green, red and black banners running the full width of the temporary structure.

Shaharani was the first to speak. There were no English translators. Five minutes into his address, everyone seated in the room stood up. I did not know what this was all about, so I got to my feet thinking that it was the respectful thing to do. Then the assembled delegates got quiet. After about a minute, the entire convention sat down.

I looked at Mantooth and said, "What was that all about, sir?" An Afghan gentleman sitting in front of me who apparently understood some English overheard my question and realized that I had no clue what was going on. He turned around and politely said to me, "The Chairman asked for all the delegates who approved of the new Constitution to stand in silence for a minute to show their approval for the new Constitution." I was shocked and embarrassed. I had just voted for the new Constitution.

The Chairman then said something else in Dari, and everyone laughed. Fearing to make a fool of myself again, I stayed motionless and did not change my expression. The kind Afghan in front of me again turned around in his chair and said, "The Chairman has just said the Constitution is written for all Afghans. Afghanistan is like a garden that has many kinds of trees, flowers and thorns. The flowers are the women." I nodded my head in acknowledgement and said, "Thank you."

Ambassador Lakdar Brahimi, the UN Secretary General's Special Representative, was the next speaker. He addressed the delegates in English with Dari translation. Brahimi said the Constitution was not perfect. He cautioned the CLJ that it would be criticized inside and outside of Afghanistan. Nonetheless, the delegates should be pleased with their accomplishment.

Brahimi mentioned two major challenges that lay ahead for the country. First, Afghanistan must have security. Not just from rockets and bombs, but also Afghans must have freedom from fear. Second, he said that Afghanistan had to improve the status of women. He called upon his own experience as a mujahideen fighting against the French in Algeria as a basis for his statement that women, more than men, suffer at a time of war.

I could not help but take notice of the fact that the children singing the CLJ anthem were separated by sex with the boys and girls on different sides of the tent. This occurrence was a curious juxtaposition to Brahimi's remarks. The CLJ concluded with an over one-hour long address by President Hamid Karzai, who flew into the CLJ by Chinook helicopter from his Presidential Palace minutes earlier. He spoke in Dari, Pashtu, and Uzbek, but not English, so I do not know what he said. Unlike a political party convention in the United States, clapping never interrupted his remarks and his introduction was greeted only with a smattering of applause.

President Hamid Karzai addresses the Constitutional Loya Jirga. Photograph by David Hoffman.

Three days later, I was invited to attend the graduation of the students from the Faculty of Law and Politics at Kabul University. Dean Wasel had arranged for me to sit with the rest of the faculty. Fortunately, Professor Amiryar attended the ceremonies and was seated next to me. At appropriate times, he provided English translation of the substance of the lunchtime conversation. Amiryar had served as the legal advisor to the CLJ.

It was apparent to me that the faculty members were giving the George Washington University Professor a hard time. They were waving their hands and raising their voices as they made their points to Amiryar. He stayed calm and addressed all their comments. When the band started to play, I looked at the Professor and asked him, "What was that all about? Can you give me an executive summary?"

"They are claiming," he replied, "that the CLJ was illegitimate because it was forced upon Afghanistan by the United States. I was trying to defend the process."

"I see," I said. "Do you feel like it was legitimate?"

"Yes," he answered. "Law professors will find fault in anything."

I had been at the Parwan Restaurant with Victor McGee for over three hours and thought that it was time to leave the graduation. I told Amiryar that I needed to get back to Kabul Compound. He grabbed my arm and stated, "You must stay. We have a special presentation for you." With that, the Professor ran off and got the Dean.

A few minutes later, the Dean appeared holding an envelope in his hand. He jumped up on the elevated stage and told the band to stop playing. In a sea of cameras, videocassette recorders, and television crews, Dean Wasel gave me a certificate acknowledging my work as a visiting professor at the University. He then asked me to speak to the over two hundred and fifty people in the dining room.

"Today," I spoke into the microphone, "you have been given a great honor. You also now have a great responsibility. You are the best and brightest young people in all of Afghanistan.

The future of your country is in your hands. Go forth and do great things for Afghanistan." After a pregnant pause for the translation, the room erupted in applause. It was one of the most special moments I experienced on the deployment.

My excitement was short-lived. The very next day we had our weekly meeting with the Afghan military judges. Lieutenant General Tahib was insisting that Mantooth and I sign our approval of the panel's draft law for the Organization of Military Courts. Based upon my conversations with Major General Craig Weston and Ambassador Khalizad, I knew that we could not endorse this draft. The proposed law retained military court jurisdiction over civilians, the police, and the national security officers.

"You have worked with us for the last three months preparing this draft law," Tahib said in Dari. "Certainly, you are now willing to sign it so that we can tell the Shura council that the United States Army has approved our proposal for organizing military courts."

I tried a diversionary tactic. "Don't you think we should take another look at the draft law to make sure it is consistent with the new Constitution before we approve it?"

"Nonsense," he replied. "The draft is entirely compatible with the new Constitution."

I was fully prepared. "Take a look at Article 117 of the new Constitution. It says the Supreme Court is composed of nine members. In this draft, it says that there will be thirteen military judges on the Supreme Court. How is that consistent?" I thought I had played the trump card. At present, the Supreme Court had over 150 judges, but the new Constitution reduced their numbers to nine.

Apparently, no one at the Constitutional Commission had bothered to tell the judges on the Supreme Court that the new Constitution meant that a lot of justices would be out of work. Tahib answered, "The nine judges will be department heads. I am the Chief Justice of the military section. I will continue to have twelve assistant judges working for me." Mantooth was speechless. If there was a way out of this one, I had to figure it out.

"General Tahib," I said, "I think we have a very fundamental misunderstanding. With your permission, I will arrange a meeting with the Legal Advisor for President Karzai to help us better understand the issues." With that statement, I averted a showdown with the Chief Justice's top advisor over constitutional interpretation. Shinwari was arguably the second most powerful Afghan in the transitional government, and I had no desire to butt heads with him or his assistant.

Two days later, Mantooth and I met with General Tahib and Enayata Qasimi in the Ark. Mr. Qasimi, a handsome Oriental, was completely fluent in English and Dari. He had lived his first twelve years in Afghanistan before fleeing to Pakistan during the Russian occupation. The prestigious Lawrenceville Academy in Princeton, New Jersey, had given him a scholarship, and from there he had gone onto college and the University of Maryland Law School. He was now receiving a salary from a USAID contractor and working as the Legal Advisor to President Karzai.

Since General Tahib spoke no English, Qasimi had no qualms about communicating with me in English in the general's presence. "Colonel Moring, the restructuring of the judiciary in Afghanistan is an extremely sensitive matter. I cannot tell the general the full ramifications of the new Constitution. This process must be well thought out and gradual. I will tell him that I will look at his draft for organizing the military courts, but both you and he should know that President Karzai is not approving any restructuring of the court system for some time."

"The Afghan military judges," I replied, "are insisting that we approve their court structure before we adopt a military crimes code. I fully understand the President's position on judicial reform, but the ANA desperately needs some form of discipline. Can we in the short term get President Karzai to approve a regulation adopting a list of military crimes and a non-judicial punishment procedure similar to our Article 15?"

"I don't see why not," Qasimi answered. "Just make sure I see it before you give it to the Minister of Defense."

I could not have been more pleased. I could not wait to tell General Weston. After six months of negotiations with the Afghan military judges, we had finally found a way to separate a quick fix military discipline system from the complex task of reorganizing the structure of the Afghan military courts and funding the prosecutor's office.

Chapter XXIV.

Nackt

Two days before I left on R&R leave, the new Constitution had its first test. An Afghan woman had sung on national television. To make matters worse, she had appeared without a veil covering her face. My friend, Chief Justice Shinwari, was outraged and fired off a letter to the Minister of Communications and Public Information. He charged that the appearance of a woman without a veil on national television was unconstitutional.

Under his reading of Articles Two and Three of the Constitution, the religion of the Islamic Republic of Afghanistan is the sacred religion of Islam. No law can be contrary to the beliefs and provisions of Islam. The Chief Justice condemned the Ministry and the woman as violating the Constitution by engaging in a public performance that was contrary to the sacred religion of Islam.

The Minister of Communications and Public Information immediately returned a letter to the Chief Justice. Citing Article Twenty-two of the new Constitution, the Minister maintained that any kind of discrimination between the citizens of Afghanistan is prohibited. The citizens of Afghanistan— whether man or woman—have equal rights and duties before the law. Since an Afghan male had appeared on television the night before without wearing a veil, an Afghan woman should enjoy the same privilege.

I had no desire to wait around Kabul until the Afghans resolved this constitutional crisis. I had ten days of authorized leave and I was going home. One of the consequences of being extended from 179 days to 270 days of "Boots on the Ground" was that soldiers were permitted to take up to 15 days of paid leave at the discretion of their unit commander. Some of the ASG staff took the position that leave was only intended for enlisted soldiers. I was not one of them.

The timing of the notice of extension created problems for the implementation of the R&R leave. We did not learn of our extension until we had already completed five months in theater. The policy stated that leave must be taken at least sixty days before redeployment. This policy meant that all 126 remaining members[93] of the ASG had to take leave between November 21 and January 21. Further, the policy stated that no more than ten percent of the unit could be on leave at any one time. With this restriction, Colonel Wagner decided to limit those soldiers electing to take leave to ten days (instead of fifteen) with four days for travel on either side of the ten-day period.

Everyone wanted to go home either at Thanksgiving or Christmas. Since such a schedule was not feasible, enlisted soldiers got to pick their leave dates first. My leave would not come until the end of January. Susan had thought it important for me to be home at this time to help the children prepare for their semester exams. I was just glad to be going back to my family at any time.

Sergeant Major Werley had arranged for me to get to Bagram Air Field by joining the convoy that was making a mail run from Kabul Compound. I was surprised to learn that General Barno's interpreter, Shams, would also accompany us. I had seen Shams around the compound, mainly at meals, but had never talked with him. He seemed a rather shadowy figure with dark skin, black hair and an unkempt beard. Unlike most Afghans, he wore a coat and tie. And yet, Shams separated himself from all others by wearing a dark brown ski hat even in the hottest weather. He always sat alone in the chow hall and said nothing.

Werley drove the Toyota Surf with a fellow enlisted man in the passenger seat. I sat with Shams in the back seats. In his usual friendly manner, Werley engaged Shams in a conversation about his work and background as we traveled down New Bagram Road. I sat back and listened, not wanting to pry into the personal affairs of anyone so close to the commanding general of the entire theater. The Sergeant Major's interview of the fifty-plus year old Afghan was fascinating.

Shams told us that he was born in Kabul, Afghanistan, to a rather wealthy family. He was educated at Kabul University and enjoyed a good living until the King was deposed and the Russians invaded. Shams then made his way to the United States via Pakistan where he received further education and became a college professor. I believe he was living in Boulder, Colorado, on September 11, 2001.

"During the Seventies," Shams explained, "Kabul was one of the most liberal places in all of the world. American college students flocked here for the drugs. Marijuana, hashish, and heroin were cheap and readily available. There were no laws and everyone lived and let live. Compared to what you see today in the ruins, Kabul at that time was a fairly modern city with a functioning parliament, strong economy, cinemas, beautiful water fountains, and public parks with green grass."

"No one thought about fundamentalism," Shams continued. "Religion was simply not a force in everyday life. The Ayatollah Khomeini changed all of that beginning in 1979. Over time, the radical philosophy coming from Iran appealed to the uneducated, poverty-stricken peoples of the rural areas of Afghanistan. The Russians and the west were blamed for all of the country's problems. Jihad was declared and the most liberal country in the Islamic world began its retreat to the Middle Ages. Over the next twenty-five years, Kabul was destroyed and turned over to the mullahs."

Then, Werley ventured into an area where I would have never gone with the General's aide. "Do you think Osama Bin Laden is still in Afghanistan?" the Sergeant Major inquired. I was dying to hear Shams' answer. Since the focus of OMC-A was reconstruction, we never discussed the hunt for the perpetrator of 9/11 at our staff meetings. Bin Laden was the focus of General Barno and Combined Forces Command-Afghanistan. I never participated in the secret briefings on Al Qaeda.

I really did not think Shams would answer the question directly. He could have easily told us that the subject was confidential. Shams, nonetheless, did not even attempt to qualify his remarks. It was clear to me that he had given the subject a lot of thought and was so well connected with the officials of the interim government of Afghanistan that he was in a position to know.

"Most people believe that Bin Laden is hiding in the mountainous region between Afghanistan and Pakistan," Shams said. "I do not think that is possible. The rural people of those areas rarely come into contact with strangers. They know immediately when someone outside their tribe has entered their territory. Rewards or no rewards, these tribesman could not keep secret the presence of such a well-known figure."

"Bin Laden is not in the mountains. He is living in a major city in Pakistan. Almost all of the leading Al Qaeda terrorists killed or captured in Pakistan during the last two years were found in large cities. Bin Laden is no different. He is under the protection of the Pakistani secret service in some big city. The intelligence agency is double-dealing with its own government and the Americans. Musharraf [Pakistan's President] knows that he stays in power only if it appears that he is using his military and secret service to search for Al Qaeda and Taliban. He also knows that when Bin Laden is found he loses all leverage on the US Government."

"Most of the Pakistanis view Musharraf as a lackey of the Americans. When, in fact, he keeps the extremists at bay and himself in power by providing refuge to Bin Laden under the watchful eye of his intelligence service. At an appropriate time of Musharraf's choosing, he will arrange for the death of Bin Laden. It will be staged as a covert shootout with Bin Laden being killed trying to escape from being trapped in some newly discovered hideout. The Americans will never be able to conduct any interviews to ascertain the truth because there will not be any witnesses."

I did not believe what I was hearing! In some ways it made sense. I recalled that when the Twin Towers collapsed in New York, most Pakistanis cheered. Only after the Bush Administration demonstrated that it was willing to use the US Air Force to destroy the Taliban, did Musharraf become America's number one ally on the war on terror. It now appeared to me that Musharraf may have developed the perfect strategy to appease Bin Laden and his Al Qaeda associates while at the same time remaining in power with the support of the Americans.

With Shams' startling words still bouncing around my brain, I arrived at Bagram Air Field. Within a relatively short time, I boarded the C-17 through its rear ramp to start my journey home. As I tried to close my eyes and catch a nap, the harsh reality of war in Afghanistan interrupted my repose.

A Signal Company had gathered at the back of the plane. One of the soldiers in their unit had lost part of a leg in a mine strike a day before and was being airlifted to Landstuhl Hospital in Germany. As the soldier was wheeled into the aircraft laying down on a gurney, nearly 120 service men and women stood at attention and saluted their injured comrade. As the ramp of the plane slowly closed for departure, tears came to my eyes. I prayed to God for a safe trip for my injured comrade and me.

Transportation to Allentown posed few problems. I flew directly from BAF to Ramstein Air Base in Germany. From there, I took a shuttle to Rhein-Main Air Base in Frankfurt only about 78 kilometers away. Specialist Howard Romans was taking leave the same time as I was, so we traveled together. Romans was only nineteen years old and was a little nervous about the transportation arrangements. He was glad to be traveling with me. After only ten hours waiting at the Frankfurt terminal, Romans and I flew to Baltimore with soldiers from Iraq on a plane dedicated to those personnel on R&R leave from Operation Iraqi Freedom.

Susan and the children met me at the Allentown airport. Leigh held a sign, "Welcome Home Daddy." We hugged and kissed like we had never hugged and kissed before. We laughed and cried at the same time. I was home and it was wonderful.

The ten days spent with Susan were some of the best of our married life. During the deployment, we had come truly to appreciate how much we meant to each other. I was so proud of my wife and children. They had weathered this ordeal and found it within their hearts to treat me like a hero. The ten months away from home had made me realize, more than ever, the awesome family that I had. Susan was wonderful (understanding, attentive, pretty, and courageous), and we celebrated each day together. The leave was too short. I wanted more time with Susan and the children.

I did not even have time to get used to the opulence and order of American life. After driving in Kabul for seven months, I was conditioned to pull out immediately whenever there was an opening in traffic. I found myself routinely ignoring traffic lights and stop signs when driving around Allentown.

While getting dressed for dinner one evening, Susan and I had the television on. We watched the "Red Carpet" interviews by Joan Rivers of actresses entering the Screen Actors' Guild Award Ceremony. As more and more cleavage appeared, I kept thinking about the woman in Kabul who was condemned by the Chief Justice for not wearing a veil. It also dawned on me that the money spent by the actresses on one evening gown would endow a chair for a professor at Kabul University for twenty years.

Susan drove me to the Allentown airport at 5:30 A.M. in the morning. The two of us were a bundle of emotions. We were thrilled with the opportunity we had had to be together. We had thoroughly enjoyed our short time as a couple. We were sad and depressed about having to say goodbye. We hated the fact that we had to be separated again. We tried to keep reminding ourselves that I would be home again after only 50 more days in Afghanistan.

Romans and I made it to Frankfurt on schedule and without difficulty. However, we got separated during deplaning, and he got off the jetliner after I did. As I exited the aircraft, I was handed a re-boarding pass and told to sit in the airport lounge for a briefing.

The Department of Defense had chartered a special jet on a commercial airline to fly soldiers on R&R leave from Operation Iraqi Freedom back to theater. After sitting for twenty minutes, the loudspeaker announced, "Will Lieutenant Colonel Moring please come to check-in desk in the main terminal." I did not know it, but I was seated with the troops waiting to re-board the plane continuing on to Kuwait. Somehow Romans had figured it out and got me paged. The Army had made no plan and had no plane for the soldiers returning to Afghanistan for Operation Enduring Freedom.

We immediately went to the Space Available Check-in desk at the Air Mobility Command Terminal. I asked, "When is the next flight for Bagram?"

The Air Force private behind the desk answered, "Where is Bagram?" With that, I knew that we were in trouble. While the Defense Department had dedicated flights for the Iraqi Freedom soldiers, those of us trying to get back to Afghanistan had to fend for ourselves.

Once I had explained that Bagram Air Field was in Afghanistan, the Air Force Private informed us that there were two flights leaving Rhein-Main for BAF at 0030 and 0230 hours, local time on Saturday morning, about a twelve hour wait. Feeling somewhat relieved, we signed up for first flight. The Private then told us we were numbers 44 and 45 on the waiting list of soldiers trying to get back to Afghanistan.

Before we left Bagram, Romans and I had been given an instruction sheet by Major Widdowson telling us that if we had any transportation problems, we should contact the CJTF-180 LNO (liaison officer), Major Dean Mings. Of course, Mings was nowhere to be found. He was not at the terminal to greet soldiers returning to Afghanistan, and no one from his four person staff was there either. I looked up his phone number on the instruction sheet and called him.

"The AMC has told us about a flight to Bagram at zero dark thirty," I said. "Is that our best option, Major?"

"I don't know why they even told you about that flight. No one is going to get on it. That is a Special Forces chartered flight coming right out of Langley," Mings responded with disgust. "When did they say the next flight was?"

I thought, *here is the guy responsible for transportation for CJTF-180, and he is asking me when the next flight is to Bagram!* "They are telling us there is another flight at 0230," I replied. "Should we try to get on that plane?"

"Yeah. And, if they can't get you on that flight, I will try to arrange for a shuttle to get you to Ramstein for a 2 P.M. flight out of there," said Mings.

Romans and I signed up for the second flight and waited fourteen hours in the terminal for the roll call. There was no briefing given by the Army's passenger liaison staff to incoming soldiers. No information about chow or lodging. No maps of post. The two guys working in the Passenger Liaison Office were playing video games and making personal phone calls. We went to the USO lounge, got a cup of coffee, and signed up to use one of the five Internet terminals.

At 0245 hours, the announcement was made: "There will be six seats available on Flash 764 to Bagram." Two planes had landed and left for Bagram, and we were not on either of them. I immediately marched into the Passenger Liaison Office. A sergeant was on night watch behind his computer and wearing headphones attached to a CD player.

"I'm sorry to disturb you," I asserted with sarcasm, "but how can we arrange for a shuttle to Ramstein for the 1400 flight later today?"

"I don't know. There won't be any shuttle service available tomorrow. It is a weekend," the sergeant answered without taking off his headset.

I was pissed. "You know, Sergeant, we don't have weekends down range. Every day is a workday in a combat zone. Major

Mings said he was going to try to get us on a shuttle to Ramstein if we could not get on one of the flights tonight. What is your plan?"

"I don't know. You'll have to ask Major Mings in the morning."

"Can you arrange for billeting for Specialist Romans and me?" I inquired.

"The Esprix Hotel outside the gate is full and there is no room for transients at post billeting," the Sergeant replied as if I was a major inconvenience to his normal routine. "Can I direct you to tent city, sir?"

"Is there any heat in the tents?

"Oh, yes, sir."

"Will you contact Major Mings first thing in the morning and arrange for someone to notify us at tent city if we can get a shuttle to Ramstein?

"Oh, yes, sir."

Romans and I carried our backpacks and duffle bags to tent city one-half mile away. The tents had cots in them and nothing else. No water. No MREs. No blankets. No help. We used the port-a-potties outside the tent and collapsed on a cot, not having slept for 40 hours.

We did not wake up until 11 o'clock in the morning. No one had come to wake us up. Romans and I walked back to the Passenger Liaison Office with all our gear. There were two new persons manning the office. There were still no representatives from CJTF-180 at the terminal. I called Mings.

"What happened to the shuttle to Ramstein," I asked.

"Oh, I did not even bother to call the shuttle service. There were only twelve seats available on the Ramstein flight, and I did not know if you were going to get on it or not," said Mings nonchalantly.

"When is the next flight to Bagram?" I wanted to know.

"There are no flights over the weekend. The next flights I got going out are to Kandahar on Monday and Manaus on Tuesday. I suggest you sign up for one of them."

By this time, I had seen three flights of Iraqi Freedom soldiers fly in from Baltimore and Dallas, wait two hours for plane refueling, and then continue on their dedicated flight directly to Kuwait. Normally, being stuck in Germany would not necessarily be a bad thing. However, our four days of allowable travel time were used up. Romans and I were now being charged with annual leave; our vacation days were being eroded while we were sitting in an air force terminal.

It was now one P.M. on Saturday, and the next roll call was not until 1330 hours on Monday. Romans and I decided to go to town and get a hotel room for the night. Maybe throw back some good German beer. We made the mistake of going to the Passenger Liaison Office to arrange for a taxi to take us to the commercial airline terminal on the other side of the airport.

"I just called a taxi for you," said the desk sergeant. "It will be here in ten minutes." Howard and I pulled our stuff out of the lockers and got ready for a night on the town. When we got to the taxi stand, there were eleven people waiting there. Some had been standing around for forty minutes. Ten minutes later the taxi came and took four passengers.

I went back to the desk sergeant. "Could you call for another taxi," I pleaded. "The last one came and only took a few people. There are a lot of people waiting for transportation."

"Oh, didn't I tell you," explained the sergeant. "There is only one taxi on weekends. Should I call to have it come back? It should be back in about thirty minutes."

"You know, when we flew from here back to Baltimore," I started to vent, "there was a Chaplain, a full-bird Colonel, and VFW representatives waiting to greet us. The USO Hospitality Desk got us a room for the night at a Comfort Suites. They made sure we had commercial plane reservations all the way back to our home of record. You people treat us Afghan soldiers like crap."

Romans had remained faithfully at the taxi stand. Fortunately, he had run into a Reserve Chaplain from San Diego stationed on post with a car. He graciously agreed to drive us the fifteen minutes to the Frankfurt terminal where we could catch a subway to the downtown Hauptbahnhof. From there, it was a quick walk to a hotel and a hot shower.

The city tour book said there were "rowdy, boisterous bars" in the Alt Sachenhausen section of town. Sounded like the perfect place for us. As we walked out of the hotel, it started to rain. Romans did not have any civilian clothes with him, so he was wearing sweatpants and a pullover I had loaned him. Unprepared for a night in Frankfurt, we got wet.

After wandering around town for over an hour, we saw no rowdy bars. In fact, we did not see anything boisterous. The whole town seemed dead. Having both exhausted our map reading skills trying to find the Sachenhausen, we walked in a Youth Hostel and asked for directions. The young German guy looked at us incredulously when we inquired about the location of the Sachenhausen. "It's right behind this building," he said laughing.

As we enjoyed our bratwurst and a liter of lager at the BierHaus, we felt like idiots, but could not care less. We were a thousand miles from Afghanistan and General Order No. 1 was not in effect. Romans enjoyed his first German beer ever.

On the way back to the hotel, we soon realized our overnight accommodations were in the middle of the "Red Light" district. This part of town was alive and getting busier. While Romans was showering, I had read in the official city tour book that this district had "Eros Centres." For thirty Euros, according to the book, one could spend a few intimate minutes with the lady of his choice. For a higher price, he could name his sexual pleasure. As I read this, I wondered how the woman who sang without a veil on Afghan television and Chief Justice Shinwari were doing. Romans and I decided to stay away from the Eros Centre. Honor First!

The next morning, we were ready for a sophisticated cultural experience. Howard and I planned to visit three museums, the Goethe House, and the Frankfurt Zoo. The best known museum was the Das Stadel, Stadelsches Kunstinstitut und Stadtische Galerie on the Main River. According to the tourist map, the best way to reach this art museum was by a footbridge. It was a cold and windy day, but the sunshine felt great as we crossed over the river. Hanging from one of the suspension towers was a huge, 25 by 50 foot, poster of a woman's right breast. After getting over the initial cultural shock to our burqa-oriented minds, we realized that it was an advertisement for the latest exhibit at the museum.

The art exhibition was entitled "Nackt!" The show included works entitled, "Eve,"[94] "Nude on a Couch,"[95] "A Nymph by a Stream,"[96] "Femme Surprise,"[97] "Venus,"[98] "Self-Portrait with Exposed Breasts,"[99] and Reclining Female Nude with Legs Spread."[100] I wanted to buy Chief Justice Shinwari a plane ticket and a season pass to the Das Stadel. By far the most bizarre exhibit was a series of five televisions and a giant screen showing old and obese naked women unknowingly filmed in a Budapest bathhouse. The tour book described the exhibit as "blatantly contradict[ing] the ideals propagated by the consumer society."[101] I wondered how Islamic society might have interpreted the presentation.

We next visited the Historiches Museum in the Romerplatz. This museum contained exhibits on the history of Frankfurt from Roman times until 1938 and from 1945 to the present. Startlingly absent was any reference to Adolph Hitler or Third Reich. *I guess they wanted to forget.* Instead, the building contained scale models of Frankfurt before and after the allied bombing of 1945. The post-war Romerplatz looked a lot like some sections of Kabul today.

After our day of sightseeing, we got back to the air base in time to take a two-hour nap in tent city before the Super Bowl kicked off at midnight. Howard was exhausted and slept through until ten in the morning. Since the Philadelphia Eagles had lost the National Football Conference championship game for the third year in a row, he had no interest in the spectacle. So, I walked the mile to the Rocket Sports Lounge by myself.

Most of the military people there were in civilian clothes. Only the stranded Afghan war veterans showed up in DCUs. The soldiers and airmen looked terrible out of uniform. Women were wearing hip huggers so low that there was backside cleavage. Tank tops were stretched to the breaking point irrespective of body fat content. Males and females had tattoos and body piercings every place imaginable. The officers in the room could be counted on one hand. The two German and one American brand beer taps were flowing all evening.

No matter how they chose to dress, one could still tell the room was full of representatives of the armed forces of the United States. When Beyonce´ began to sing the National Anthem, the raucous, circus atmosphere suddenly ended. Everyone in the bar stopped talking and stood at attention. I glanced at the three big screen televisions displaying the American flag and then looked around the room and said to myself, *Honor First.*

The first twenty-five minutes of the game created little excitement and only sporadic applause. The final five minutes of the second quarter and the half-time show were an entirely different matter. Twenty-four points were scored in 300 seconds, and then MTV presented its entertainment for a worldwide audience.

Janet Jackson and Justin Timberlake were provocatively dressed for the final number, "Strip Me Naked." As the song ended, Justin ripped Jackson's outfit in a maneuver he would later call a "wardrobe malfunction." When Janet's right breast with nipple piercing was exposed to the entire globe, the Rocket Sports Lounge exploded with pandemonium and excitement. Soldiers were on their feet, yelling with outstretched arms. It was then when I thought that the US needed a Chief Justice Shinwari to condemn the two American singers and their MTV producers to death.

By noon the next day, Romans and I were back at the air terminal checking on the status of the Air Force flight to Kandahar. The Military Airlift Command announced that 54 seats would be available. We got our boarding passes, and I turned in my two duffle bags for loading on the aircraft. Two hours later and forty-five minutes after the scheduled boarding time, the airman on the loudspeaker stated, "Flash 474 to Kandahar is experiencing mechanical problems, and the flight will be delayed until 1430 hours tomorrow. Those persons needing overnight accommodations please check in with the Passenger Liaison Service."

I could not get my personal belongings. They were already on the plane. We immediately went to see the friendly guys at Passenger Liaison. "Do you think it would be best for us to try to get on the 1030 flight to Manaus tomorrow instead of the 1430 to Kandahar?" I asked.

"If you do," the staff NCO responded, "then you go to the end of the space available list."

"What do you mean?" I inquired, starting to get even more irritated. "Major Mings told me that priority on the flight list is determined by the time when you signed up at the Space Available Desk."

"Well, that's the case," he explained, "only if you were not issued a boarding pass. If you change flights after being issued a boarding pass, then you go to the bottom of the list."

Disgusted, I said, "Where do we go to see about billeting for the night?"

"Check in with the 64th Replacement Company."

Romans and I then walked over to the billeting office. Three uniformed persons were sitting behind the desk watching a movie on the computer. No one bothered to stand up when a Lieutenant Colonel entered the room.

"Can we help you?" asked the Caucasian senior sergeant, obviously perturbed that someone was disturbing his late afternoon cinema.

"There was an announcement made at the terminal that any passengers seeking accommodations should come to this billeting office," I replied politely.

"Do you need directions to tent city?" came the response.

Starting to boil over, I spoke sternly, "We were just told at Passenger Liaison that the 64th Replacement Company had plenty of rooms available."

"Are you on emergency or medical leave?" questioned the sergeant.

"No," I replied brusquely.

"Then you will have to stay at tent city. All our rooms are reserved for the contingency that there will be surge of medical or emergency leave personnel."

Lowering my voice volume, I stated, "I understand," underscored with sarcasm. "The soldiers returning to Afghanistan and going down range are not a priority of this office."

After spending the night at tent city with no change of underwear, no bedding or blankets, and no water, we ventured back to the air terminal. The flight to Kandahar was called right on time, and we boarded the bus to take us out to the C-17. After spending six days in Germany trying to return to our Afghan bases, it appeared we were on our way. Then, the bus came to a complete stop 200 feet away from the plane. We waited for 15 minutes. A crewmember stepped onto the bus and said, "We are not ready for you yet. Please come back in one hour."

A buck sergeant from the 18th Airborne Corps seated in the middle of the bus stated in a loud voice, "I'm glad the Air Force is fucked up as bad as the Army. It makes me proud to wear the uniform of the armed forces of the United States."

Sixty minutes later, we were wheels up and on our way to Kandahar. Finally.

CW3 Jim Mayer, the crew supervisor, was on the loudspeaker of the C-17 within minutes. "On behalf of Air Mobility Command, we apologize for the delay. Welcome to the flight to Candyland. We have about eight and one-half hours flying time ahead of us. There is a latrine in the forward area of the aircraft. Air Force regulations prohibit smoking. Anyone wishing to view the galley, just ask me and I will check with the pilot. Enjoy your flight."

I tried to sleep, but couldn't. Other soldiers had found space on the floor and used a poncho liner as a blanket. Some guys were resting with their backs up against HUMMV hard shells that the Air Force was transporting to the combat zone. The Major sitting next to me pulled out his laptop and had a program that allowed him to design the home he was going to build when his active duty ended.

After reading and then putting down my book, my butt was getting sore. I had spent two hours on a canvas seat with no legroom, and I was getting bored. Warrant Officer Mayer was sitting in his swivel chair at the front of the plane, monitoring his screens. I thought it was the perfect time to ask him if I could climb the stairs to the galley.

"Colonel Clayton," Mayer radioed to the pilot, "we got an Army lawyer down here who would like to come up."

"Do you think that is a good idea? We don't like lawyers," came the reply jokingly.

"I don't know, sir," answered Mayer not knowing if Clayton was serious. "It's your call."

"Send him up," instructed Lieutenant Colonel Tom Clayton, USAF. He is a tall, thin pilot with graying hair from the 300th Airlift Wing. Clayton pointed to a pair of headphones sitting on the rear seat of the flight deck and told me to put them on. Talking into the mouthpiece, LTC Clayton introduced himself and the co-pilot and asked my name.

"Platte. Is that like the river in Nebraska?" he inquired.

"Yes. Same spelling," I volunteered.

"Ever been in a cockpit of a C-17 before?"

"No, first time. It's fascinating. I had no idea that there was that much room up here."

Clayton proceeded to point out the controls. He showed me the odometer that indicated that we were flying at 365 miles per hour. The altimeter read 35,000 feet. "Where are we?" I asked.

"I don't know," said Clayton.

I thought to myself, *you're the pilot and you don't know where we are? That's comforting.* He looked over to the co-pilot and said, "Get out the map. Figure out where the hell we are."

The co-pilot traced his finger along the flight path on the map and then stopped. Clayton said, "Somewhere over Romania. Hey, do you want to see an aerial refueling? You'll see the tail of a DC-10 about twenty feet away right outside this window."

"I would love to."

"Great. We will call you back up when its time. Chief Mayer will let you know."

As I walked down the stairs to the broad belly of the plane, I knew that I was in for a real treat. After stepping over soldiers spread out all over the floor of the aircraft trying not to wake anyone, I found my seat and waited for the call. It came less than an hour later.

"Colonel Moring," Chief Mayer announced on the loud speaker. It was time. I once again climbed the stairs to the galley. A sergeant with a video camera was already seated behind light colonel Clayton and his co-pilot.

Colonel Clayton pointed to the headphones and seat belt. "Are you ready for the AR?" he asked.

"AR?" I responded quizzically.

"Aerial Refueling. We are only a few minutes away," he explained. It was night, but there was a full moon. In addition to the big windows for the pilot and co-pilot at the front of the C-17, there was a set of windows right above my head. The moonlight shone brilliantly through the overhead window.

I quickly looked at the control panel. We had slowed to 275 miles per hour and dropped to 21,000 feet of altitude. An air traffic controller speaking Russian was audible on my headphones.

"Where the fuck are they?" blurted out Clayton. "We are here at the right time. We are in the right place. They must be this blip on my screen," pointing to the radar. "Do you have a visual?"

The co-pilot answered, "No. Now wait a minute, white light at two o'clock."

"Yeah, right there. Got him," said Clayton happily.

"Do you have radio contact?" questioned the co-pilot.

"No, I haven't even asked for it," Clayton informed. "Put the seat belt sign on. It's going to get cold in the cabin. We're closing. One mile out."

All of sudden the white light disappeared. The entire sky was black again except for the moon. "Where the fuck are they now?" Clayton shouted seemingly alarmed.

Fortunately, the co-pilot quickly answered. This experience had gone from super exciting to frighteningly scary. I did not want a front seat pass to a mid-air collision between two multi-ton planes. "They are at 12 o'clock."

Within a minute, I could see the tail of a DC-10 just a football field away. "O.K. Let's slow it down," commanded Clayton. "Closing. Closing. Sixteen feet." The huge plane was right above my head. It was so close I could read the words painted on underside of the rear wings, "Kansas Coyotes." The other plane's pilot was speaking on the radio. It was a female.

"You the man!" shouted the co-pilot triumphantly. "Here comes the boom."

I could see a man looking out the window on the back of the DC-10. He seemed to be controlling a long shaft that exited from the rear of his airplane in our direction.

Clayton stated, "I bet that boomer's eyes are wide open now." It appeared to me that the pilot was flying manual now. He had his right hand on the joystick and was moving his fingers back and forth. His concentration was apparent. "Keep those fingers loose," he said.

"Ready. Latch."

After hearing one light tapping noise, I heard another. Clayton seemed very upset. "What the hell happened? We're disconnected. We got a ready and then a latch light. That's not supposed to happen." Pointing to the co-pilot, he said, "You fly the plane. I will take a look at the manual."

My heart started racing. We were sixteen feet away from disaster and the pilot was reading the instruction manual. I looked at the co-pilot's left arm and then at Clayton paging through a book. *Come on now*, I thought.

"We're okay," said the Colonel. "Probably just had contact with no lock. Let's try again." He again took over control of the plane and within seconds there was a firm tap. "Done," Clayton stated obviously pleased with himself. He turned to the Sergeant seated at my left and inquired, "Did you get all of that on tape?" The enlisted soldier seemed too panicked to respond.

"Okay, steady now. Hey Chief, what's the temperature like down there?"

Mayer answered, "You could hang meat down here."

Within minutes, the DC-10 had transferred 65,000 pounds of fuel and we disconnected. The female pilot's voice came on over the radio. "Please stop by when you are in Kansas."

Clayton replied, "I sure will." He then turned to me and asked, "So, how did you like it?"

"I was scared to death."

"So was I," said Clayton expressionless.

"Where are we now?" I wanted to know.

"Captain, paint the shoreline for the Colonel," Clayton instructed his co-pilot. He then compared the outline of the green light on the radar screen to the map he was holding in his hand. "We are at the eastern edge of the Black Sea."

Having had my adventure, I returned to my seat after thanking Clayton and his co-pilot for the experience. After a few more hours, we were on the ground in Kandahar. Romans and I would have to wait another day to get a flight back to Bagram. R&R was over.

Chapter XXV.

The Streamlined Code, Part Two

When I finally got back to Kabul after eight days travel from Allentown, everything had changed. It seemed that I had been away for six months instead of twenty-two days. And, most of the change I did not like.

Colonel Mantooth had been asking for a meeting of the Chiefs of staff of OMC-A and CFC-A[102] to discuss the reorganization of Judge Advocates on Kabul Compound since November. Within two days after my return, the new Chief of Staff of OMC-A, Colonel William Babcock, assembled the lawyers in his office. Colonel Snukis, attended for CFC-A.

Babcock, the bald-headed, grisly Vietnam veteran spoke first. "Colonel Snukis and I in consultation with our general officers have made a decision concerning the placement of you lawyers. Colonel Mantooth, you will serve as the Staff Judge Advocate of CFC-A. Lieutenant Colonel Moring, you will formally become the SJA of OMC-A. Lieutenant Colonel Goerke, you will remain at MOD/GS reform and continue to mentor the General Counsel and Judge Advocate General of the Ministry of Defense. Colonel Medvigy, you will assume responsibility for judicial sector reform for both CFC-A and OMC-A. All of you are your own bosses, and no one works for the other. Are there any questions?"

Yeah, I had a lot of questions. Did this mean that I would be stripped of all my responsibilities for civilian and military judicial reform? Had Babcock and Snukis cleared this new position for me with

Colonel Wagner? Did this mean that Mantooth would have a staff and would not have to place such heavy reliance on me? Would I now be accorded the same respect that Colonel Gordon had as SJA of OMC-A?

It was clear that the Chiefs had made up their minds. Everyone, for the most part, stayed silent. The good news was that I was now officially the SJA of OMC-A after performing the duties of that position since November 5, when Colonel Gordon left. The bad news was that I lost the leadership of judicial reform after having served as the action officer in that sector since I arrived in theater. Having played second fiddle to Gordon and Mantooth, I would now take second chair to a five-foot, six-inch prosecutor from Sonoma County California, who had just pinned on the Colonel's eagle a few months before.

What made matters worse was that my power base at the Embassy for launching judicial reform projects was gone. The USAID Director in Afghanistan had decided to fire his Democracy Officer, Ana Klenicki. In her place, USAID would bring in a temporary replacement from its El Salvador office, Sepida Keyvargan. Ana had authorized the defense counsel training program and had given me the go ahead for the recruitment of a Master's Level Professor from the United States to direct a legal aid clinic at Kabul University. Now she was terminated. Her part-time fill-in knew nothing about these initiatives. Moreover, she knew nothing about Afghanistan.

Combined Forces Command-Afghanistan had conducted its stand-up ceremony while I was gone. LTG David Barno was now supreme commander of the coalition joint operational area. Colonel Bridge's prediction had come true. The center of gravity had moved from Bagram to Kabul. CJTF-180 would no longer tell OMC-A what to do. Instead, CFC-A would tell General Austin in BAF what General Barno would like him to do.

It was a mess. CFC-A had the power, but no personnel. General Barno wanted to assemble a staff equal to that of a corps commander. In reality, he commanded less than a division in all of Afghanistan and Uzbekistan. That apparently did not matter. The only unit from which he could get that kind of manpower quickly was from CJTF-180. The Tenth Mountain Division, however, did not want to give up its war fighter staff. Nonetheless, scores of officers came from Bagram to Kabul, and there was nowhere for them to live.

Back in June 2003, General Eikenberry and Colonel Bridge had anticipated the influx of personnel to Kabul. These men of vision had the engineers draw up plans for a "Super Compound" to be built by February 2004 in the mountains just outside the city. By September of that year, CJTF-180 Commander, LTG Vines, had decided that he did not want to make the thirty-minute drive into Kabul to attend meetings at the Embassy. So, he scrapped the idea of a super compound. As a result, LTC Janze and SGM Werley suddenly had to find work and sleeping spaces for the expected 353 new arrivals for CFC-A and the eighty new personnel at OMC-A.

It was not just a question of locating more safe houses for soldiers to live. General Barno wanted a PX, expanded gym, chapel, and new joint operations center. CFC-A would need new vehicles, computers, office furniture, and a bigger chow hall. What we hoped would be the last three months of the ASG's time in Kabul would not be steady as she goes. Base operations would have to plan and execute a major expansion plan and acquire new land for Kabul Compound.

Barno was putting pressure on the warfighters as well. In an exclusive interview with the BBC, he vowed that the coalition would catch Bin Laden and Mullah Omar during calendar year 2004.[103] The Commanding General said that the 11,000 American soldiers in Afghanistan would focus their attention on combating Al Qaeda and the remaining members of the Taliban. "The sands in the hourglass of all of the Al Qaeda senior leadership is running out. You can be assured that we're putting a renewed emphasis on closing this out and bringing these two individuals to justice, as well as the other senior leadership of that organization. They represent a threat to the entire world."[104]

Another new development in Kabul was that Janze had lost his girlfriend and was not in a good mood. Since November, he had enjoyed a May-December relationship with a twenty-four year old First Lieutenant who directed the finance office. While I was gone, 1LT Wiley had decided that she did not want to be seen in the presence of Ferd while on the compound. Wiley had been the subject of a violent attack by a female subordinate who was now in the process of a courts-martial for assaulting an officer. The attractive, blond Lieutenant had received enough public attention and did not want a relationship with a Lieutenant Colonel adding to the stir. Janze felt bitter and lonely.

The only good thing that happened while I was on R&R was that Lieutenant Colonel Kyle Goerke had made progress with the military justice code. Kyle told me that General Nooristani and General Shir, the new General Counsel and Judge Advocate General of the Ministry of Defense, respectively, had reviewed the proposed non-judicial punishment regulation. With only minor changes, they were ready to present it to the Minister of Defense for adoption.

A few things that I had expected to change did not. There were supposed to be meetings of the Gardez Rule of Law Project to discuss a public awareness campaign connected with the opening of new courthouses. The committee meetings had been postponed. USAID contractor, Management Systems International ("MSI"), and its Chief of Party, Dennis Gallagher, were supposed to have conducted national security checks on the Kabul University graduates selected to participate as defense counsel in the Four Courts Initiative. Nothing had been done. The streamlined code was supposed to have been entered into law by Presidential Decree, and then the Italian Justice Project was supposed to have commenced the training of the Mobile Court Team. The Ministry of Justice, however, was still reviewing the translation of the code into Dari.

Needless to say, I was not pleased. I immediately sent out an e-mail to the Gardez group scheduling a meeting at the Italian Justice Project in three days. We could not afford to lose momentum. The new people at USAID were inexperienced and clueless. Presidente DiGennaro had fired his chief of staff, Dr. Palmisano, who had gone home to Trieste. The embassy was trying to set up something known as the Afghan Reconstruction Group ("ARG") and another organization called the Embassy Inter-Agency Planning Group ("EIPG"). It looked to me like more layers of bureaucracy with increased reporting requirements and no action agents.

DiGennaro was glad to see me again. As between Medvigy and me, there was no doubt in his mind as to who was most knowledgeable between us. Presidente took a seat at the head of the table. Since Italy was the lead nation on judicial sector reform, I was glad to see him take charge of the Gardez Rule of Law Project. Shortly after the start of the meeting, he directed his attention to me and said, "Now, Platte, it is absolutely imperative that we get the interim code before the Council of Ministers this Monday. You must talk to your Ambassador about this."

Medvigy, trying to assert himself, stated, "Mr. Presidente, would it not be more appropriate if your Ambassador spoke with President Karzai and got the code on the agenda?" If he had only bothered to ask me, then I would have filled Medvigy in. But, he was way too busy to receive a briefing from a subordinate.

DiGennaro and Ambassador Giorgi were feuding. Presidente did not think that his Ambassador had done enough to support the streamlined code or judicial reform. DiGennaro intended to replace Giorgi with another Ambassador of his choosing. He had the power in Italy to do so. There was no way that Giorgi was going to go to bat for Presidente on the streamlined code.

The old man turned to Medvigy and said, "I do not think that would be effective," trying to be polite. "The Ambassador is not quite committed to this project."

"Presidente," I interceded, "Colonel Medvigy and I will do everything in our power to bring this issue to the attention of General Weston and the US Ambassador." Thinking that I had satisfied DiGennaro for the moment, I continued, "Now, can we discuss the training of the mobile court team?"

"If there is to be no code, then there will be no training," replied DiGennaro.

Once again trying to take over the meeting, Medvigy said, "Sir, I think that it is safe to assume the code will be enacted based upon all my conversations."

Conversations with whom? I thought. If Medvigy had some inside knowledge that adoption of the code was imminent, he certainly had not bothered to inform me.

"Well, that is very good news Gary," chirped DiGennaro. Turning to his new chief of staff, Vincenzo Lattanzi, Presidente asked, "When can we start the training, Vincenzo?"

Lattanzi squirmed, looked at his watch, and replied, "A week from Saturday."

"Very good," announced DiGennaro. "Then we will start the training of the mobile court team of distinguished judges, prosecutors, judicial police, and defense counsel a week from Saturday."

Medvigy continued to swim in waters unknown to him. "Presidente, have you given the Chief Justice a written document explaining your plans with respect to the deployment of the mobile court team to the provinces?"

DiGennaro looked at Medvigy incredulously. "Do you really expect Shinwari to read a written plan? The only document he reads is the Koran."

I once again jumped into the conversation. "Colonel Medvigy and I would be glad to arrange a meeting with Chief Justice Shinwari to obtain his consent to deploy the mobile court team."

Leaving the meeting, I needed some questions answered by Medvigy. As we returned to the Kabul Compound in the JAG mobile, I asked, "Sir, are you going to speak with General Weston on getting the streamlined code on the agenda of the Council of Ministers?"

"Yes, and I will also speak to my contacts at the embassy," stated Medvigy. I had no idea who these "secret" contacts were at the embassy, and he obviously had no desire to tell me.

"Don't you think that we should also pay a visit to see the Minister of Justice, just in case? I am not at all certain the code will get presented to the Council of Ministers without Minister Karimi as its proponent. Have you met him yet?"

"No."

"Well, this will be a good reason for you to meet him."

The next day, I made an appointment at the ministry. Karimi was as buoyant and as self-assured as he had been on my last meeting with him. However, this time there were no television cameras. Remembering that he was focused on getting security for his building at the time that Colonel Mantooth and I last met with him, I started the conversation with reference to this subject. He seemed delighted.

The interview next turned to the streamlined code. He assured us that President Karzai and the Supreme Court supported the code. "The only trouble is with the Saranwali," his translator, Mr. Monsoory, interpreted for us in English. "The Attorney General is controlled by the warlords. He feels that this new code will cut off his power with some factions. President Karzai favors this law. He will sign the code even without the approval of the Attorney General."

His Excellency further stated: "I must ask your help in getting it on the agenda for this week's meeting of the Council of Ministers. Last week's meeting of the Council was cancelled and, for that reason, the agenda for this week is actually last week's agenda. The code is not on the agenda for this week."

I sensed trouble. Both DiGennaro and Karimi were putting the fate of the Interim Criminal Procedure for Courts in the hands of the American ambassador.

"I will be leaving Wednesday," Karimi continued, "for Germany for two weeks. So, the code must be placed on the agenda before this Sunday for Monday's council meeting."

Medvigy, Mantooth, and I all nodded with acknowledgement. I had one more matter for the Minister's attention. "Your Excellency, it is my understanding that your Ministry maintains a list of certified defense counsel pursuant to the Law for Organizing the Affairs of Defense Attorneys. As I mentioned at our last meeting, I taught a seminar on the role of the independent defense counsel at Kabul University Faculty of Law and Politics. Of my 85 students, 63 expressed an interest in becoming defense counsel. I personally interviewed 35 of the graduates and have selected 17 of the very best. In accordance with your guidance at our last meeting, I offer these seventeen graduates for certification by your ministry as defense counsel."

Without comment, he accepted my folder filled with resumes and pictures. Karimi then paged through the folder and asked, "No women?"

"Yes, your Excellency," I replied, "there is one. Naseema. She was the top graduate in the class."

"Good," emphasized Karimi. "I welcome all reforms that signal progress for Afghanistan. One thousand years ago, the East and the West were very similar. Progress was made in the West only after religion was separated from the affairs of the state. The East has not separated religion from government and, for that reason, has not advanced in technology, culture, or wisdom." I left the meeting thinking that I was glad that this man was in control of the "MOJ."

Back in the JAG mobile, Medvigy said he would speak to General Weston and his contacts at the embassy to ensure that the code was placed on the agenda for the Monday meeting of the Council of Ministers. He was now in charge of judicial reform. My role had been diminished. There was little to do except sit back and see what happened on Monday.

CENTCOM had insisted that OMC-A receive a team from the Defense Institute of International Legal Studies ("DIILS") for technical assistance on judicial reform. My initial reaction to this proposal was negative. By December 2001, the US had obtained control over Afghanistan. Colonel Gordon had been working on judicial reform since October 2002. I had spent seven months on the job. *And now, Central Command thought it was appropriate to send a technical assistance team to Kabul?*

I soon realized that I could not fight it. DIILS was coming to OMC-A. The responsibility fell on my shoulders to serve as its escort officer for a week and introduce the team to the judicial reform players in the US government, coalition, Afghan ministries, and NGOs. I figured that at least I could keep the DIILS group from disrupting the progress we had made on judicial reform.

They arrived at noon on Monday, just before the meeting of the Council of Ministers. Colonel Paul Holden, Captain Felipe Paez, and Captain Chris Martin all fell asleep during my initial briefing. The DIILS team had spent the last four days traveling from the States, and they were exhausted. Their substantive work would have to wait.

While they rested, I gave an interview to a Major from EIPG. The embassy had insisted that I was the "SME" (subject matter expert) on judicial reform, and EIPG needed updated information to brief the Secretary of State. It was a good thing. The data the State Department had obtained on judicial reform was miles away from the ground truth.

Early Tuesday morning, the newly self-proclaimed SME, Colonel Medvigy, had gone to the Ministry of Justice without me. Medvigy was on his way out of the MOJ building as I arrived there with the DIILS team. He had learned that the Council of Ministers had considered the code, but had taken no action. The Colonel said he could not stay at the meeting because he had another mission--to make sure some Afghan police officers received their pay.

I introduced the team to the MOJ Director of Legislation and to Mr. Mansoory. The Minister's executive assistant did not wait for us to ask. As soon as we sat down, he said, "I bet you want to know what is the status of the streamlined code."

"Yes, we do," I replied eagerly.

"The Council of Ministers considered the code yesterday at its meeting. The Attorney General and Supreme Court opposed the new law. President Karzai directed the Minister of Justice to meet with these ministries and try to obtain their consent. There will be a meeting today in this office with representatives of the Attorney General and Supreme Court, and we will work hard to gain their approval of the code. If the code is not adopted as a law, then I will resign my post here at the ministry."

I did not like what I was hearing. The code was supposed to be a done deal. The Minister of Justice himself had said Karzai would sign it even if the Saranwali still opposed it. Now, the Supreme Court was voicing opposition. Chief Justice Shinwari was the most influential mullah in all of Afghanistan. Now it appeared that there was some uncertainty about the passage of the code.

As the DIILS team made their pitch about all the wonderful lectures and seminars they could bring to Kabul for legal training, I barely listened. My only thought was developing a strategy to get the code signed by Karzai. I needed to find a way that pressure could be applied at a level way above my pay grade.

The next stop was the Italian Justice Project. Vincenzo Lattanzi met us at the door. He was not his usual grinning, affable self. His hair was a mess, and it was apparent that he was greatly disturbed. "Presidente DiGennaro will not be meeting with you today. He is on the phone with Rome," explained Vincenzo. Colonel Holden, leader of the DIILS team, was noticeably disappointed. He had wanted to meet the legendary Mafia Prosecutor.

As it turned out, Holden and his crew never had an opportunity to make their presentation. Lattanzi would not let them. He was not in the mood. Vincenzo wanted to vent. "We met with the Minister of Justice on Sunday. He said the code would be signed on Monday. It was not. I am tired of this shit. Presidente DiGennaro has written a letter to the Minister of Foreign Affairs in Rome stating that he is resigning as head of the justice project if the code is not signed by the close of business today."

"Certainly, Vincenzo," I offered, "it is just a matter of time until the code is signed. We must all be patient."

"You know Presidente. He has no more patience," Lattanzi said angrily.

"Will Italy continue as the lead nation?" I asked meekly.

"I do not know. That will be up to Rome. I am leaving with DiGennaro tomorrow. The mobile court team training is cancelled."

Due to the abrupt nature of the meeting, I got the DIILS group back to Kabul Compound forty-five minutes ahead of schedule. Our next interview was not until 3:30 P.M. I felt it was imperative to get an e-mail to all the important people in the USG involved with judicial reform about what had happened a few minutes earlier at the Italian Justice Project.

Not thinking that I was being the least bit over-dramatic, I entitled the message: "Italy Status as Lead Nation in Jeopardy." The report contained all the information I had just learned from Vincenzo and Mr. Mansoory. In addition, it stated that Mr. Qasimi, Karzai's legal advisor, was advocating delay in adopting the code because of grammatical errors in the English version of the code. I noted in the e-mail that Qasimi was an employee of MSI and, as such, was being paid with USAID funds. I wrote: "An effort needs to be made with Qasimi, and someone should reassure the Italians. If there is any way to get a message to President Karzai concerning the code, then this should help resolve the impasse."

Time was of the essence. I had no idea when General Weston or Mr. Sedney would read the message. The Italians were leaving town if the code did not become law by Wednesday night. Washington's directive to preserve the status of Italy as the lead nation on judicial reform would not be fulfilled. I needed to act.

I walked over to the Corner House hoping to find Colonel Medvigy at his office with the "CMCOORD" ("Civil-Military Coordination"). He was sitting at his desk working on the computer. With what I am sure appeared to him as a panicked expression, I explained what had just happened at the Italian Justice Project. Medvigy kept his eyes on the computer screen and was unmoved.

"Yeah, I know the Italians are upset," the Colonel said. I

spoke to them last night. They just need some calming down. Do you want to get lunch?"

This was unbelievable. The very foundation for judicial reform in Afghanistan was the streamlined code of criminal procedure. DiGennaro and the Justice Project had been delaying all reform initiatives pending the adoption of this code. It had been eight months in the making. The whole house of cards was ready to collapse, and all Medvigy could think about was his stomach.

"With all due respect, sir," I said as my blood began to boil, "I do not think that I have time for lunch. You may be the lead on judicial reform now, but I am still the personal legal advisor to General Weston. I have an obligation to inform him on critical events that impact upon his command. I am going to try to see him right now."

Shrugging his shoulders, Medvigy replied nonchalantly, "Do what you like. I was thinking about seeing the Italians after lunch. I really don't think anything else needs to be done."

Without offering a salute, I left the CMCOORD and walked quickly to the second floor of the Rose House. The General's aide was gone, so I went right to Weston's office and knocked on the door. He was inside. "Sir, may I have a moment of your time," I pleaded.

"Yes, Platte," Weston replied, "What's on your mind?"

I laid it all out for him. The General was obviously concerned and fully engaged on the issue. Thanks to my late December PowerPoint briefings to him on judicial reform, the scope of the problem with the Italians needed scant explanation. As Weston was about to give me my marching orders, Medvigy walked in the room unannounced. Apparently, he had decided to delay his lunch. I am certain that he could not stand the fact that I was getting face time with the General all by myself.

"Come on in, Gary," Weston said, waving his long, bony arm. "Platte was just explaining to me what is happening with the Italians. Apparently, there was a breakdown in coordination of this program between the ministries. Here is what I would like for you to do."

Medvigy interrupted the General. He avoided eye contact with me. "Sir, with your permission, I have somewhat of a different focus from Platte. I would like to explain. . . ."

"Be quick," snorted Weston obviously perturbed with Medvigy's interjection as he was about to give his command guidance. "I only have a few minutes until my next meeting."

"Well, sir," Medvigy began with the arrogance of a Prosecutor with an open and shut case, "All I think we need to do is calm down DiGennaro."

"This is what I want you to do," said Weston, cutting off Medvigy. "I want you and Platte to meet personally with Minister Karimi, the Supreme Court Justice, and the Attorney General and get them to sign a paper stating their support for the streamlined code. If necessary, meet with all of them in the same room to insure that there is personal contact and agreement on the code. The Ambassador is meeting with Karzai this afternoon, and I will make sure that he gets the word to raise this issue with the President."

I was grinning inside. This was a total rejection of the Medvigy plan of inaction. General Weston realized the urgency and importance of the adoption of the code, and he preferred my strategy. Now was the time to execute the plan.

Medvigy still wanted his lunch. He also thought that our first visit needed to be with DiGennaro. I thought there was some merit to this approach, but did not think that Medvigy was the best person to deliver the message to the Presidente. While Gary ate lunch, I went for Colonel John Mantooth. If there was anyone that DiGennaro would listen to from the USG, it was the gray-haired municipal judge from Pursell, OK.

Mantooth had begun to spend most of his time on the legal work of CFC-A. Ever since the Judge Advocate meeting with Babcock and Snukis, he had slowed down his activities with judicial reform. He was just returning from lunch when I caught him at the Ark.

"Grab your hat and your "IBA" (Interceptor Body Armor), sir. We are going to the Italian Justice Project," I said in the tone of voice of an order, rather than a request.

"What's up?" he asked.

I gave the executive summary. "The streamlined code was not approved yesterday, and DiGennaro is threatening to quit. But, I think he will listen to you. Medvigy is waiting in the JAG mobile."

Within minutes, we arrived at the Italian compound. As we pulled into the gate, DiGennaro and Lattanzi came out of the house and onto the marble deck to greet us. From the hugs and the kisses on both cheeks, it seemed like a family reunion. The Presidente was clearly overjoyed to see all three of us calling upon him.

Fortunately, Medvigy did not insist on taking the lead. The bond between DiGennaro and Mantooth was simply too strong. Mantooth started the dialogue. "Presidente, we want you to stay. You are just too important to the work of judicial reform in Afghanistan to leave the country at this time."

"But John, when will we get the code? This is such an important tool to ending the crime and corruption in this country. I have written Rome telling them I am going home if the interim criminal procedure code is not adopted into law by tomorrow."

"The American Ambassador has a meeting with Karzai today," explained Mantooth. "I am sure that he will do everything in his power to see that the code becomes law."

These words seemed to appease DiGennaro. I did not need to say a thing. Colonel Mantooth's positive attitude and reassurance had done the trick. Presidente was no longer talking about leaving. Instead, he spoke for twenty minutes on his plans for the future of judicial reform. He was fully committed to his work. For the first time, we heard his vision about a national judicial training center, bar association, and legal aid for the poor.

Mantooth had to get back to a meeting at CFC-A. There were more kisses and hugs, and we were off to Kabul Compound. After dropping Mantooth off and picking up Parwaiz, I insisted that our first stop be the Ministry of Justice. We needed to find out the result of the meeting between the Director of

Legislation and the representative from the Supreme Court and Attorney General.

Minister Karimi and Mr. Mansoory were not there. No one seemed to know where they were. Parwaiz began making inquiries to persons in the hallways about the Director of Legislation. Through several intermediaries the word came that he could not see us. I was not satisfied with this answer. General Weston's order was unequivocal. I asked Parwaiz to ask the Afghan ministry official to find out the status of the meeting on the code that morning.

Medvigy and I waited in the hall of the fourth floor offices. No one offered us tea and pistachios today! Finally, the messenger emerged from behind a curtain serving as an office door. He spoke in Dari. Parwaiz translated: "The Director of Legislation met with the Attorney General and Deputy Chief Justice this morning. They have both signed a letter approving the code. He is now preparing a letter on the code that he will deliver to President Karzai this afternoon. It should be signed into law later today."

I felt relieved. All of our work had not been in vain. The streamlined code would finally become law. Medvigy liked what he heard, but he was still skeptical. As a criminal prosecutor, I assumed that he had heard all sorts of untruths. He wanted to visit the Attorney General next.

Medvigy had never been to the offices of the Saranwali. I had been there many times since July when I went there for the first time to present my lecture on the American military justice system. Behind the wheel of the JAG mobile, I led the way. My leadership, however, ended at the iron gates in front of the ministry. The guards said we would have to keep our weapons in the car. Since we could not leave our pistols unattended, Medvigy told me to stay with the car while he and Parwaiz met with the Deputy Attorney General.

After a full hour, the Colonel and my translator emerged from the ministry. "How did it go?" I asked hopefully.

"Not well," answered Medvigy. "The AG would not give me a straight answer as to whether he has signed off on the code.

We had to listen to a forty-five minute speech as to why they are adamantly opposed to the reform. They see no reason to change the existing criminal procedure code. They are quite content with all 500 articles."

I was crestfallen. "How do you account for what we were told at the MOJ?" I wanted to know. "Do you think that President Karzai will sign the code into law without the approval of the Attorney General?"

"I don't know," said Medvigy.

Something that DiGennaro had told me months ago kept resonating in my mind--"*The Afghans are totally incapable of telling the truth.*" I wondered if that really was the case or whether the Afghans were just so anxious to please the Americans that they would say anything that they thought we would like to hear.

We had one more stop to complete the mission that General Weston had given us. "Let's see what the Supreme Court has to say," directed Medvigy. It was now 3:35 P.M. As we pulled into the gates, the normally busy grounds surrounding the building were lifeless. The guard said the court was closed.

I had left word with Lieutenant Colonel Goerke to get the DIILS group to the embassy by half past three. Colonel Medvigy and I decided to join them there. We found the team talking to the new USAID Democracy Officer, Sepidah Keyvanshad, in the second floor lobby. Colonel Holden and the boys were making their pitch.

I hadn't even found a place to sit down when a secure metal door opened, and out walked Ambassador Khalizad with three assistants. He came to the door of the office near where I was standing apparently with some purpose other than talking with me. "Good afternoon, sir," I said, not at all sure of myself. I had about three seconds to evaluate potential courses of action.

Had General Weston gotten him the message to speak to Karzai? Did he know that DiGennaro was about to quit and go home? Was it appropriate to question the US Ambassador as to what he was going to say to the President of Afghanistan? I had seen his armored vehicle out in front of the embassy when we walked in. I knew that he was leaving for his appointment with Karzai.

Throwing caution to the wind, I blurted out, "Sir, are you going to talk to Karzai about the streamlined code?"

"No, I had not planned on it," he replied, staring at me. I could tell he was wondering who was this Army officer addressing him in this manner. Suddenly, his face softened as he gained recognition of me. "We are going to talk about the restructuring of Security Sector Reform."

"Sir, do you know that Presidente DiGennaro is threatening to resign and go back to Italy if the interim criminal procedure code is not signed into law by tomorrow?" I continued impudently.

"He is, is he? Well, I guess we ought to talk to the President about the streamlined code then." He turned and looked at the entire crowd from DIILS, OMC-A, and USAID in the lobby. Everyone seated and standing nodded. The Ambassador then walked briskly down the steps to the first floor and left the embassy.

The DIILS team was now caught up in the saga of the streamlined code and wanted to know all the details of our earlier meetings. Colonel Medvigy and I recounted the day's ups and downs. At the same time, it was clear to me that Sepidah wanted to react to my e-mail about Mr. Qasimi delaying the adoption of the code. She had been working in El Salvador with USAID prior to coming to Afghanistan and was unaccustomed to dealing with Army lawyers on judicial reform projects.

"Wouldn't we better off without DiGennaro?" she asked. "From everything I have heard he is impossible to deal with, and he has done nothing." *I wondered who was filling her head with this stuff.* From her next comment it became apparent. "You know that Mr. Qasimi is not an employee of MSI. He is an independent contractor. At some point, I am going to have to sit down with you and explain the relationship between USAID and its contractors."

Someone from MSI, most likely Dennis Gallagher, had gotten to Sepidah. MSI had supplied the personnel that constituted the support staff for the Judicial Reform Commission through a subcontract with The Asia Foundation. When the

JRC initially opposed the streamlined code, DiGennaro had tried to shut the commission and its staff down. MSI held the Presidente personally responsible for discrediting the work of the JRC and, by implication, the work of its consulting firm. Gallagher would have preferred to see DiGennaro go away. If President Karzai's legal advisor opposed the code, then that was fine because its rejection by the Afghans would undermine DiGennaro's program.

I was beginning to seethe. I was prepared to explain to Ms. Keyvanshad that I was a Philadelphia torts lawyer, and I fully understood the difference between an independent contractor and an employee. Instead, I held my fire.

"The point is, Sepidah," I explained calmly, "that the USG is paying the salary of Mr. Qasimi, and Mr. Qasimi is taking a position contrary to the USG on the streamlined code. Also, I think Afghanistan needs DiGennaro in spite of his personality. There is no one in this country who can command the respect of the United Nations and their funding agencies as well as he can."

At that moment, the Ambassador returned to the second floor of the embassy after meeting with Karzai. He did not stop. As he walked by our group, he uttered, "Tell DiGennaro to stay patient. President Karzai needs 48 hours to have the code read by the Minister of Justice." Medvigy and I looked at each other. We were both thinking the same thing. *What the hell did that mean?*

Back at Kabul Compound, I was concerned. The Ministry of Justice had told us something that was not true. The Saranwali were not going to sign off on the code. We did not get to see anyone at the Supreme Court. Certain people at the embassy did not care if DiGennaro stayed or left. I sent a long e-mail to General Weston detailing our efforts to accomplish his mission and explaining the reasons why Afghanistan needed the Presidente.

Wednesday brought new information. Dennis Gallagher was fighting back. He had copied me on an e-mail he had sent to Mr. Sedney about Mr. Qasimi. While acknowledging that

Qasimi was under contract with MSI, Gallagher emphasized that he worked for President Karzai. He then revealed Qasimi's version of what had occurred at the meeting of the Council of Ministers on Monday.

According to Gallagher, the streamlined code had come up at the very end of the session. Minister Karimi had advocated for the adoption of the interim criminal procedure code. Karzai expressed impatience that the matter was not resolved. Karimi said that he had obtained signatures of approval from the Supreme Court and Ministry of Justice, but not from the Attorney General. Karzai then directed Karimi to finalize the process and get the code to him immediately.

I was not pleased with Medvigy. He had copied me on an e-mail he had sent to General Weston Wednesday morning in response to my long e-mail providing the situation report from the day before. Gary had told Weston, "I do not understand Platte's focus. But, rest assured, I will carry on with the mission." I thought to myself, *Thank God, General Weston has Gary Medvigy, because his own SJA has somehow lost his focus.*

Fortunately, the General knew exactly where I was coming from. I wanted to let Weston know that there were some people at the Embassy who might urge the Ambassador to let DiGennaro go home. If that was US policy and the embassy opposed DiGennaro's code, I needed to know that. I did not want to press the Supreme Court Chief Justice and government ministers for their signatures on the streamlined code. By return e-mail, General Weston assured me that the USG wanted the code and the Presidente.

Armed with that knowledge, I urged Medvigy to make our first stop that morning at the Ministry of Justice. We needed to know whether, in fact, the Saranwali had signed off on the streamlined code. Medvigy and I were very surprised to find Karimi in his office. We had thought that he left the day before to attend a seminar sponsored by the Max Planck Institute in Germany.

At first, Karimi did not want to talk streamlined code. He knew why we were there, but he wanted to talk his agenda first.

Karimi demanded to know from Medvigy where the USG was in providing protection for his ministry as he began the process of registering political parties for the June elections. The Colonel gave some non-committal answer. We were then ready to talk interim criminal procedure code.

Speaking through Parwaiz, Karimi said, "The code will be signed by President Karzai in the next few days."

Medvigy was not satisfied. We had heard this before. "Has the Attorney General signed his approval for the code?" he asked.

"The Attorney General is a communist," answered Karimi. "He opposes all change. We got his attention, however. Mr. Saleh, Karzai's national security advisor, called Daqueeq and told him he would close down his Attorney General's office and merge its functions with the Ministry of Justice if he did not sign off on the criminal procedure code. Shortly thereafter, he signed it."

I had no idea that the streamlined code had generated this level of power politics. Nonetheless, it appeared the code would become law. *Mission accomplished or was it?* DiGennaro was apparently satisfied. He agreed to start the training of the mobile court team on the third Saturday in February. I resumed my duties as escort officer for the DIILS team. Medvigy would report our success to General Weston.

The final stop on the weeklong tour of Colonel Holden and his group was to meet with the President's Legal Advisor, Mr. Qasimi. Even though Kabul Compound was only a stone's throw from the Presidential Palace, I had never been there. Karzai and his administration worked out of a medieval looking castle topped by a huge Afghan flag. I was pleased to see that ANA soldiers had replaced the militia as the gate guards. I was surprised to see that the interior guards were all Americans from a private security company.

We walked through a large central arch below the gothic tower into a large courtyard with modest landscaping. From there we entered a three story, white stucco building that housed the President's staff. Mr. Qasimi greeted us at the door to his office. He could not have been more gracious.

Immediately the conversation turned to the streamlined code. "I know that I have received a lot of criticism in some circles for my work on this interim criminal procedure code," said Qasimi. I started to become uncomfortable, but it did not appear to me that he knew that I was one of his principal critics. "Nonetheless, I have tried to do my best for this country. I met for two hours with the Attorney General this morning, and I finally convinced him to sign his approval for the code. I have a meeting with the President later this afternoon, and I will present him the code for his signature."

I did not know if Qasimi had actually closed the deal as he reported or whether he was just the clean up man after the National Security Advisor put the screws to Daqeeq. I really did not care. The streamlined code was an improvement over the 1974 criminal procedure law, and judicial reform could now begin in earnest. The Italian lead had been preserved.

Two days later, Medvigy learned that Karzai had signed a Decree proclaiming the streamlined code the law of Afghanistan.[105]

Chapter XXVI.

Death Without Honor

R oll Call," shouted Army Captain Russ Turner. All personnel assigned to OMC-A and a few attached to CFC-A had gathered on the concrete slab adjacent to the Rose House. Folding chairs were set up in neat rows. A cold breeze interrupted the cloudy, overcast day. A pair of desert boots rested on the pad next to an inverted M-16 rifle topped by a Kevlar helmet.

"Chief Thompson," yelled Turner.

"Hooah!" answered Thomson, officer in charge of General Weston's PSD.

"Specialist Juno," Turner continued.

"Hooah!" responded Juno with a lot less volume than Thompson.

"Specialist Smith," barked Turner.

"Hooah!" replied Smith.

"Specialist Hall," announced Turner in a somewhat louder voice. There was no answer. A minute passed. There was still no answer. David Hall would not report to roll call on February 28, 2004. The young man, barely over twenty years old, had died two days before in a senseless motor vehicle accident.

"Butchy" as Hall was nicknamed, had been out drinking with General Weston's aide-de-camp, Air Force Lieutenant Todd Doughty, at the German compound of ISAF. Coalition forces were not subject to General Order No. 1A. Beer flowed freely at the ISAF compounds and the Germans did not bother to ask whether any particular soldier was subject to the US prohibition on the consumption of alcohol.

The night of the accident General Weston had attended a dinner with Farooq Wardak, Chief of Staff of the reformed Ministry of Defense. The General had taken his PSD with him. Each member of the PSD had one day off duty per week. It was Hall's day off. Having turned his job over to a new Air Force Captain, Doughty was supposed to be getting ready to redeploy to the United States in two days. Instead, he had taken Hall to the German compound.

Before General Weston had arrived at Kabul Compound, Doughty and the PSD had assembled quite a track record. Two armored SUV's had been totaled in accidents caused by the PSD driving at an excessive rate of speed. Several members of the PSD had been investigated for purchasing steroids in downtown Kabul and selling them to the Marines at the US Embassy. One such transaction had resulted in a member of the PSD being pushed off a roof and ending up hospitalized.

By far the worst incident prior to Hall's death was the fatal motor vehicle accident involving a local national on Halloween. The two-vehicle PSD had refused to allow a car occupied by American contractors to pass them to the right. Instead, the PSD trail vehicle had executed a blocking maneuver and forced the civilian contractors off the road and into an Afghan riding a bicycle. He died on the spot.

Doughty was in the lead vehicle of the PSD at the time of the accident. Brigadier General Prasek was not in the car because he was waiting at Task Force Phoenix for the PSD to pick him up and take him to Bagram. Doughty, the muscular and almost bald General's aide, stopped the convoy long enough to get his picture taken by the Afghan police. He was standing over the body of the dead Afghan like an African big game hunter. Doughty did not bother to report the accident until after the General's PSD arrived in Bagram.

An informal investigation of the 31 October accident conducted pursuant to Army Regulation 15-6 was inconclusive. The Investigating Officer could not determine responsibility for the death as between the PSD and the civilian contractors. The Criminal Investigation Division ("CID") found insufficient evidence to press charges. A subsequent Internal Affairs investigation of the CID officers who performed the automobile accident investigation found no wrongdoing or cover-up.

Clearly, something was wrong with this PSD. General Weston had inherited this bunch and Doughty from Prasek. He had no knowledge of the steroid purchases or any prior violations of General Order No. 1A. During his tenure, the PSD had performed faithful service to him. On the night of the tragic motor vehicle accident involving Specialist Hall, Weston was on official business.

These facts did not stop Lieutenant General Barno from launching a Commander's Inquiry of Weston's supervision of the PSD. The scenario I had contemplated back in November when Mantooth came to the compound had come true. There was a conflict of interest in one lawyer representing both generals. Each flag officer needed his own counsel.

At the request of General Barno, Colonel Mantooth drafted the Letter of Appointment for the investigating officer. I prepared myself for the representation of General Weston.

Around dinnertime a few days after the memorial service, General Weston summoned me to his office. At that time, I learned that the investigating officer, John Murphy, a full-bird Colonel and civilian lawyer, had already been to visit General Weston. Without providing any notice to me, Murphy had scheduled an interview of the Chief of OMC-A for later that evening.

I prepared Weston for the interrogation as best I could. I had represented many medical doctors and some corporate chief executives before, but this was different. As a rule, General Officers do not make good clients.

To avoid any surprises, I obtained the Military Police traffic accident report from the Provost Marshall. The report chronicled the high blood-alcohol content of Doughty, the presence of beer in the car, and the excessive rate of speed of the vehicle prior to the accident. Apparently, Doughty had swerved the car to avoid something in the road and the car had hit a drainage ditch on the side of the pavement. Hall had not fastened his seat belt. As the vehicle began to roll sideways, his head became severed from the rest of his body. The photos were horrific.

Included in the MP file were two photographs seized from Doughty's room following the accident. They depicted the Lieutenant and two other OMC-A officers, one past and one present, drinking Heinekens at a Kabul restaurant. The photographs were taken some three months before General Weston's arrival at Kabul Compound. Apparently, some people on the compound knew of Doughty's ongoing violations of General Order No. 1A.

I was seated next to General Weston as Colonel Murphy entered the Chief's office. As soon as he saw me, blood rushed to his face. The General very politely introduced me to the investigator as the Staff Judge Advocate of OMC-A. It was very clear to me that Murphy was not pleased.

He barked, "Well, I do not know if that is proper or not and I do not care. I only have a few questions and this should not take long." I had been around enough lawyers to know that Murphy was at the same time trying to intimidate me into silence and lull the General into thinking that this was just going to be a living room conversation among friends.

It did not take long for General Weston to realize that this was not just a perfunctory meeting. Murphy started out slowly and then started throwing hardballs. The Colonel was conducting an investigation of a two-star general, and he was taking this assignment very seriously. He handled the interview in the same manner as would a criminal prosecutor interrogating a "perp."

At one moment, I interrupted the questioning to ask if General Weston had seen the "SOP" (standard operating procedure) for the PSD. I thought Murphy was going to take my head off. It was testing his patience for me to be present during the interview. His angry smirk in my direction signaled strongly that any participation by me in this session was intolerable to him. I said nothing else during the interview. Murphy's smug arrogance in questioning the general officer made me sick.

After Murphy finished his inquisition, General Weston and I reviewed what had just transpired. Twenty minutes later, I was ready to call it a night. I walked from the general's office back to the School House where Janze, Werley, and I shared an office. As was my custom when I left for the evening to travel by car to my safe house, I opened the door of the second floor dayroom to say good-bye to Janze and Werley. Usually, at this time of night, they were watching a movie.

The light was on in the dayroom. There was no movie. Murphy was interrogating Janze, the Garrison Commander. I quickly excused myself and shut the door. Murphy shouted to Janze, "What the hell was he doing here?" Ferd told me later about his exchange with Murphy after my exit. Janze explained that I always stopped by the dayroom to say good night. To which Murphy remarked bluntly, "Well, that was awfully coincidental and suspicious."

I was certain that General Barno had asked for the commander's inquiry simply to explore the command climate at OMC-A and make recommendations to prevent future accidents. Murphy, apparently, had another idea. The close encounter at the School House dayroom led me to believe that the following day would be trouble.

Colonel William Babcock, OMC-A Chief of Staff, asked me to sit in on his interview with Murphy. I was resting on a couch across the desk from Babcock as the Florida attorney entered the room. His Irish temper went to 10 on a scale of 10 as he eyeballed me. "What are you doing here?" he demanded.

"The Chief of Staff has asked me to be present for the interview," I replied sternly, but politely.

"You have no right to be here. I am going to have to ask you to leave," Murphy insisted with his veins bulging in his neck.

"Sir," I interjected, "Are you telling me that you are going to deny Colonel Babcock his right to counsel?"

"Well, if you do not like it, then you can call General Barno," Murphy snipped.

I was not going to take this. Instead of providing me with a substantive explanation as to why Babcock could not be represented by counsel, Murphy thought he could make me back down simply by invoking the name of the supreme commander. I knew that Colonel Mantooth was the legal advisor to the commander's inquiry. General Barno did not need to get involved.

Speaking very slowly and deliberately, I stared Murphy in the face and said, "I am not going to call General Barno. I am going to call General Barno's legal advisor. Let's see if Colonel Mantooth thinks that you can deny a field grade officer his right to counsel."

Realizing that I had called his bluff, Murphy said, "Go ahead and call Mantooth. I will wait right here until you reach him."

In the adjacent room, I got Mantooth on the phone right away. I soon learned that the kind and gentle soul from Purcell, Oklahoma, had learned how to deal with strong-willed counsel from his many years on the municipal bench. After listening for two minutes to my spirited insistence on the right to counsel in a potential criminal investigation, Mantooth forcefully stated, "Platte, be quiet. Now, I want you to listen to me. Here is my ruling. If you and I were civilians representing our clients, I would do exactly the same thing that you are doing. However, this is the military. A commander can ask questions of his subordinates without counsel being present. Colonel Babcock can refuse to answer the questions without counsel present, but he has no entitlement to counsel."

Pig-headed and refusing to admit defeat, I thanked the CFC-A Staff Judge Advocate for his ruling. There was no way I was going to let Murphy know that he had won without exchanging a few words. I marched right back into the Chief of Staff's office and said, "Colonel Babcock, it is up to you. If you like, you can terminate this interview unless I am present. You do not need to answer his questions in the absence of counsel."

Murphy did not wait for Colonel Babcock to answer. Ignoring me, Murphy said to the Chief of Staff, "You are not entitled to counsel. Should we proceed with the interview? Colonel Moring, your presence is not needed here."

I could not believe how mean-spirited Murphy was. Apparently, he had missed the television commercials about "The Army of One" and the "One Team, One Fight" concept. He was not going to let me be present for his interview of Babcock under any circumstances. Entitlement or not, as a matter of common courtesy I thought any reasonable officer would have let the Chief of Staff have counsel present during the interrogation.

"Why don't we let Colonel Babcock decide," I said angrily. "You let me sit in on General Weston's interview. It would seem that you would allow the same consideration for his Chief of Staff."

"I won't do that, especially after last night. You were teetering on the edge." Murphy did not explain what he meant. He did not need to. I knew exactly what he was saying. He was accusing me of putting words in the mouth of my client. I was pissed.

Babcock could tell the tension was escalating to an unacceptable level. Without waiting for me to unload on Murphy, he said rather nonchalantly, "Platte, I'll do the interview. It will be all right."

"Yes, sir," I replied quietly and left his office. I did not speak to Murphy again. Within five days, he finished his tour and redeployed to the states. The results of his commander's inquiry were never shared with me.

A few days later, I got a phone call from Captain McKay once again summoning me to General Weston's office. I had become, all of a sudden, a traditional judge advocate dealing with military justice matters. General Weston told me to come into his office and have a seat. Mike Martin, the MPRI chief of party, was already in the room. The retired full bird colonel from Virginia was holding a paper with several photographs attached to it.

"Well, Platte," said General Weston, "when it rains, it

pours. You know Mike Martin from MPRI. He has just brought a matter to my attention. I will let Mike explain."

Mr. Martin handed me his document with the heading, "Probable Cause for Search." "I have just learned that two MPRI employees may be involved in taking food from Camp Phoenix and selling it to people over at the UN," he explained very solemnly. It was readily apparent that he was at great pains to make these revelations. He felt dishonor as a consequence of the misconduct of these retired military professionals.

I looked at the photographs. There were huge ice chests filled with T-bone steaks, a storage room stacked with canned goods, and boxes of government rations still in their original shipping packages. General Weston wanted me to get the Provost Marshall involved and launch an investigation that evening. He gave me one hour.

The Provost Marshall, Captain Andrew Barrow, had just that day received an email from the CID based in Bagram. CJTF-180 was once again playing power politics with Kabul Compound. It just did not seem to matter to 180 that Kabul now housed the three-star general and the higher headquarters. CID issued an order stating that the Provost Marshall in Kabul could not conduct any criminal investigations. Criminal investigations were the exclusive province of CJTF-180.

Barrow, a Reading, Pennsylvania, policeman, told me that he could not investigate this food scandal without specific authorization from Bagram. While he prepared a SIPRNET message to CID at CJTF-180, I researched the law to determine whether seizure of the food would require a search warrant. An hour later, Barrow had permission from CID to seize evidence only.

I was impressed with the firepower Barrow had assembled for this mission. The Provost Marshall had organized a convoy of five vehicles including three Toyota Surfs and two heavy armor Hummers with standing machine gunners on top. We drove through the streets of Kabul looking more like Taliban hunters than food retrievers. Mike Martin led us to the MPRI safe house.

Private security guards from the United States opened the gate to the house. I was immediately surprised by the size and quality of the safe house. It was far grander than anything occupied by soldiers assigned to Kabul Compound. I was further shocked to learn that American tax dollars were paying to rent a twelve room, two-story house for just three persons. Each MPRI employee had a private room with separate bath on the second floor. The first floor contained offices and a full kitchen.

Mike Martin led the fully armed Military Policemen and me down the stairs to the basement. Three of the four basement rooms were filled with food. One room housed canned goods and a medium-size meat locker. Another room had cases of Heineken and other beverages. The third room contained two commercial size refrigerated freezer containers spanning the length of two walls.

I had asked Bill Bradigan, a thirty-one year Army veteran and present day supervisor of Kellogg, Brown and Root Services, to accompany us. It was the responsibility of this Halliburton subsidiary to manage the food rations of the United States Government in Afghanistan. Bradigan's assignment was to determine whether the food was, in fact, Army rations. After one look inside the meat coolers, Bill did not hesitate to voice his opinion.

The MPRI safe house contained approximately $3000 worth of USG rations. The freezers were filled to capacity with every type of meat served to troops in theater--T-bone steaks, tenderloin, meatballs, hot dogs, hamburgers, lobster tails, and crab legs. There was enough food to feed a platoon for a year.

It took the MPs almost two hours to carry all the food up the stairs and out to the vehicles parked in front of the safe house. The two MPRI suspects came back to the house while the seizure was in progress. Mike Martin immediately suspended them and confiscated their cell phones and computers. They had the audacity to ask why Martin was restricting them to quarters.

When we got back to Kabul Compound, I instructed Barrow to make sure the seized food was placed in a sealed, refrigerated container, inventoried, and photographed before any of the MPs went to bed. I also directed that the Provost Marshall prepare sworn statements concerning the search and confiscation. It was 10:30 P.M.

The next day, the CID from Bagram arrived at Kabul Compound in the middle of the morning. I deliberately separated myself from their investigation so as not to influence it in any way. By mid-afternoon, I learned that they had completed their inquiry. The CID agents had made the "brilliant" tactical decision to interview the two MPRI suspects as their first witnesses. These men stated that the mess hall sergeant at Camp Phoenix had given them the food in June 2003. The explanation apparently satisfied this crack team of investigators, and they went back to BAF stating that Barrow's case was "full of holes."

I knew that General Weston would not be satisfied with this lackluster police work. I got on the phone with Colonel Pede in Bagram the following day.

"The CID was here yesterday," I told Chuck. "They spent two hours investigating the alleged crimes and another four hours criticizing the probable cause affidavit of the MPRI chief of party and the seizure conducted by the post MPs. They did not interview anyone at Camp Phoenix. They did not bother to speak to the eyewitness who saw the MPRI employees unloading the food in the safe house twenty-four hours before the seizure. The CID agents did not speak to the gate guards at the safe house. No one questioned the legality of the notion that USG rations could be given away. The investigation was a farce."

"What can I tell you, Platte?" replied Pede. "You are now experiencing the same problems with CID that I have been dealing with for the last eight months. They are totally incapable of conducting a thorough investigation. I recommend that General Weston appoint his own investigating officer and launch his own AR 15-6 investigation." That is just what I did.

Colonel Mantooth had a very annoying habit of shaving with his electric razor while driving the JAG mobile from our residence at the Pink House to Kabul Compound. This morning was no exception, but for the fact that we had other passengers.

The newly renovated courthouse in Gardez was ready for its grand opening. In many ways, it was the culmination of the Gardez Rule of Law Project and symbolic for extending the reach of the central government outside Kabul. The embassy had arranged a convoy to inspect the site in advance of the US Ambassador and Karzai coming there to dedicate the courthouse.

Colonel Medvigy and Lieutenant Colonel Pitts picked up Mantooth and me at the Pink House just after daybreak. Within seconds, Mantooth had his razor out, grinding away with the most irritating sound. The buzzing continued as we entered into the gates of the US Embassy to meet the rest of our group. The sound was so loud we could not hear each other talk. I hoped he would stop his personal hygiene soon.

Some nine months after I had first stepped foot on the embassy grounds, the area had been totally transformed. No longer was the State Department's presence in Afghanistan limited to a few mobile homes and a small two-story building riddled with rocket holes. Construction crews were working twenty-four hours a day building a brand new, five-story embassy building. A new perimeter wall provided greater standoff distance from a bomb attack. Across the street and connected by an underground tunnel was a new housing area for USAID and other government employees. Two and one-half years after 9/11, it appeared that the USG was serious about Afghan Reconstruction.

David Hoffman and the rest of the new embassy team for governance and the rule of law were waiting in front of the old building as we drove up. Thankfully, Mantooth put away his razor as we exited the vehicle and greeted our travel companions for the day. I was immediately struck by the appearance of the embassy public affairs officer, Kathy Brown. The petite twenty-something brunette was wearing a black pants suit with high heels and a very tight spandex top giving emphasis to her ample bosom. The perfect outfit, I thought, for driving two hours through Indian country in order to meet Afghan judges and prosecutors.

The Embassy Regional Security Officers ("RSO") wanted our unarmored SUV leading the four-vehicle convoy. Shortly after we pulled out of the embassy gates, Mantooth resumed his shaving. If that was not enough of a bother, the RSOs insisted on blaring their car sirens whenever the flow of traffic slowed down to twenty miles per hour or less. Medvigy, seated in the front passenger seat, remarked, "Why don't we just put a sign on front of our car—WE ARE FROM THE US EMBASSY. PLEASE SHOOT US."

I was not proud to be an American at this moment. There was no need for us to travel faster than the rest of the traffic. Every eye in Kabul was trained on us. Every man, woman, child and donkey cart had to get out of the way. It was truly embarrassing and needless. Much more importantly, it was dangerous.

Our route took us southeast across the snow-covered Hindu Kush Mountains on a one-lane road in poor repair. I reached for my seatbelt. Afghanistan was a war zone, but the Taliban and Al Qaeda never posed as great a threat to my personal safety as this drive through the country.

"You missed one," Medvigy said to Pitts, driving the SUV.

"What do you mean?" questioned Pitts.

"You have hit every damn pothole in the road since we left Kabul. Could you drive more carefully?" barked Medvigy. The scenery was absolutely breathtaking, but the tension in the car was mounting. Mantooth seemed totally removed from the driving drama. He kept rolling down his window to take photographs of the stunning geological formations. Anywhere else in the world but Afghanistan, this beautiful mountain area would have been prime real estate.

Gardez was even poorer than Kabul. And yet, someone must have had a good sense of humor. As we entered the town, a sign in English on the side of the dirt road read, "Welcome to beautiful downtown Gardez." Unlike Kabul, I could not imagine that this city had ever been a nice place to live. The dirt streets were nothing more than open sewers with three feet deep ruts in the middle of the road filled with trash and human waste. Dust permeated the air restricting visibility to about fifty feet. Carcasses of dead goats and sheep covered with flies hung from meat hooks in the open air market.

We drove straight to the Provincial Reconstruction Team ("PRT") just south of the city. It was my first trip to a PRT. An American flag flew from a turret at the corner of the twenty feet tall perimeter wall. The PRT Commander, a US Army Lieutenant Colonel, greeted us at gateway and took us into his mess hall for a briefing. After the hair-raising convoy, I was just glad to sit down and drink a bottle of water.

The PRT was working in an austere environment. It was worse than Bagram. They were situated in what was once a stronghold of the Taliban with little force protection and even less resources. Everyone lived in hastily assembled plywood shacks. There was no gym, PX, or other form of amusement. It looked like the most exciting thing that had happened here were visits by Donald Rumsfeld and the Army Chief of Staff.

The Commander told us that the denizens of Paktya province were no different than other Afghans living in rural areas. They wanted schools, deep-water wells, and mine clearance. We were shown a PowerPoint slide with all the projects completed to date. Surprisingly, the new courthouse was not one of them.

Back in the vehicles, we drove through the center of town to the offices of the provincial governor. Two months ago, I would have led the discussion with the government officials. However, with the new embassy interest in judicial reform and the presence of Medvigy and Mantooth, I was just a spectator. I was glad to see that Kathy Brown had deferred to local culture and placed a scarf on her head which matched her pants suit and dirt-covered high heels.

Dennis Gallagher of MSI had told us that the judges and prosecutors in Gardez wanted nothing to do with the streamlined code and the mobile court training team. We were pleased to find out otherwise. I was particularly taken by the comments of a middle-aged prosecutor, whose name I cannot remember.

Through use of a translator, he said, "We have nothing here, but we are smart people. We want to have courts and the rule of law. We can learn. We need your expertise and your training." As we toured the renovated courthouse, I felt a sense of hope for the future. Even though the freshly painted, stucco building had empty offices, wood stoves, and no running water, it was a start. We picked out a spot for the US Ambassador to dedicate the new courthouse. It was under a thirty feet tall tower with a clock face painted on it locked in time at ten minutes after two.

COL Mantooth and author meet with Afghan judges and prosecutors outside their new courthouse in Gardez.
Photograph by COL Medvigy.

The RSOs said we had to leave right away if we were going to get back to Kabul before nightfall. The convoy mounted up with our vehicle in the lead once again. With sirens blaring, we worked our way faster than we should have through the clutter of people, animals and vehicles on the road leading out of Gardez. Pitts panicked as the SUV fell into a two feet trench in the middle of the dirt street and lost control of the vehicle. Medvigy yelled at Pitts, "What the fuck are you doing?" as the vehicle hit an elderly Afghan man walking in the road.

The sudden stop of our vehicle caused the third vehicle in the convoy to smash its front against the rear of the second vehicle. Immediately, one of the RSOs was on the outside loudspeaker shouting, "Don't stop. Keep moving" at a volume that everyone in Gardez could hear. I looked out the window to my right only to see the old Afghan struggling to regain his feet. At least, he wasn't dead. It was inexcusable, but the RSOs were not stopping to find out his condition.

Three miles down the road, the third vehicle came to a complete stop. The collision had burst the radiator and water was running out. As a result, the entire convoy came to a "tactical halt." We dismounted and established an armed perimeter around the vehicles. The RSOs said we needed to return ten miles to the PRT to drop off the disabled vehicle. Haste had made waste.

The next day back at Kabul Compound, Janze was in our office checking his computer program that tracked the days, hours, minutes, and seconds we had been in theater. "In one week we will have been one year on active duty," Janze announced. "In two weeks, we will have 270 days boots on the ground. When the Army brought us here, they said we would be here for 179 days. They lied and extended us. Then, they said we would be here no longer than 270 days. They lied again. It will be mid-April before we get out of here."

We were all getting jaded. It was not fun anymore. I used to get up in the morning excited about the day's activities. Not anymore. The ASG was just going through the motions. It was time to go home. The problem was that no one knew when we were going home. Our replacements, the 33rd ASG, were still at the mobilization station at Fort McCoy, Wisconsin, going through training. We would have to wait until they got to Afghanistan before we could leave.

It was getting annoying. The Air Force guys had four-month tours. The command started working on their officer evaluation reports and award packages after they were in theater for only two months. The individual augmentees, like Mantooth, had orders limiting them to 179 days on the ground. They knew when they were leaving down to the week. The ASG continued to in-process new soldiers only to be there when they out-processed. We were looking at fifteen months on active duty.

Susan was about ready to scream. She had had enough. The school year had been incredibly difficult for both children. Will was continuing to be bullied by his classmates. What made matters worse was that the Middle School Director had told him that he expected too much from the school. "Just because your dad is away in a war you should not expect any special attention." This callous disregard for the welfare of my child was shocking and made my blood boil.

Patriotism and self-sacrifice had its limits. The children needed their father. I was going to miss Leigh's performance in the annual school play for the second consecutive year. Will said he did not even want to read my e-mails anymore because it only reminded him that his dad was not home. I had had enough. I had run out of gas. I needed to get home to be with my wife and return to my real job.

The deployment, however, was not over. The work continued. I tried to find some satisfaction in my judicial reform activities. The Italians held a Gardez Rule of Law meeting at their offices. Twenty-four people attended the session representing the UN, USG, ISAF, and NGOs. Presidente DiGennaro chaired the meeting and laid out his vision for erecting a national judicial training center, creating a bar association, and developing public defenders. I did not say a word at the meeting. I was pleased. After nine months of pushing and prodding the Italians to do something, they had finally seized control and had an agenda.

Later that week, Mantooth and I took DiGennaro to the Italian Compound of ISAF to eat wood oven baked pizza. We celebrated the adoption of the streamlined code and his eightieth birthday.

After the January reorganization of Judge Advocates on the compound, I had left the reform of military justice to Kyle Goerke. Apart from the DIILS trip, I had had no involvement in the process to get the draft regulation on military offences and non-judicial punishment approved by the Ministry of Defense.

Two days after I had reported to General Weston at the weekly Command and Staff meeting that the regulation was stalled at MOD, Lieutenant Colonel Goerke sent me an e-mail. "Defense Minister Wardak signed the non-judicial punishment regulation today," he announced. I sent him a quick reply: "Terrific. Good job. After nine months of painstaking work, we finally achieved the mission that General Eikenberry had given us in June 2003." It was not a comprehensive Uniform Code of Military Justice comparable to the one used by the US Armed Forces. However, it was finally a "Band-aide" for military justice for the ANA." I copied Colonel Gordon on the e-mail.

"Let us now hear from Colonel Moring on his work at Kabul University," said Tom Berner of the ARG a few days later. As the new lead at the embassy on judicial reform, the New York City attorney had called a meeting of all the actors in the US government involved in the rule of law. Berner lauded my defense counsel seminar at the Faculty of Law and Politics and wanted me to discuss the efforts to create a Master's level program on the independent (non-government) lawyer.

I addressed the fifteen people assembled in the embassy conference room. "Dean Wasel of the Faculty of Law and Politics, and Professor Qadir Amiryar, the advisor to the Minister of Higher Education, desired to have a Master's level program at the university. They asked me to recruit a professor and find a funding source for such a program. After an exhaustive process of contacting the American Bar Association, the Association of American Law Schools, the International Bar Association, the Max Planck Institute, Lawyers without Borders, and the International Legal Foundation, I identified a professor who wanted to come to Afghanistan to teach a Master's level program and establish a legal aid clinic. USAID agreed to fund Dr. Christine Warren, a law professor at William and Mary, to begin a program in August 2004."

"I have just recently learned that the university has rejected Dr. Warren. This is a major disappointment for me."

Sepideh Keyvanshad, the Iranian-American replacement for Ana Klenicki, had opposed my idea of a Master's level program ever since the date I first introduced her to this initiative. I was not sure why. USAID had gone in a different direction ever since she took over the helm.

"Afghans," she interjected, "like most other people, do not want to say 'No.' They simply say 'Yes' to American ideas just to appear friendly and cooperative. "

"I am not sure you understand the background of my work on this project," I responded rather sternly. "The Dean and Professor Amiryar personally reviewed the resume and qualifications of Dr. Warren. I explained that USAID would pay her salary. At the graduation ceremony for the Faculty of Law and Politics, Dean Wasel announced to the graduates and their families that Kabul University would have a Master's level program this year."

Sepideh would not leave it alone. She seemed determined either to run me into the ground or defend the right of Afghans to change their mind. I did not know which. She retorted, "It is my understanding that she was rejected because she was not trained in Islamic law."

It is one thing to take a position based upon philosophical differences. It is quite something else to maintain a stance based upon false information. "Dr. Warren," I rejoined, "is one of America's leading legal experts on Shari'a law and a lecturer on Islamic law at William and Mary." I thought that would shut her up, but I was wrong.

"When you want to start a new program in a foreign country, it is important to find out what the local officials want and cater to their needs," said Sepideh. "You just cannot tell them what is good for them and expect them to accept it."

I lost it. "I take considerable umbrage in that remark. You have no idea what I did to set up this program. I asked the Dean and the advisor to the Ministry of Higher Education what they wanted. I recruited an Afghan judge to teach the Master's level course. They rejected him. They wanted someone from the West to teach the course. They readily endorsed Dr. Warren. The Faculty Senate held a vote on this matter. Professor Amiryar and Dean Wasel voted for the master's level program. The majority of the Senate voted against the initiative. The Senate includes both the shari'a law faculty and the statutory law faculty. The Islamic law faculty killed the project. I do not know the real reasons, but I fear that it was because she is a woman."

Berner realized he had to play peacemaker. He tried to make a joke. "Well, Dr. Warren may be able to teach both the common law and Islamic law, but she surely cannot change her sex. I guess the Master's level program will just have to wait."

Eric Fisher, the new Second Secretary at the Embassy, seemed particularly intrigued by my defense counsel seminar. He turned to me and said, "Colonel Moring, do you think you could arrange a meeting of your law students with me? I would love to find out what they are thinking about the upcoming Presidential and Parliamentary elections."

Five days later, I had eight of my students meet with the embassy officials working in the political/economic section. I had selected my top student, Naseema, a female, and two each from the Pashtun, Tajik, and Hasara ethnic groups. I could not have been more proud. The men showed up at Kabul Compound wearing coats and ties. During the questioning by the embassy policymakers, each one of my students was articulate, well mannered, and smart. According to my "kids", it was okay for the USG to postpone the presidential election from June until September 2004. In their view, the legitimacy of the election as measured by full and fair participation was more important than its timing.

Chapter XXVII.

"Generals Do Not Ride Subways"

Mantooth was going home. It did not seem fair. I had been in theater for almost ten months and had greeted him when he arrived in November. As an individual augmentee on six months' orders, the Oklahoma lawyer could punch out after only five and one-half months. He would leave theater before me. My departure date was not until a week later. So, I had to arrange another farewell party for a senior Judge Advocate.

The Colonel and I went to the Supreme Court to say good-bye to General Tahib. He was one of the most gracious Afghans we had met in our efforts to bring military justice to the ANA. Once he learned that we were leaving Afghanistan, he wanted to entertain us for the last time. The General invited us to have lunch with him on "Juma" (Friday) at his ancestral home in Kanakan Province, north of Kabul. He insisted that we wear traditional clothes. The day before the picnic, Tahib arranged for his sons to purchase and deliver to the compound "pajamas" for Mantooth, Medvigy, and me to wear.

It was a picture perfect Afghan day when General Tahib met us at the compound early in the morning. The temperature was 65 degrees with brilliant sunshine and not a cloud in the sky. Tahib had invited eight of his sons and his four-year old daughter to accompany us on the picnic. Two of his sons were judges and a third was a medical doctor. All spoke a little English. There were no wives.

The three American attorneys were tickled to forego our uniforms and leave the compound wearing our colorful pajamas and Tajik flying saucer hats. Despite having been in Afghanistan for over nine months, it was my first trip up old Bagram Road. It was so much more scenic and heavily populated than the new Bagram Road that the Soviets had built to avoid ambushes by the mujahideen.

As we traveled north on the Muslim holy day, I was struck by the number of Afghans working alongside the road. They were down on their knees probing the ground with long sticks. Each person had a clear plastic shield protecting his face. I asked out loud, "What the hell are they doing?"

Medvigy answered. As a civil affairs officer, he had seen this type of activity before. The Afghans were clearing mines along the road on their day of worship. Apart from the face shield, they were not wearing any other protective gear. White rocks marked the areas that they had cleared. Red rocks identified unexplored territory.

Tahib abruptly turned his SUV off the hard ball onto a dirt road. The three-vehicle convoy bounced and turned on a narrow path between sun-dried mud buildings. We then came to a solid blue gate surrounded by an eight feet perimeter wall. The General dismounted and signaled for us to drive our vehicles into the compound. Even in this beautiful country dwelling nestled in a mountain valley, security was an issue.

The presence of water and lush green fields of spring wheat and grapes immediately struck me. There were few places in Afghanistan like this. Tahib had a pump house operated by a gasoline generator bringing water to the surface in a volume equivalent to a fire hydrant. Drainage ditches funneled the water to various parts of the field in a steady current. Farm workers erected mud barricades to redirect the water through alternative canals to irrigate other sections of the land.

Without saying a word, Tahib smiled and pointed to a shady place under a large Sycamore tree in the middle of the field. His older sons dutifully carried hand-made carpets to the location and rolled them out on the dry ground. His younger male children carried pillows, bread, and our breakfast meal. Other sons started a fire to boil water for green tea.

Apart from "Tash Okur" (thank-you), we never spoke directly to Tahib. Everything we said had to be translated by his sons whose English was broken. In law school, Mantooth, Medvigy, and I had all studied the famous real property case of the "Fertile Octogenarian." The sons informed us that we were in the presence of one. The General had four wives and thirty children. The kids ranged from age 60 to four years old. He explained that the Muslim faith allowed men to have up to four wives.

LTG Tahib and his sons gather with COL Mantooth, COL Medvigy, and author at their ancestral family home in Kanakan Province. Photograph by Captain Sean McGarry

After breakfast, Tahib motioned for us to follow him. We walked in the muddy area between drainage ditches in the direction of wall surrounding the remnants of what appeared at one time to be a large home. Tahib led us to a dirt mound covered with stone markers and flags. In unison, his entire clan stopped and silently held out their hands in front of their chests as if they were holding an imaginary bowl. I soon realized that they all were at prayer. The General's eldest son explained that this was a family and mujahideen graveyard.

Without saying a word, Tahib showed us a part of his life. The house had once been three stories tall and contained over twenty-five rooms. We observed a one-story shell of a building littered with bullet holes and tank rounds. Holding up his bony finger, the General pointed at his family homestead and said, "Russians." His second eldest son, the judge, explained that General Tahib had permitted the mujahideen to occupy the home as a hideout, and he and it had suffered the consequences. Tahib spent six years in prison during the Soviet occupation of Afghanistan.

After our long walk and a short discussion about the other judges in the military justice working group, Tahib once again treated us to an Afghan feast. We had kabobs, rice with carrots and raisins, mantu, and fresh bread. For some reason, the General did not want us to tell General Esmat and Hassan that we had visited his country estate. I told Tahib he could trust us to remain silent about our good fortune. "After all," I said, "they are both communists." The General did not have to wait for the translation. He pointed his crooked finger at me and laughed heartily.

The following morning was Mantooth's last day in Kabul. As the compound judge advocates gathered in his office in advance of his award ceremony, Lieutenant Colonel Goerke rushed in and explained that the new Dutch Colonel, Huig van Duijn, would not be joining us. "Huig has been shot at in his vehicle while leaving the Pink House," Goerke said catching his breath.

Since Mantooth and I both lived at the Pink House, we were shocked. It was right outside the US Embassy wall and within fifty meters of a Marine watchtower. "Is he okay?" I inquired.

"Yes, but the Marine Lieutenant Colonel who was driving the car took two rounds in the back of his body armor."

I immediately pieced it together. "You are not going to tell me that the Marine sentry fired on another Marine," I asked Kyle incredulously.

"Yes, that's what we believe happened," responded Goerke.

"I can just see it now," I volunteered. "The Marine was sitting in his tower pretending to take aim at the bad guys, thinking his weapon was on safe. Instead, when he squeezed the trigger he fired a burst directly through the rear window of a vehicle and into the back of a fellow Marine. We Americans are truly our greatest danger here in Afghanistan."

General Weston was leaving the compound to attend the Afghan Donor's Conference in Berlin. Captain Turner had scheduled an award ceremony for the OMC-A personnel leaving theater during the time period Weston would be away. Somehow, I had never made his roster. As a Pennsylvania Guardsman from the Area Support Group, I was never considered a part of OMC-A, even though I had served as its deputy or Staff Judge Advocate for over nine months. Weston pinned six service members with medals and posed for pictures with each of them. I was not recognized in any fashion, and Weston left for Germany immediately after the ceremony.

I spoke to Medvigy outside the OMC-A offices at the Rose House. He said, "I cannot believe I missed Mantooth's award presentation yesterday. Snukis gave me the wrong time."

"Well," I replied, "at least he had an award ceremony." Medvigy got the message without my saying anything more. He sprung into action. Within twenty-four hours, the commander of Task Force Phoenix, Brigadier General Mancino, was pinning the Bronze Star Medal on my chest.

BG General Mancini awards the Bronze Star Medal to author at the Kabul Compound. Photograph by Tom Berner.

David Sedney, the Chargé d'Affaires at the Embassy, sent me an e-mail:

Platte:

I wish you well as you depart and I know that your family and friends back home will welcome your return. But, from Kabul it is with great regret that I bid you farewell. You have made an incredible contribution towards the building of a new Afghanistan – towards helping some of the longest suffering, most dispossessed people in the world in their struggle for peace and prosperity. Few people have the opportunity to both change individual lives and to make key contributions to building the foundations of a nation. Fewer still seize those opportunities. You did both. You leave here with the gratitude and respect of your colleagues both Afghan and American (and even Italian). You will be very, very missed. All the best (and I hope to see you in Afghanistan again).

David

The e-mail meant more to me than the medal.

I should have realized it after the night at the Steinberger Airport Hotel in Frankfurt, Germany. This trip was going to be different from all others. I had finally left Afghanistan for good, but my duties at OMC-A were not over. General Weston had requested that I serve as an escort officer for two Afghan generals on their first trip to the United States.

The two Afghans could not have been more different. Major General Abdul Nooristani looked like the actor, Chaim Topol, in the James Bond movie, For Your Eyes Only. He talks with his hands, and his lips never stop moving. He is both warm and bombastic. Islamic culture and norms are easily disregarded when they get in the way of his personal pleasure. Nooristani always had to be the center of attention.

In contrast, Brigadier General Shir Muhammad ZaZai was quiet and demure. He deferred to Nooristani. At all times, he waited for the appropriate time to make his statements. He is a strict follower of his religion and of his culture. General Shir was always on time and well-dressed. He played by the rules.

We were supposed to leave Kabul for America at 0830 hours. Nooristani kept the three-vehicle convoy waiting at the Ministry of Defense for almost ninety minutes as he said good-bye to each and every officer in the department. Apparently, he thought the Americans would hold the plane for him. That was not happening.

We were an hour late for roll call at Bagram Air Field. Ultimately, it did not matter. I had called the Movement Control Team in advance and they had us already manifested to Germany as priority passengers on the C-17. We had to wait eight hours before boarding the airplane. Nooristani was not pleased.

Four months after I had last passed through Frankfurt on my way home on leave, Major Mings was still the CJTF-180 liaison officer at Rhein-Main Air Force Base. I had called him earlier in the week and informed him of the Afghan VIPs coming to his station. He had no recollection of me. Once again, he had no rooms on post and we had to find accommodations at a hotel near the airport. Tent city, which had been my German home for five nights, was not an option for the Afghans. Mings checked them into the Steinberger Hotel.

"Your rooms are all on the seventh floor. Take the elevators located in the first hallway to your left past the telephones," said the hotel clerk in English. Nooristani, Shir, and my 22 year-old Afghan interpreter, Parwaiz Barkzai, gathered their luggage and followed Lieutenant Colonel Goerke and me down the hall. Parwaiz approached the doors of the elevator and then came to an abrupt halt. He watched several times as the elevator doors opened and closed. All the while, he was not moving.

"Come on, Parwaiz," I said, "let's get moving. We are all tired and we need our rest." He did not budge. "Let's go Parwaiz," I implored. Sensing a problem, I asked in a more sympathetic tone, "What's wrong, Parwaiz?"

"I have never seen an elevator before," he replied somewhat sheepishly.

I smiled and said, "Get on, let's go for a ride."

The culture shock continued the next morning. The Afghans apparently thought that the US Government would spare no expense for their entertainment and comfort. They had spent half the night at the first class hotel making long distance phone calls to Kabul. At checkout, the Steinberger presented me with a 340 Euro ($450) bill for hotel room phone calls to Afghanistan. The Afghan generals, like most everyone from their country, had no credit cards. No one had any Euros. To avoid an international incident and get out of the hotel, I had to charge their expenses to my personal credit card.

"Welcome to the diaper run," said the steward. We had left the "comfort" of a C-17 for the luxury of a commercial jetliner. In-flight meals and movies. I was really on my way home. It was a good feeling. Then the babies started to cry. It was the week before Easter and the soldiers and their families permanently stationed in Germany were on their way to America for the holiday and Spring Break.

Upon our arrival in Baltimore, the United States Air Force had its act together. Two non-commissioned officers met us at the gate shortly before 8 P.M. and took us to the front of the line at Customs. The Judge Advocate General of the US Army had arranged for one of his field grade officers to meet us in the terminal, and we were off to the nation's capital. None of our Afghan guests had ever been in the United States before.

When we checked into the Marriott in Crystal City, Virginia, I asked for the hotel to turn off all services for the Afghans. No telephones or movies. I had learned my lesson. Central Command would only pay for airfare, hotel and $51 dollars per diem. Everything else was supposed to come out of the Afghans' pockets.

It was now past 11 P.M. and I was exhausted after three days of international travel across nine time zones. I quickly got out of my uniform and prepared to go to bed. As I was brushing my teeth in my underwear, I heard a light and repeated knock at my door. It was Nooristani.

"Who team leader?" demanded the General in broken English after I opened the door. "You," pointing at me, or "Goerke?"

Not wanting to be responsible for any of his complaints, I responded, "Goerke."

"Goerke no here," replied Nooristani. I walked across the hall to Kyle's room and knocked on the door. There was no answer. With that, I realized that I was team leader at least for this night.

Nooristani, realizing that I had been unsuccessful in passing the buck to Goerke, sternly uttered his request. "I need Chai." I could not believe it. We had been up for twenty-fours hours straight. It was almost midnight. I was standing in the hallway of the hotel in my underwear. And he wanted a cup of green tea!

I tried to explain in broken English that we could not purchase Chai in Washington, D.C., at that time of day. He did not understand. His hotel room door was open, so I walked in. Fortunately, I found a coffee pot and a tea bag in the bathroom. I boiled the water and made the Earl Grey English tea. It was not Chai, but it pacified the General. I finally got to bed.

We had agreed to meet in the lobby at 9 A.M. for breakfast the next morning. The buffet closed at 9:30. Goerke, Parwaiz, Shir, and I waited until half past nine and there was no Nooristani. We decided to go to breakfast without him. At 10 A.M., he finally appeared dressed in a three-piece suit.

Our VIP party had arrived in Washington a day ahead of schedule. This meant that we had an extra day to tour the city before the Generals began their formal interviews with government officials. It also required that we change hotels. The Arlington Sheraton had no vacancy for the day prior to our scheduled arrival.

Shortly after breakfast Captain Chris Martin of the Defense Institute of International Legal Studies arrived at the Marriott. He had developed the agenda for the week and, more importantly, he had the government credit card to pay for the lodging and meal expenses of the Afghans. Martin went directly to checkout to pay the bill.

Parwaiz and Shir had heeded my instructions after the night in Frankfurt. There were no additional charges on their bills. Nooristani was another story. Martin came to me and remarked, "Sir, as a matter of policy on these VIP trips, I have the hotel services turned off for our guests. I see that General Nooristani made $160 in phone calls last night. The government will not pay for these expenses."

I was flabbergasted. I immediately went to the hotel clerk and demanded to know why my request that all phone and movie services be turned off for the Afghans was not honored.

"Colonel Moring, we did turn off services in rooms 412, 414, and 416 last evening," the clerk stated.

"Then why is there a $160 phone bill for room 416?" I inquired heatedly.

"We received a phone call last evening from the occupant of Room 416 demanding to have phone services restored," he answered.

"The occupant of Room 416 does not speak English. How did you know what he was saying?" I asked, thinking that I could argue that there was a miscommunication.

"Mr. Nooristani made his request through an interpreter," said the clerk, smiling broadly.

Martin was not much for diplomacy when it came to the taxpayer's money, and, unlike me, he was not going to charge the phone calls to his personal credit card as a service to our foreign guests. He stared at Nooristani and said, "You owe the hotel $160 for phone calls. The US government is not authorized to pay for these expenses."

I thought Nooristani was going to explode. He turned to Parwaiz and apparently gave him a Dari tongue-lashing. The interpreter did his best to explain the situation. Ultimately, Nooristani pulled out his wallet and counted out eight $20 bills. I had no idea where he got the cash.

Captain Martin next explained that the government van would not be available for pick up and use until the following day. We would travel by subway. I suggested the Arlington Cemetery as a first stop. I thought it would be appropriate for the Afghan Generals to see the rows and rows of grave markers—the price of American freedom. We walked to the Pentagon City Metro and took the Yellow Line to Arlington Cemetery. As usual for a Saturday morning, the subway had only a few passengers, and everyone got a seat.

Shir was immediately taken by the expanse and majesty of the cemetery. He was wide-eyed and speechless. Nooristani, on the other hand, seemed fascinated by only one landmark--the JFK gravesite. He asked 25-30 tourists to step away from their positions around the marker so that he could have his picture taken alone with the eternal flame.

It was a sunny but brisk April day. The cherry blossoms were in full bloom. As we walked down from the cemetery and across Memorial Bridge toward the Mall, Nooristani clasped my hand. When I was working as a trial attorney for the Justice Department in the 80's, you would not have caught me dead holding the hand of another man on the streets of Washington. However, this day it did not bother me. It was customary for Afghan men to kiss each other on the cheeks and to hold hands. It was a normal gesture of friendship. So, I walked from the Lincoln Memorial to the National Air and Space Museum hand in hand with Nooristani. It was all in the nation's service.

As we traversed the Mall, I was shocked to see how the nation's capital had changed since I had last been there prior to 9/11. As a law student, several of my classmates and I had driven a car within 100 yards of the Washington Monument and taken our golf clubs out of the trunk. We then hit golf balls with nine-irons at the monument. That act of foolishness was not possible today. There were jersey barriers and barricades everywhere. A fifteen feet wall encircled the lawn around the stone pillar from Independence Avenue to Constitution Avenue. The street in front of the White House was closed to traffic. Concrete walls blocked off all government buildings.

This was not the Washington I once knew. Unfortunately, the need for security in my own country was as great as it was in the third world country I had just left. Except for orderliness, cleanliness and upkeep of the buildings, Kabul and D.C. were a lot alike. It struck me that the capital of Afghanistan and my nation's capital were both victims of the Global War on Terrorism. Americans and Afghans had lost some of their freedom.

After waiting in line for forty minutes to undergo a security check with the other tourists, we entered the Air and Space Museum. The Afghans seemed fascinated by the exhibit on the Wright Brothers and asked for a translation into Dari of everything written in English about the historic pair. I then suggested that we take a look at the Apollo 11 exhibit.

"What is Apollo 11?" asked Parwaiz.

"You know, when man landed on the moon for the first time," I explained.

Parwaiz's normally quiet excitement turned into amazement. He uttered incredulously, "You mean to tell me that man has landed on the moon?" I could only laugh. Here was one of the most intelligent Afghans I had had the pleasure to meet, and somehow the Taliban had failed to educate him about one of man's greatest accomplishments. It was great fun showing him the command module and explaining the various stages of the lunar space flight. I felt like a parent taking an eight-year old child to Disney World for the first time.

The Yellow Line took us back to the Pentagon and the Arlington Sheraton. Unlike the subway trip in the morning, the train was extremely crowded with Cherry Blossom Festival celebrants returning home. Nooristani and Shir could not find a seat and had to stand with the rest of the commuters. The senior general was not happy.

"Where is Nooristani?" I asked Parwaiz the next morning.

"Sir, he is in his room," replied Parwaiz respectfully.

Parwaiz was on time and simply doing his job as an interpreter. Nonetheless, this status did not prevent me from punishing the messenger.

"Does he know we were supposed to meet in the lobby at eight-thirty for breakfast? This is not a play day. Today, we have appointments with important government officials. This is not a personal vacation. He is on official business for the Government of Afghanistan," I said somewhat perturbed.

"Sir, he knows the time," answered Parwaiz. "He is refusing to leave his room. He said to go about our day without him."

I was mad. And yet, I knew that I was too emotional to confront Nooristani. All I could think about was how discourteous and ungrateful this Afghan was. He was different from General Tahib and the other Afghan military leaders I had met. Goerke volunteered to talk to Nooristani. I sat in the lobby and waited with Captain Martin.

"Do you have any biographical information on these Afghans," I asked Martin.

"Yes, sir, I do," replied Martin. "Would you like to look at it?" With that, he provided me with two typewritten pages of data he had prepared to present to the government officials with whom the Afghans would be meeting. As I reviewed Nooristani's bio, the picture became clearer.

Major General Mohammad Amin Nooristani had served as a regimental commander in the Afghan army prior to the Soviet invasion in 1979. The Russians attacked his unit and took him captive that year. After three months in Bagram as a prisoner at the airfield, he agreed to collaborate with his conquerors. The Soviets sent him to Leningrad for four years of training at their Ground Artillery Academy. After spending one year as a regimental commander in the Russian Army in Balkh Province, Afghanistan, he spent two years at the General Staff Academy in Moscow. Nooristani then served the Russian Army for four years as a division and then corps commander in Afghanistan.

Unlike Tahib, Nooristani was no freedom fighter. In fact, he helped the Soviets combat the mujahideen. He was a product of the Russian military machine where officers are treated like royalty and enlisted soldiers are considered their servants. No wonder he fled to Pakistan from 1993 until 2002. Nooristani was not welcome in his own country.

Now that he was in the United States, he expected the same treatment he had received from the Russians. Goerke had the responsibility of telling him that was not going to happen. Somehow Kyle had convinced the two-star general to come down to the lobby after almost two hours of listening to his complaints and telling the prima donna how important he was. As Nooristani attempted to telephone his brother who was supposedly living in Florida, Goerke told me the entire story.

Kyle said, "He kept shouting. Generals do not ride on subways." Nooristani had expected to be met at the airport by a motorcade. He was disappointed that our itinerary did not include lunch with President Bush at the White House. Waiting in lines at museums and taking subways was an embarrassment to a flag officer. He wanted to be treated in a fashion commensurate with his rank and status in Afghanistan.

Goerke tried to explain that the American army is different from the Russian army. The purpose of the US Army officer and non-commissioned officer corps is to take care of the troops, not the other way around. American generals ride subways and live in modest homes. It is a rare occurrence for a Major General to have any contact with the President or the Secretary of Defense.

We promised Nooristani that we would not subject him to any more subways and that he could sit in the front passenger seat of our government van. Fortunately, Senator John Warner of Virginia, Chairman of the Armed Services Committee, had cancelled his appointment with the Afghan Generals that morning. His office had called Captain Martin and stated that the Senator had gone out of town for the Easter holiday and could not meet with us. After much coaxing by Kyle, Nooristani said he would resume his appointment schedule after lunch.

Martin drove the van to Capitol Hill and dropped us off at the Russell Office Building for our 2 P.M. meeting with the Majority and Minority Counsels to the Senate Armed Services Committee. We were early so Goerke and I waited with Shir and Nooristani in the majestic entranceway to the large marble building. The Afghans were nattily dressed in three-piece suits. Goerke and I were wearing our desert camouflage uniforms with newly sewed on combat patches on the right shoulder.

As we paused for a picture in front of the marble statue of Senator Russell of Georgia, in walked Senator Warner. He sauntered by within two feet of where our foursome was posed without saying a word and without acknowledging our presence. Goerke said, "Platte, is that Senator Warner?"

I answered, "Yes, it surely is. Can you believe it?"

"These people forget who they work for," Kyle remarked disgustedly.

Parwaiz realized what was going on. I asked him not to translate. After the morning we had just had, I did not want Nooristani to know that the Senator most responsible for determining the budget for Afghan military operations had snubbed him. Instead, we hurriedly left the entranceway for the offices of Warner's staffers. The Majority and Minority Counsels acted as if they were meeting the Afghan Generals against their will. They constantly looked at their watches as Nooristani spoke and asked no questions when he finished his remarks. It was painful for me to observe the absence of hospitality by these civil servants after experiencing the kindness of General Tahib and all other Afghan government officials.

After the meeting, I was dying for some seafood. Since Afghanistan is a land-locked country with little to no capacity for refrigerated transportation or storage, seafood is unknown to them. In an effort to expand the horizons of the Afghan generals and satisfy my own palate, I took them to Phillips Seafood Restaurant on the Washington waterfront. I had previously arranged for my old boss, Colonel David Gordon, to drive up from Fort Bragg to dine with us.

Another miscalculation. Shir politely said, "I cannot eat any of this food." He ordered chicken as he had done for every meal since we had arrived in the United States. Nooristani, on the other hand, ordered the most expensive item on the menu—fillet mignon and a shrimp cocktail. He had already exceeded his government per diem for the day so I wondered how he would pay for it. Kyle and I ordered the all-you-can-eat seafood platter special.

"I no like this food," said Nooristani gruffly. He had taken one bite of shrimp and a taste of the steak before pushing it away. The senior general then stood up and motioned for a waiter. The young black man waiting on our table was obviously nervous and upset. He had no idea what to expect from this large man who spoke little English. Nooristani said, "Give me chicken."

Parwaiz was having a great time. He considered himself off duty during meals and was enjoying the show. Our interpreter asked Kyle and me if he could try everything on our plate—crabs, oysters, clams, shrimp, and mussels. The young dog was learning new tricks and continuously commenting about how good the food was in America.

Gordon, meanwhile, listened to all my stories about how much OMC-A had changed since he had left. He wanted to know whether he should ask the JAG Corps for permission to return to Kabul. I said, "No. It is not much fun anymore. The embassy is now fully in charge of judicial reform. Military lawyers are no longer running the show."

The next day included trips to the United States Supreme Court, Department of Justice, and Court of Appeals for the Armed Forces. Nooristani once again missed breakfast, but was dressed and ready to go when the van left the hotel for our first appointment. After listening to the loud-mouthed Afghan pontificate all day, Kyle and I laughed about how we could now give the General's stock presentation:

AFGHANISTAN HAS BEEN AT WAR FOR 25 YEARS. EVERYTHING WAS DESTROYED BY THE TALIBAN. I AM VERY SORRY ABOUT 9/11. WE NEED MORE MONEY FOR THE AFGHAN NATIONAL ARMY. WE NEED TRAINING FOR OUR PERSONNEL. PLEASE SEND OUR PEOPLE TO YOUR COUNTRY FOR SCHOOLING.

Brigadier General Shir Mohammad ZaZai, Major General Mohammad Amin Nooristani,and Parwaiz Barkzai along with author outside the United States Supreme Court. Photograph by LTC Kyle Goerke.

The following morning we checked out of the hotel because we were taking the Afghans to Charlottesville, home of the Army's Judge Advocate General's School. Nooristani delayed the trip by spending one hour at the registration desk arguing with the clerk about his phone bill. By this time, Captain Martin had driven the message into the General's head that the US government was not paying. Nooristani proceeded to argue with the clerk about the amount of the bill. The senior Afghan somehow once again came up with $300 in crisp twenty-dollar bills and we were on our way.

Kyle and I had had enough of Nooristani. As soon as we checked into the JAG School, we left the generals in the hands of Captain Martin. Goerke and I were taking advantage of the beautiful sixty-degree day in Charlottesville. We changed into our civies and headed off to Birdwood, the University of Virginia golf course. For the first time in ten months, I felt like a normal person again. The sense of freedom and the release of the feeling of responsibility were awesome.

On the way back to D.C., Nooristani chose to make an announcement. He had arranged to meet with his brother from Florida that afternoon at the Sheraton National-Pentagon City. I just shook my head in exasperation. We had given Nooristani the itinerary for the trip on our first day in America. That afternoon we were scheduled to take a tour of the Pentagon and meet with William Haynes, III. Apart from being Nooristani's counterpart in the US government as General Counsel to the Department of Defense, Haynes had been nominated to take a seat on the US Court of Appeals for the DC Circuit. There was no way we could blow off this appointment.

I looked at Kyle and said, "Your turn, team leader." I was now totally disgusted with Nooristani. I could not engage the senior general without losing my temper. While looking out the window of the van at the beautiful green grass and blossoms, I constantly checked my watch. Nooristani kept blabbing about his brother for eighty-four of the ninety-eight minutes it took to make the drive from UVA to D.C. I would not be holding hands with this Afghan again.

As soon as we reached the Sheraton, Nooristani bolted out of the van and walked directly to guest registration. Parwaiz went with him. The clerk said, "I have no record of your brother checking in. When did you expect him to arrive?" This dialogue continued for another twenty minutes before Nooristani was satisfied that his brother was not there. Kyle and I watched this theater taking place at the check-in desk and then shook hands smiling at each other.

As I waited for the elevators to take me up to my hotel room, an attractive middle-aged woman approached me. She was conservatively dressed and had a broad smile. "I hope you don't mind me asking," she stated, "but are you just home from the war?"

I replied, "Yes ma'm, I am. Just finished ten months in Afghanistan."

"Could I give you a hug?" she queried affectionately.

"Why, yes, of course," I answered as she wrapped her arms around me. "I have been in the United States now for eight days. I have been all over town in my dress camouflage uniform on the streets and in government offices. And, you are the first person to welcome me back. I really appreciate it."

"Thank you for all that you have done," she said softly.

It had been fifteen years since I had last been in the Pentagon. The Justice Department had sent me over there in 1989 to review some Top Secret documents requested by a plaintiff as discovery in a claim against the government. Security was much tighter now. All visitors required an escort. The building had been completely remodeled. There was no vestige of the damage done by the terrorists.

The Pentagon tour took us to an exhibit for 9/11. As we looked out the window toward Arlington Cemetery, the guide explained that the hijacked plane had just cleared our hotel, the Sheraton National, and rotated at a ninety-degree angle. The wing of the jet then touched down in the parking lot, sending the airplane in a cartwheel motion into the south wall of the Pentagon. As the guide spoke, I glanced over at the Afghans. They appeared interested and serious. I could not help crying.

We were then shown into a beautiful conference room set aside for the Offices of the General Counsel. The interior wall contained photographs of every DOD General Counsel from the Second World War to the present. I recognized many of the names as these individuals had gone on to become federal judges, cabinet members and elected officials. After waiting fifteen minutes, Mr. Haynes entered the room. He was gracious and extremely polite to the Afghans. However, the good-looking attorney never bothered to say hello or shake the hands of Kyle and me. Once again, a top government official ignored the combat veterans.

Nooristani gave his standard speech. Just as my mind was wandering off to the UVA golf course, the senior Afghan stood up and presented Haynes with an Afghan flag lapel pin. I was not ready for this. Nor was I prepared for what came next. General Nooristani asked the DOD General Counsel if he could do him a favor. Haynes replied, "I will do my best." The senior Afghan then requested the US government to extend his stay for one week and pay the airfare for him to visit his mother in California.

Haynes was now team leader. He did not flinch. The Defense Department's top lawyer said he would look into it for the General. I was sure he was just being polite.

The Sheraton had no information on the arrival of Nooristani's brother. The general was visibly upset. He needed something to lift up his spirits. Kyle had the perfect solution— dinner at an Afghan restaurant. Shir and Nooristani had traveled half way around the world to become acquainted with the judicial institutions and culture of the United States. And yet, their happiest day in America was at the Afghan restaurant in Arlington, Virginia. Nooristani ordered almost everything on the menu, liquor and food. His own bill came to $125. He put the $42 left of his per diem on the table and refused to pay a penny more. Shir, Nooristani and Parwaiz had had such a good time, neither Kyle nor I wanted a confrontation. We paid the difference. Parwaiz, the least financially able of our group, was so embarrassed by Nooristani's conduct that he used his own left over per diem to help defray the tip.

In my twenty-five years of military service, I had never met The Judge Advocate General ("TJAG") of the United States Army. For army lawyers, his position is an echelon above reality. Major General Thomas Romig could not have been nicer. Just a few months earlier, he had cancelled a trip to visit the Army lawyers in Afghanistan after a rocket attack brought down a helicopter carrying his Sergeant Major and other top aides in Iraq. General Romig knew first hand the horror of the Global War on Terrorism.

He invited us into his beautiful offices in Rossyln, Virginia, overlooking the Potomac River and the nation's capital. The Army's top lawyer made certain that Kyle and I had a seat in a circle that included his two top assistants and the Afghan Generals. He briefly explained his job and the top issues impacting upon the JAG Corps. General Romig then turned the discussion over to the Afghans.

General Shir was meeting his counterpart in the US Government. I would have thought that Nooristani would have permitted Shir to take the lead in at least this interview. It did not happen. Nooristani proceeded to give his stump speech, leaving little time for Shir. Ultimately, all agreed to explore ways of training Afghan lawyers in the Army JAG School in Charlottesville and elsewhere.

With the Afghans safely out of his office and being entertained by one of the General's assistants, Romig motioned for Kyle and me to come over to him. I approached TJAG, thinking that he was about to compliment me on my work in Afghanistan. He whispered, "I got a call this morning from Bill Haynes over at the General Counsel's Office. He asked me if I could find a way to extend the visit of the Afghans so that Nooristani could visit with his mother." I was speechless and flabbergasted.

After enhancing the name of the JAG Corps by working on the Afghan Constitution and co-authoring the criminal procedure law as well as the military justice code, there was no recognition by the top Army lawyer for my work. In fact, Romig had no information at all about my duties. Lieutenant Colonel Pede, my colleague back in Afghanistan, had written a report to TJAG stating "Nothing Significant to Report" on non-traditional army lawyer activities. Pede had used four pages of his report to talk about courts-martials and claims in Afghanistan, but provided no data on the work of OMC-A judge advocates. Now, I was being asked by TJAG to do personal favors for an arrogant and ungrateful Afghan general.

Since Captain Martin was controlling the funds, I summoned him into our conference with TJAG. Martin explained that the unexpected hotel stay in Germany and the early arrival in the United States had exhausted the budget. However, there were no flights out of Baltimore on Saturday, so that the visit would have to be extended another day to Sunday. TJAG seemed pleased. He said, "Well, at least now I can report back to Haynes that we tried to extend the trip and got them an extra day."

I had had enough of Nooristani. My orders stated that I was to report to Fort Dix for out-processing on Saturday, April 10, 2004. As much as I enjoyed the company and good humor of Parwaiz, I did not want to spend another day playing nursemaid to Nooristani. After dinner on Friday night, Parwaiz and I exchanged gifts and said our good-byes. He gave me a beautiful, hand-made Afghan sweater. We shook hands and hugged. I thought that this was my last contact with my friend.

He surprised me the next morning at 7 A.M. when he greeted me in the hotel lobby. Parwaiz said he wanted to accompany me to Union Station. We said good-bye again at the train station. I cried and said I hoped to see him again, knowing that in all likelihood I never would.

Chapter XXVIII.

Welcome Home 213th!

Fortunately, there was a staff sergeant on duty at Bravo Company headquarters when I arrived at Fort Dix late Saturday afternoon. I was hoping to check in and then get a pass. Due to several incidents of misbehavior with returning troops, Dix had a rule that one had to be in garrison for three days before he qualified for a pass. I explained to the sergeant that I had already been in country for ten days and requested an exception to policy. I just wanted to be with my family for Easter Sunday. He signed the pass.

I couldn't wait to get home. The last two months of active duty seemed like an eternity. Shortly after I turned into the driveway of my suburban home, Susan, Leigh and Will smothered me with hugs and kisses. I was the lucky one. While the rest of my unit performed a relief in place with the 33rd ASG in Afghanistan, I was home with my loved ones for the holiday weekend.

Not much had changed at Fort Dix. Major Giblin and the rest of the JAG officers I had shared space with at the Staff Judge Office were still there. They had spent almost two years on active duty as reservists called up to perform garrison support for troops deploying out of Dix. Colonel Velez was still commanding the garrison support unit, bullying those soldiers who were seeking weekend passes and drinking alcohol in their temporary barracks. The weather was cold and rainy just as it had been in April and May of 2003.

One week after I had arrived at Dix, my unit's plane touched down at Maguire Air Force Base. Some family members had made the drive from Allentown and waited until 11 P.M. on this Sunday night to spend just a few minutes with their returning service member at Timmerman Theater. I shook the hands of each and every soldier as they made their way into the theater and gave them a hearty "welcome home." New post rules mandated that no one could leave post or consume alcohol in the barracks. At least the "no travel rule" was obeyed that night.

Services at Fort Dix had not improved much since our deployment ten months ago. We were told that we could not even begin the steps necessary to out-process for two days. Everyone was dying to go home and, instead, we were forced to endure Dix for seven more days. More anthrax shots, fifteen hours of waiting in lines to get discharge certificates, and a half day of sitting around doing nothing waiting for a five minute medical exam by a physician's assistant.

Finally, the big day came—April 25, 2004—the date when we were going home for good. In typical Army fashion we were awakened at 3 A.M. so that we could clean up the barracks. The cleanup was completed by 4 A.M. and we waited another four hours for the Dix inspectors to arrive. By 9 A.M., three buses had arrived for our journey home. Suitably, they were red, white, and blue. The officers took the first bus, the non-commissioned officers the second, and the enlisted soldiers the third. The sun was shining brightly as we boarded the buses for home.

As soon as we crossed the Pennsylvania state line, a State Police escort greeted us and took positions in their patrol cars at the front, rear and sides of our convoy. No traffic was allowed to pass our three vehicles on the Northeast Extension of the Pennsylvania Turnpike. Suddenly and without warning, all three buses and our police escorts came to an abrupt halt on the shoulder of the interstate highway just south of the Quakertown exit. We all feared the worst—mechanical breakdown within 15 minutes of home. Instead, we were greeted with the most awesome display of civilian patriotism I had ever seen.

The Lehigh Valley Veterans' Committee had asked a local motorcycle club to supply up to 213 bikers to escort the 213th ASG into Allentown. On this Sunday, the Rolling Thunder Motorcycle Club showed up with 487 bikers, mostly Vietnam Veterans, to bring us home. All were wearing or displaying red, white, and blue. We all pressed our faces to the windows of the buses and returned the thumbs up of the bikers with salutes of our own. The motorcycles entered the turnpike at the Quakertown interchange and the convoy measured over three miles long as we approached the Lehigh Valley exit.

Colonel Wagner had made arrangements for us to visit the Our Lady of Hungary cemetery ten miles north of Allentown. One of our members, Sergeant Christopher Geiger, had died of a heart attack at Bagram Air Field shortly after our arrival in Afghanistan. He was only thirty-eight years old. He had answered his nation's call, but found the intense heat and high altitude of the war-torn country a burden his body could not bear.

As we entered the cemetery grounds, each one of us carried a rose. We passed one-by-one in front of the grave marker for Chris and paused to give a salute to our fallen comrade. Those unit members who had been closest to him could not hold back the tears. The weather had suddenly turned cold and stormy. Of the original 132 soldiers of the 213th Area Support Group that deployed for the Global War on Terrorism, all had returned home safely save one.

American flags flew from the four corners of the armory at 15th and Allen Streets as the buses made their way to the welcome home ceremony. My son, William, braved the rainy downpour and stood outside the Armory, waving to me as we walked off the buses. Red, white, and blue bunting adorned the building I had previously only known as a place for once-a-month weekend drills. Children and adults all carried our nation's flag.

Susan Moring welcomes home her husband at the Allentown, PA Armory of the 213th Area Support Group. Photograph by the Parkland Press.

Some of the families had not yet seen their loved ones. Sheltered from the rain, people were standing shoulder to shoulder as we made our way into the armory. As faces were recognized for the first time in ten months, shouts of joy created a near panic in the normally staid military headquarters. Kisses and hugs abounded for the Pennsylvania National Guard.

Wagner had told the politicians to keep their remarks short. And for the first time in my lifetime, the pols heeded the request of a military leader. Every government leader from the State Adjutant General down to the local state representative limited his or her comments to less than five minutes. The most eloquent of which was the Mayor of Allentown, Roy Afflerbach. The Mayor had been present on the day in March 2003 when we had departed the city for Operation Enduring Freedom. He said, "When you were deployed, it was sunny outside and rainy inside as many choked back tears. Today, it is sunny on the inside and rainy on the outside."

At the close of the ceremony, Wagner summoned all the children in attendance to come to the podium. Thirty or more children came to the center of the drill floor and lined up across from the four rows of soldiers spanning the old gymnasium. All recited the Pledge of Allegiance to the flag of the United States of America. As the children slowly made the way back to their seats, Will hesitated and remained on the floor in the center of the troops within feet of the First Sergeant. He then raised his hand to his head in a salute and shouted, "Thank you 213th!"

EPILOGUE

I had no idea how long it would take me to return to the role and mindset of a citizen. There are no days off in a combat zone. I had accumulated 22 days of leave. Government ethics laws prohibited me from representing private clients while I will still on the Army payroll. So, I decided to use my entire leave period to try to get my family and home life back together.

After spending a wonderful week together as a family at my father's condo in Myrtle Beach, South Carolina, I started doing the things that had been left undone or otherwise needed to be done to begin the path back to normalcy. The house gutters were clogged with leaves. The water softener had no salt pellets. My car that had been left idle for 15 months would not start. The kitchen faucet was spraying water everywhere.

The remaining days of my leave went quickly. Susan and the children patiently adapted to having a husband and father back in the home again. Nonetheless, I still could not get the events which sent me to Afghanistan out of my mind. When Leigh and I traveled by car to take her to golf camp just outside Pittsburgh, I insisted on stopping in Shanksville to see the location where United Flight 93 had crashed on September 11, 2001. As I stared at the abandoned open strip mine that was now a large field of tall grass, I paused and reflected on the fact that the global war on terrorism had begun in the skies above this ground.

When I returned to my desk at White and Williams a week later, I started making phone calls to clients and friends letting them know that I had returned to work. The Litigation

Department Chairman, Tom Goutman, had done a wonderful job of keeping the Allentown office running in my absence. His once a week visits from Philadelphia made certain that the regional office met the needs of clients. Unlike some of the less fortunate lawyers with whom I had served in Afghanistan, I did still have a law practice when I returned from the combat zone.

In some quarters, the "welcome home" was warm and uplifting. I received a standing ovation after I made a formal presentation on Operation Enduring Freedom to the members of the Allentown Rotary Club and the Lehigh Country Club. White and Williams gave me the seat of honor at the biennial firm "Prom" held at the new National Constitution Center in Philadelphia. All the local politicians showed up at the Allentown Armory three months after our return to home station for a two-hour "Freedom Salute" to honor the soldiers and their families. Some people that Susan and I had hardly known prior to the deployment ended up being the most appreciative of our sacrifices.

One of these persons was newly elected Congressman Charles W. Dent. Charlie telephoned in early January 2005 to ask me if Susan and I would like tickets to the Commander-in-Chief's Ball as part of the second inaugural of President George W. Bush. We jumped at the opportunity. The normally four hour drive from Allentown to Washington, D.C. took eight hours due to a snow storm that brought I-95 to a standstill. The long car ride did not dampen our enthusiasm for the event--especially when the Chairman of the Joint Chiefs of Staff, Richard B. Myers, shook my hand and thanked me for a job well done on judicial reform in Afghanistan.

But in other ways the homecoming seemed unnoticed. There were no parades for my unit or dinner parties for my family. I suppose there were many reasons for this lack of recognition for our service. Some Americans did not believe that the United States should send troops overseas for any purpose. I supposed that they preferred that we sit back and wait to be attacked. Other people held all soldiers accountable for what they believed was a misguided foreign policy in invading Iraq. Some people simply did not realize that the United States was at war and uncaringly went on with their daily lives.

For almost a year, I found it hard to concentrate on my legal work. The first personal injury file I opened was a slip and fall at a Uni-mart in the Pocono Mountains. I stared at it for hours. As hard as I tried, I could not overcome the inertia. As a soldier, the United States Government had entrusted me with the responsibility of rebuilding a war-torn nation. As a civilian, I was helping an insurance company decide how much a 55 year-old fat man should be paid for a bruised knee.

Although I continued to follow the events in Afghanistan with interest, I tried to put the war behind me. And yet, the news from Central Asia kept drawing me back. While I prepared for trials and took depositions, I monitored the successful Afghan Presidential election in October 2004 and parliamentary elections in September 2005. I pondered how the work we had done at OMC-A had made it possible.[106] I noted that the war fighters had not been as successful in their hunt for the masterminds behind the tragedy of 9/11 as we had been in reconstructing the embattled country. At the end of his term as commander, General Barno was no longer predicting that Osama Bin Laden would be captured by the end of the year.[107] General Eikenberry, the architect of reconstruction, had returned to Afghanistan to take his place as the two-star general commanding CFC-A.

Believe it or not, there were even times when I thought about what it would be like to return to Central Asia as Eikenberry had done. I missed the interaction with the Afghans and the Italians. Moreover, putting on a business suit in the morning did not give me the same feeling of pride as when I donned the Desert Camouflage Uniform of the United States Army.

Even though I considered the practice of law an honorable profession, I knew that many did not think so. In the months following my return from Afghanistan, I realized that some Americans did not even see any honor in military service in a combat zone. Ultimately, I came to an understanding that honor is a personal thing.

Do not look to others to bestow honor upon you. Honor comes from within and stays with you as long as you live in an honorable way. No one can take your honor away from you. Honor lets you sleep peacefully at night and propels you to righteousness during the day. Honor First!

Endnotes

[1] I recommend "Jarhead: A Marine's Chronicle of the Gulf War and Other Battles," by Anthony Swofford, Scribner Press (2003) for that purpose.

[2] Mobilization

[3] State Area Command

[4] National Guard Bureau

[5] Forces Command

[6] System for Identification of Personnel

[7] Fort Dix, New Jersey

[8] U.S. Army Central Command

[9] Not an acronym. An Army expression for approval, acknowledgement, or acclamation.

[10] Privately Owned Vehicle, also known as a car.

[11] Mandated Table of Organization and Equipment

[12] High Mobility Multi Purpose Wheeled Vehicle

[13] Preventative Maintenance and Care System

[14] Pre-Menstrual Syndrome (not Army acronym)

[15] Bachelor Officer Quarters

[16] Bachelor Enlisted Quarters

[17] Unit Administrator

[18] Common Task Training

[19] Battle Dress Uniform

[20] Load Bearing Equipment

[21] Kevlar Pot (helmet)

[22] Weapons of Mass Destruction

[23] Nuclear, Biological and Chemical

[24] Single Channel Ground and Airborne Radio System

[25] Operations Order

[26] Operational Security

[27] Soldier Readiness Processing

Clothing Issue Facility
Physical Training
Individual Physical Fitness Uniform
American slang (vulgar)
Intermediate Staging Base
Nuclear, Biological, and Chemical equipment
Semi-automatic rifle
Lubrication for Small Arms, also known as oil.
Mission, Equipment, Time, Terrain, and Training
Intelligence Preparation of the Battlefield
Military Operations Protective Posture Level Four
Mission Readiness Exercise
Meal Ready-to-Eat
Tactical Operations Center
Rucksack Deployable Law Office
Military Decision Making Process
Missing in Action
Enemy Prisoner of War
Personnel Evacuation Holding Area
Shit out of luck
Unit Basic Load
Ammunition Transfer Point
Ammunition Supply Point
As soon as possible
Opposition Forces
Night Vision Goggles
Civilians on the Battlefield
Command and Control
Global Positioning System
Area Support Group
Headquarters and Headquarters Company
After Action Report
Command Sergeant Major
Battlefield Operating System
Echelon Above Corps
Division Support Command
Corps Support Command

65 Combat Service Support
66 Commander's Critical Information Reports
67 Theater Support Command
68 Southwest Asia
69 Reception, Staging, Onward Movement and Integration
70 Desert Camouflage Uniform
71 To Accompany Troops
72 Tactical Land Area Network
73 Time-Phased Force Deployment List
74 Pretty Darn Quick
75 Absent Without Leave
76 Bullshit
77 After four months in Afghanistan, SSG Blue allegedly locked and loaded an M16 rifle and threatened to "Kill the Bitch", referring to MSG Susan Brown, and was sent back to Fort Dix for disciplinary action.
78 The seminar was sponsored by the Judicial Reform Commission. Mr. Baha, the Chairman of the Commission, was the opening speaker of the program, and most of the members of the Commission were in attendance at one point or another. Mr. Karimi, the Minister of Justice, was personally invited to attend the seminar, but chose not to simply because it was held at the Office of the Attorney General.
79 Afghanistan: Re-Establishing the Rule of Law, Amnesty International, 14 August 2003.
80 Title of a song, "Abraham, Martin, and John," performed by Dion in 1968, words and music by John Hollins.
81 By February 2004, Brahimi would become the Secretary General's Special Envoy to Iraq.
82 National Defense University, 1998.
83 Air Point of Departure
84 Coalition/ Joint Operations Area
85 Combined Forces Land Component Commander
86 The term "Haji" was not intended to be a racial slur or putdown. It simply referred to one of the five pillars of the Islam faith requiring all followers to make a pilgrimage or "Haj" to Mecca.

[87] A few months after we took this flight, one of the planes in the fleet of Uzbekistan Airways crashed killing all passengers in a flight to Tashkent.

[88] Uzbekistan: The Golden Road to Samarkand, Colum MacLeod and Bradley Mayhew (2002).

[89] New York Times, October 26, 2003

[90] "Sept. 11 Panel to Issue Subpoena Seeking Documents From FAA," Wall Street Journal, October 16, 2003, by Scott J. Paltrow.

[91] Office of the Secretary of Defense

[92] Forward Operating Base Salerno

[93] By this time, the unit had sent home six members, including Specialist McFadden, for medical or personal reasons.

[94] Auguste Rodin, 1881.

[95] Gustave Caillebotte, 1880.

[96] Pierre-Auguste Renoir, 1869

[97] Edgar Degas, 1890

[98] Lucas Cranach the Elder, 1532.

[99] Suzanne Valadon, 1931.

[100] Auguste Rodin, 1906.

[101] Svenja Kriebel, Visitors' Guide, Nackt!, Das Stadel, Stadelsches Kunstinstitut und Stadtische Galerie (2003).

[102] Combined Force Command-Central Asia ("CFC-CA") had been renamed Combined Forces Command-Afghanistan ("CFC-A") apparently for political and diplomatic reasons.

[103] "General vows to catch Bin Laden," BBC News, January 26, 2004, by Andrew North.

[104] Id.

[105] In 2006, Presidente DiGennaro informed me that an Afghan judge cited a provision of the Streamlined Code requiring the government to file formal written charges of a criminal offense as his authority to release from prison a former Muslim citizen being held without formal charges on the allegation that he had converted to Christianity, thereby ending a diplomatic controversy for President Karzai.

[106] Almost two years later, the US Army presented the Joint Meritorious Unit Award to twenty-two members of the 213th Area Support Group who had served with OMC-A.

[107] General Suggest Bin Laden is Alive, Associated Press October 20, 2004.